Ten Times More Beautiful

Ten Times More Beautiful

The Rebuilding of Vietnam

by Kathleen Gough Aberle

Monthly Review Press
New York and London

Copyright © 1978 by Kathleen Gough

Library of Congress Cataloging in Publication Data
Aberle, Kathleen Gough, 1925–
   Ten times more beautiful.

   Includes bibliographical references.
   1. Vietnam –Description and travel–1975–
2. Aberle, Kathleen Gough, 1925–   I. Title.
DS556.39.A23   959.704   78-14890
ISBN 0-85345-464-7

Monthly Review Press
62 West 14th Street, New York, N.Y. 10011
47 Red Lion Street, London WC1R 4 PF

10 9 8 7 6 5 4 3 2 1

Manufactured in the United States of America

Our mountains, our rivers, our people will always be; the American invaders defeated, we will rebuild our land ten times more beautiful.

—Ho Chi Minh

Contents

Preface

In November 1976, I spent ten days in Hanoi and nearby provinces as a guest of the Women's Union of Vietnam. As a socialist and supporter of the antiwar movement, first in the United States and later in Canada, I had looked forward for twelve years to this visit. While the notes I kept grew day by day under the watchful and sometimes amused eyes of my interpreter, the idea took shape of writing an account of my whole visit. "Would it be ridiculous?" I asked my women friends from Hanoi, "After all, I'm only here ten days." "No, no," they replied, "everyone has her own *aperçu,* and after working with such passion, you ought to do something with it." I decided that although I am no scholar of Vietnam, what I was experiencing meant enough to me to try to convey it to others. I was encouraged by the fact that K. N. Raj, the Indian economist, had written an account of a week's stay in Hanoi in November 1974.[1] Perhaps mine may be read as a sequel, two years later.

Going to Vietnam in late 1976 held a special interest for me. For ten months previously, I had been studying two villages in Thanjavur District of Tamilnadu State in southeast India as a social anthropologist. The work was a re-study: I had lived in the same villages for eighteen months in 1951–1953. Now I had been back to see what had changed there, especially in the relations of landlords, tenants, and agricul-

9

tural laborers and in the economy of the district as a result of Tamilnadu's land reform acts and of the "green revolution" of the last ten years. I was also, of course, deeply concerned with the effects of the Emergency instituted by Indira Gandhi's government in June 1975.

Thanjavur is a paddy-growing district, the delta of the River Kaveri. It has close similarities with the Red River delta of Vietnam. I wrote to my friends in Hanoi that I wanted especially to learn about agriculture and to compare agrarian relations and methods in southeast India with those of north Vietnam.[2] I left Thanjavur at the beginning of the autumn harvest (delayed by drought) in late October and reached Vietnam on November 10 to find the same harvest, also delayed, in progress. Although my view of it was necessarily superficial, I could not help seeing a stark contrast between the living conditions of the Vietnamese peasants working in state-run cooperatives and those of the tenant cultivators and landless laborers who form the large majority of the farmers in Thanjavur. In most respects the contrast favored Vietnam, in spite of thirty years of intermittent warfare and of the devastating bombing raids carried out by the United States from 1965 to 1973. My account of my Vietnam journey is thus written partly against the backdrop of south India as well as of the antiwar movement in North America from 1965 to 1975.

For ten days a small group of women from the Foreign Affairs section of the Women's Union of Vietnam gave all or most of their time to showing me their country, answering my questions, and carefully explaining to me the goals and character of the revolution they are committed to serving throughout their lives. I am especially grateful to Nguyen Lê Khanh, my chief interpreter, who left her four-month-old son and worked to exhaustion to fulfill all my requests, to Vu Thi Liên and Tran Thi Hoan, who came with me on my tour and shared with me many of their thoughts and feelings, and to Vô Thi Thê, my senior hostess. To Nguyen Bich Liên and

Duong Thi Duyên, and to Quyên, the young man who drove us on our tour, I am grateful for many practical tasks carried out efficiently and with much kindness. To these and all the other friends who gave of their time, their work, and their affection, I give my deepest thanks for showing me what they mean when they say that their revolution is based on the combination of reason and love.

Vancouver, B.C.
October 1977

CHINA

Viet Bac

Red River

Black River

Ha Bac

Haiphong

Quang Ninh

Dien Bien Phu

Hanoi

Hong Gai

Thai Binh

20°

Nghê An

VIET

GULF OF TONKIN

HAINAN

Vientiane

Ha Tinh

LAOS

Mekong River

Quang Tri

Hue

THAILAND

NAM

Da Nang

15°

KAMPUCHEA

Binh Dinh

Phnom Penh

Ho Chi Minh City

10°

GULF OF SIAM

Tra Vinh

SOUTH CHINA SEA

International boundary

Railroad

River

Con Son Island

One inch equals 95 miles.

SOCIALIST REPUBLIC OF VIETNAM

1

Rangoon to Hanoi

November 10, 1976. I slept very badly in the Hotel Than-
ada (President Hotel) in Rangoon last night—a pity, on such a
momentous day. At U.S. $10 a day including food, the hotel
is reasonable, but my room was small and airless and the
climate sweltering. Over coffee with spam and eggs I revive
somewhat and exchange greetings with a young man from St.
Paul, Minnesota, my husband's home town. He and his wife
(who is down with malaria) are touring South and Southeast
Asia on their honeymoon. He seems awestruck to know that
I'm on my way to Hanoi. Like the others I have met since
Calcutta—a Canadian volunteer worker from Borneo, an
Indonesian diplomat, and a Burmese taxi driver—he respects
the Vietnamese and seems almost afraid of them for their
courage and victory. "You must be an important person to
be going there," he says. "Not at all," I reply; but I do rather
feel that I am!

The ride to the Rangoon airport is a lovely journey of grass
and trees, past the gold-domed pagoda and several august,
British-built mansions with faded paint. My porter, aged ten,
wants a ballpoint pen or a U.S. dollar, but I haven't any, so
he gets five chaks.

The Aeroflot personnel beam at me; they had given me up,
for I am four days late. On November 6, British Airways
cancelled its flight to Rangoon for the winter season without

informing my travel agent, and I have been pleading and fuming in Calcutta for three days. Foreign flights to Hanoi enter only from Vientiane, Peking, or Phnom Penh. This means that from Calcutta there are three flights a week via Dacca or Rangoon, both of which require formalities and visas for transit. In Rangoon I board a Russian jet flying from Moscow to Vientiane, and from there a four-engine Ilyushin suited to Hanoi's small airport.

Gert Christensen, a Danish development officer, talks to me in Rangoon and Vientiane. Gert advises on development programs in Kenya, Tanzania, Egypt, Bolivia, Ecuador, Sri Lanka, the Philippines, Bangladesh, India, and Vietnam. A new project will open in Burma in 1977. Altogether these programs total £60,000,000 sterling a year, half of which is spent in India and another third in Bangladesh and Vietnam. The Vietnamese projects concern fisheries, agriculture, and the provision of drinking water. Only gifts are given in the three main recipient countries; the rest receive soft loans, repayable without interest over thirty years.

My companion has a "liberal" attitude to the countries he works in. He stresses land reform as the key to agricultural development in Third World countries. In this respect, he says, India forms a glaring contrast to Vietnam, for in India the numerous acts have never been properly implemented, whereas in North Vietnam the land reform of 1955 was thorough and was followed by collectivization in 1959. Bangladesh, he says, is even worse than India: the landlords own the countryside, and private lawlessness and corruption prevail. There are still 850,000 refugees who live in pitiable conditions in three camps near Dacca left over from the war of 1971. I remind him that there are still four million refugees in Calcutta, mainly from the Indo-Pakistan war of 1946-1947, who live on the pavements or in one room shacks in slums.

In Vietnam the collective farms come directly under the state, but with peasant participation in their government and with informal guidance by units of the Workers' (Communist) Party. Vietnam's irrigation, Gert says, is far superior to India's because there are no hangups from private owners, small or big. Fields are large, their size rationalized to suit the needs of crops, irrigation, and transport. Both water supply and drainage are well organized. The building and operation of irrigation works are done mainly by hand but are excellent.

I contrast this silently with Thanjavur, where I've accompanied district development officers on visits to irrigation projects and have been told, and shown, how hard it is to build a path into the paddy fields, straighten a channel, or move a ditch two feet, because of the near impossibility of persuading private owners to yield an inch of land. For that reason, it is only on large and illegal private estates which far exceed the official ceiling of fifteen acres that projects which coordinate irrigation, transport, power, and optimal seeds and fertilizers can be implemented successfully. One such estate, for example, was locally reputed to cover 3,335 acres and was being developed with government subsidies during 1976. Such integrated projects have the advantages of scale of a Vietnamese cooperative, but they are very few, and their profits, of course, go only to a small number of landlords.

The south is more industrialized than the north, Christensen confirms. At the time of the revolution of 1945, what was then North Vietnam had a very few small industries, and in all of Indochina there were only about a quarter of a million modern wage workers, about a third of them on plantations. Since 1945, the north has been geared to war and to survival, although about 650,000 peasants were transferred from their villages to work in industry, construction, or transport between 1955 and 1965.[1] Now the Vietnamese want above all to industrialize rapidly in both north and south, a fact I know from reading First Secretary Lê Duân's Report to the First Convocation of the new National Assembly in Hanoi on June 25, 1975,[2] and from the current

Vietnamese slogan, "All for Production, All for Socialist Construction." To this end, Christensen says that the government is seeking World Bank loans and Western government aid as well as private investment, provided it can choose the projects and obtain desirable terms. Denmark, Sweden, and Norway provide aid to Vietnam; France, perhaps, soon will do so, and some French personnel have remained in, or are returning to, plantations and industries in the south. In October 1976 a Norwegian firm made a contract with the Vietnamese government to explore for offshore oil, and other Western firms are interested. Christensen thinks all this is badly needed, although he says that the Soviet Union, currently the most prominent aid donor, will not like it. He thinks that United States aid will eventually be forthcoming, and that it ought to be, as reparation for the war. He asserts that some "clearing up" has been done already: United States Marines partially de-mined Haiphong harbor as part of the Paris Agreement of 1973. Christensen says he saw them drinking one evening in a Haiphong bar. I am surprised and decide to ask about this in Hanoi.

Christensen confirms my impression that Soviet aid to Vietnam is now much more prominent than Chinese, and the presence of Soviet personnel is also greater. After the Paris Agreement of 1973 and the Thieu regime's refusal to implement it, Soviet military aid helped to hasten the Vietnamese victory. Although they maintain an official stance of equal relations with both powers, the Vietnamese, Christensen says, often praise the Soviet Union but do not nowadays praise China. He thinks that Soviet and perhaps West European influence will be more prominent than Chinese influence in Vietnam in the foreseeable future. I cannot assess this statement, although I know from several sources that Vietnam is seeking certain kinds of Western investment, both public and private.[3] I suspect, however, that my companion may be unconsciously exaggerating this because he has a stake in it. In Delhi at the Vietnamese embassy I have already encountered the characteristic Vietnamese refusal to discriminate between the Soviet Union and China. When I asked a diplomat there about the reports of Western aid, he replied that they were true but that Vietnam would rely chiefly on its own efforts and secondly on aid from the socialist camp. "Does that mean mainly the Soviet Union?" I asked. "From the socialist countries," he replied. "Or perhaps from China?" I pressed. "Well," he said gently, "from the socialist camp."

The big, shabby Aeroflot jet to Vientiane is almost full. About ninety percent of the passengers are Russian; they include a few women and children. The stewardesses are neat, plain, and plump—a contrast to the Indian and North American sylphs to whom I am accustomed. We are not overfed; only soft drinks are served on the five-hour journey to Hanoi. Near Rangoon all is lush and green, the paddy fields like carpet moss, the trees like sphagnum. From noon to one-thirty we pass through spectacular peaked white clouds. As we cross from Thailand to Laos there are low brown mountains, forests, and rock outcroppings, with sparse habitations. Approaching Vientiane, big yellow and green paddy fields appear amid the forest and rolling hills. The Mekong River is winding, tawny, and reddish, the city quite small and square, with scattered houses.

Incongruously, we touch down to the accompaniment of American pop music over the Aeroflot intercom, and I see the Laotian flag with its red and navy bands and white central circle. The airport is almost deserted. Two slightly built young soldiers guard it and a group of young women in white blouses and black pajamas usher us into the transit lounge. One of them makes the announcements in French, Laotian, and English in a soft, caressing voice. The airport hall, built by the French, is beautiful in stained wood with a delicately carved screen between the two main sections. There is a store with magazines in several languages and tourist bric-á-brac, but it is locked.

The Russians are tired, having traveled nineteen hours. They carry heavy hand baggage with fur wraps and coats. The men wear lounge suits, the women pants or short dresses with nylons and neat shoes. Some of them have permanent waves, and some have dyed hair. Most of them seem big and stout. There is a slender, glamorous girl in a black sweater and bell-bottomed pants. I go over to her and ask, "Are you French?" No, Roumanian. Now for the first time Gert points out a few Vietnamese, including a soldier who laughs for joy and throws his olive-green helmet into the air. At Vientiane the weather is still hot and humid and there is a heavy thunder shower.

Our Ilyushin follows the Mekong part way to Hanoi, then leaves it at 4 P.M. Beyond Vientiane there is a beautiful, wide plain with trees and fields, I think just south of the Plain of Jars of military fame. After we leave the Mekong come hills and forests again and, at last, the Red River (but from here brown, or slaty gray) and around it, vast lakes of paddy fields, some half yellow to the harvest. We cross the river and touch down.

The airfield is large, with about twenty Soviet and Vietnamese planes, but the green buildings seem tiny and defenseless, somewhat like the Leeds-Bradford airport in Yorkshire or Cochin in South India. Our entry is easy. A few young soldiers in olive uniforms stand around; one of them collects our passports and drops them onto a table behind him in the doorway. I see my friend Võ Thi Thê of the Women's Union smiling welcome, holding a large bouquet and surrounded by an eager group of women. For a few minutes it is all hugs, kisses on both cheeks, and laughter. They tell me they will have my visa extended as I am late and a full program has been prepared. This will be interesting, too, they say, as the provincial party congresses begin on November 15 in preparation for the Fourth Party Congress in Hanoi from December 10 to 20.

Six of the women will often accompany me. All are

married, all are members of the International Affairs branch of the Women's Union, and I think that all are members or probationary members of the Workers' Party.[4] Each of them speaks two to five languages in addition to her own. Their work involves guiding foreign delegates; writing and translating stories, poems, histories, and news articles on Vietnam for foreign distribution; and forming a liaison between the Women's Union and women's liberation and peace groups abroad. Vô Thi Thê, a tall, dignified woman of fifty-six, attended the Indochinese and United States women's conference in Vancouver, B.C. in 1971.[5] A professor of literature and the daughter of a scholar, she comes from Hue but moved north with the regroupment of Communists during Ngô Dinh Diem's repression of 1955–1956. Her father and two brothers had already been killed in the late 1940s during the war against the French invaders. Her mother remained in Hue and after the liberation last year Thê went south to visit her for the first time in twenty years. Since we last met ill health has driven Thê into retirement, but she continues to help guide the Women's Union and to meet foreign guests. Both Thê and Duong Thi Duyên, an attractive, energetic woman of about forty, have elder sons in universities in the Soviet Union. Thê's younger son and Duyên's daughter study sciences at the Hanoi Polytechnic, and Thê's daughter is in high school.

Vu Thi Liên, or "Big Liên," warm and gentle, is fifty and has three grownup daughters in the Hanoi Polytechnic. Until three years ago Liên taught high school mathematics. She left that on being asked to work for the union. She speaks French and German well and English moderately well. In her spare time she studies Marxism-Leninism and hopes to become a member of the party. Liên's husband is still away in the army and is able to meet her only two days a month. Nguyen Bich Liên, or "Little Liên," twenty-eight, is shy and eagerly helpful; she transports my luggage, reclaims my passport, obtains my visa extension from the Ministry of Foreign Affairs, runs errands, and makes me comfortable. Liên has a girl of five in kindergarten and a boy of eight in school. Nguyen Lê Khanh, a sturdy, bright-faced young woman, is my main interpreter; she is twenty-six and has a four-month-old son of whom she is laughingly proud. She is friendly and full of fun, seems highly intelligent, speaks excellent English rather slowly, and is very patient. Tran Thi Hoan, in her forties, has two older sons in college near Hanoi and a daughter in the tenth standard in school. She lives with her two younger children, for her husband is a hydraulics engineer in the army stationed in Ho Chi Minh City (formerly Saigon). Hoan has been in the Women's Union since 1945. Like Vô Thi Thê, she speaks excellent French and halting English. Small and slender, she has a delicate, porcelain beauty and an air of fragility, and is chic in her Parisian-style pale blue knitwear and black satin pants. In fact she was a fighter with the Vietminh, undertook dangerous missions, and more recently has done hard physical and organizational work among the peasants.

Hoan and Little Liên go off to organize my baggage while the rest of us pile into a Volga for the trip to Hanoi. Although I have previously met only Thê, all the women know the names of my husband and son and are eager with questions in French and English. Quyên, a shy, handsome youth of twenty-two, is driving us on our tour. The women tell me he comes from Nghê An, like Ho Chi Minh, and he grins with pleasure.

There are more cars and far more heavy trucks on the road than I had expected. Most of them come from the Soviet Union, some from other Eastern European countries or from China. Private people do not own cars; they belong to one or another branch of the government and are loaned out for periods of time or for special events. On either side of the road we pass yellow paddy fields, some of them already cut, and large tracts of potatoes, tomatoes, green vegetables, sugarcane, and maize. The road forks, with branches to Hanoi and Haiphong. There is a tall pile of rubble at the fork, and I am told it is one of the few places near Hanoi where evidence of the bombing is still visible. The rest has been cleared away, and Liên tells me they have rebuilt all eleven million houses and other structures in the north that had been destroyed by "the U.S. aggressors." Much new building is in progress. A modern, planned industrial city, New Hanoi, is going up about twenty kilometers west of the capital, which will now be called Old Hanoi. A large bridge is being constructed across the Red River to serve the new city.[6]

We are approaching Long Bien bridge, the old Red River bridge to Hanoi. It spans two wide branches of the river, divided by a fertile strip of vegetable fields. In the southwest monsoon of July and August it normally floods the strip and the surrounding plain to a width of about two miles. The remaining countryside, and Hanoi, are protected by dikes—long, straight earthen walls from about six to twelve feet high. "Did the U.S. airforce really bomb the dikes?" I ask, for bombing the dikes was an atrocity the American peace movement had feared would flood vast areas and create catastrophic famines. "Of course!" says Khanh, "We were mending them all the time." The dike on the far side of the river which protects Hanoi was bombed repeatedly but each time was rebuilt immediately so that the damage to crops and homes was never devastating. Liên says that this year the river did not flood because of the drought which has affected all of South and Southeast Asia, so the crops are poorer. Even so, the alluvial fields of maize and paddy (rice in the husk) look lush to me; they belong to cooperatives which provision Hanoi. Liên adds that the Red River floods more and is less stable than the Mekong because its delta is less ancient: it was formed after the Vietnamese of the Neolithic Age had settled in the region, and took its present shape toward 3,000 B.C. The River's instability creates severe drainage problems, but the red silt which gives it its name is richly fertile.

At 5 P.M., rush hour, the bridge is crowded. There is a railway in the middle with opposing streams of motor traffic on either side. Hundreds of cyclists crowd the paths beside the traffic lanes. The trucks and cars move slowly, among them an occasional oxcart. Most of the carts and plows here are drawn by single oxen similar to the humpbacked beasts of north India; they are much larger and sturdier than south Indian draft cattle, which go in pairs. The bridge was built by the French in 1904, Liên says, but it has been rebuilt many times in the recent war, sometimes throughout the night. The worst damage came in Nixon's Christmas bombing of 1972, but even then the bridge was rebuilt in a month. Bombing was not allowed to halt the traffic flow, for dozens of small motor ferries bearing vehicles, goods, and passengers ply constantly across the many branches of the river between here and the coast. From the bridge we can also see the partly covered houseboats of fishermen, along with small rowboats, ferries, and punts. Beneath the bridge on the alluvial strip lies a tangled heap of iron, "the debris of war," says Thê. Khanh points to the lofty parapets and tells me that antiaircraft fighters stood on them, shooting at bombers.

The road into Hanoi is lined with small wooden houses, teashops, and other stalls. Similar streets could be seen almost anywhere in India, except that here the roads are swept bare and washed clean, there are no open sewers along their edges, and no one sits on the pavement, lounging or begging. Further into the city come handsome avenues with trees and large French-style houses. Many have been taken over as party, trade union, or government offices, and some as small factories and workers' recreation halls. We pass a large building which Liên tells me is a children's palace, for play and organized activities after school or on Saturdays.

My hotel is on such a street. It is an old French building, like most of the Hanoi hotels apart from the Victory, a new, modern tourist hotel built and donated by Cuba on a lake some miles outside the city. Mine is called the Hotel of the Restoration of the Sword. A young woman sits writing at a table inside the door; Khanh tells me she is preparing for the party congress, when the hotel will be filled with delegates. About 150 are expected from the communist parties of foreign countries. We enter a large room divided by screens into dining room and bar-lounge, and sit down to discuss my program.

The proceedings are somewhat ceremonious. After tea is poured into small, dainty cups, Thê greets me with a short speech of welcome, thanking Canadian women for their "valuable aid to Vietnam" and me for making the long journey, and wishing me a successful visit and my whole family health and happiness. The program, typed in Vietnamese and English, is then produced. It is full and varied but not too laborious, leaving time for walks and rest. I am asked if I want to add anything, and I request a longer period in an agricultural cooperative, an interview on ideology with some leading member of the Workers' Party, and a visit to the Bach Mai hospital.

The hotel is named for a nearby lake. In 1427 a Vietnamese king was fighting foreign aggressors, after a ten-year invasion. "Were they Chinese?" I ask. "Yes!" says Khanh, laughing. The king lost his sword, but a tortoise came out of the lake and gave him another. The king slew his enemies and the tortoise returned, reclaimed the sword, and disappeared in the lake. "And the moral of that," says Khanh, "is that even Heaven helps the Vietnamese when they are invaded by foreigners."

The party breaks up with handshakes, hugs, and farewells, and Khanh and Little Liên install me and my luggage in an upstairs room. They arrange my flowers, ply me with cigarettes, and offer to help me unpack. More hugs and farewells from these delightful, affectionate young women, and I am left to a quiet dinner and a restful evening.

My room is big, with an entry porch. The French-style window with an arch and small leaded panes open onto an upstairs courtyard decorated with potted plants. Below in the yard is a pump near the kitchen. I hear laughter or singing when young men and women come to draw water. The room is clean and plain, with yellow walls, a blocked fireplace, and a mantelpiece. The two double beds have mosquito nets. There are two blue plastic armchairs, a big wardrobe, an occasional table with pretty tea things and a large thermos of very hot water. There is a massive desk, a bedside table with reading lamp and nightlight, a floodlight in one wall, and an old ceiling fan with a light bulb hung from its center. The bathroom is large and old, the plumbing ancient but operational. Only one tap—cold—in the washbasin works, so I bathe from a bowl in the bath, shivering, for Hanoi is cool after Rangoon and after the sweltering months in Thanjavur. There is a large, empty refrigerator from the Soviet Union stored in the bathroom.

Downstairs, two smiling young women serve dinner. Like my hosts from the Women's Union they wear flowered print blouses and black pants; one has pink curlers in her hair. I am alone at the table but a group of youths drink beer in the bar and a young man irons shirts at a corner table. At another table a girl is arranging flowers. The waitresses talk to me in Vietnamese to make me feel welcome, although they know I don't understand it. The table is set with knife and fork placed on a wooden stand—French style, I think. The meal is plain and very good: tender beef chunks, thick slices of firm white bread, rice, cabbage, and spiced meatballs, with a choice of lemonade, wine, or beer. Bananas and pineapple follow.

At 9 P.M. the door is half open and I wander into the street. Across the road is a dingy one-story factory making automobile parts. Lights are on, machines run softly, and through the darkened panes I can see white figures sitting at work tables. As in most industrial enterprises there are three shifts, and the factory runs all night. Now the street lamps are lit and around me everything is calm. I look up and down the avenue of trees and think of the women I have met. How soft and feminine they are!—how lovable, and how disciplined and competent. Two Hondas, no doubt from the south, purr softly by; then a group of boys appear, talking quietly, and a couple of young men, whistling, on the seat and carrier of a bicycle. I wonder how on earth they all managed through the war and the bombing, and how they can be so cheerful, so relaxed yet orderly. I am happy, and feel at home as I go in to bed.

2

History of the
Workers' Party

November 11. The Women's Union operates from a pleasant house on Hàng Chuối Street, another tree-lined avenue a few blocks from my hotel. There is a pile of rubble in the yard, not from bombing but from a disused air-raid shelter. Bombs did fall on Hàng Chuối Street, but the ruins have been cleared away. Downstairs, the reception room contains glass cabinets with art objects and bric-à-brac from women's groups in many countries. Upstairs are the offices where typing and printing are carried on.

At 8:30 A.M. Professor Van Tao, a quiet-voiced, slender man in his forties who is deputy head of the Institute of History at Hanoi University, arrives to give me a lecture on the history of the Vietnam Workers' Party; it turns into a three-hour seminar. After tea and thanks for "help in the struggle against the U.S. aggressors," we start in with Khanh interpreting. Here is a slightly edited version of her translation:

"Our Workers' Party was founded in February 1930. In our encounter with French colonialism, the first shot was fired by the French in 1847, and in 1858 France invaded Vietnam. The first attack came at Da Nang in South Vietnam; later they invaded the North. They wanted mainly to rob our country, for Vietnam is rich in resources and its people are clever. It took the French thirty years to conquer our people.

"Most Vietnamese were Buddhists then, although the Portuguese had introduced Christianity in the seventeenth century. The French colonialists, however, brought in numerous Catholic priests in the nineteenth century and converted a small population favorable to them.

"Before the conquest, Vietnam had been unified under a feudal dynasty with its capital at Hue. Laos and Cambodia were separate kingdoms. The feudal princes formed two wings, one favoring negotiation with the French and the other, continued fighting. Some of the princes helped to lead rebellions against the invaders, but most of these struggles were led by commoners. At Yen Thê in Bac Giang province there was a continuous thirty-year peasant war; the people used country weapons and rifles, though they had no cannon.

"Dê Tham and Phan Dinh Phûng were famous leaders in this period—all our people know about them. Their followers learned to make weapons in imitation of the French, in addition to those they already had.

"One may wonder why the French were successful. I think it was because of the feudal dynasty. It was backward and corrupt and was not developing the country's natural resources and economy. If the French had not come we would have had to turn against the princes anyway. As it was, most of them allied with the French against the people. In the kingdom of Minh Mênh, there had already been a hundred popular uprisings against the Nguyen dynasty. The Nguyen betrayed the people's interests, and they fought back.

"French colonialism gave birth to our working class. By 1929 there was a total of 220,000 workers, including those in transport and on the plantations. About 80,000 of them were in industry, including mines and transport. Our total population was then about 20 million, whereas today it is about 50 million according to the census of 1975. The percentage of workers is even now very low, but Vietnamese workers have special qualities. Having been created by imperialist industry, they were oppressed both as a class and as part of the nation. This gave them a double hatred of imperialism.

"The Vietnamese bourgeoisie developed after the first

World War. They were a merchant bourgeoisie at first, and then came some industrialists. They were mainly in mining, especially coal and tin. The agricultural capitalists mainly grew rubber, tea, and coffee, especially in the south.

"The working class was highly concentrated in certain industries. Five to seven thousand of them were miners and about three thousand were transport workers. Twenty thousand rubber workers were located in a single place. This gave them advantages, for the capitalists were fewer and more scattered.

"Altogether our people suffered from three kinds of exploitation—from imperialism, capitalism, and feudalism. The feudal lords were closely involved with imperialism both in the extraction of resources and in their relationships, although on Vietnamese farms the French colonialists drove out the feudals whenever they wanted land for their plantations. Among the Vietnamese there were many kinds of landlords, large and small. The bigger landlords cultivated mainly with tenants, and on paddy lands they took two-thirds of the crop as rent; in addition the tenants had to pay their own cultivation expenses. The tenants also had to give forced labor on the landlord's demesne as well as gifts at festivals. Smashing feudalism meant smashing imperialism too.

"Our working class derived from the peasantry. We have no big cities in Vietnam; even Hanoi has only 1,400,000. Of 100 workers in 1956, 99 came directly from the peasants. Peasants and workers thus are closely linked, but this also means the workers have the peasants' weak points—their slowness and lack of organization and the formal, ceremonial manners of the countryside. At harvest time our workers would leave the factories to go and harvest with the peasants—they were really half workers, half peasants. We had no tradition of worker families but only of peasant families, for there were very few cases in which both father and sons were workers.

"Our working class came into being just at the time when

Marxism-Leninism was being introduced into Vietnam. Ho Chi Minh had returned from France with a proletarian viewpoint and he transmitted Marxism-Leninism to the Vietnamese. The Second International betrayed Marxism-Leninism but Ho followed the Third International, thus giving leadership to the workers of Vietnam.

"So the Party was founded in 1930 and gave its members a training in Marxism-Leninism. Marx said that the proletariat of the world must unite, but Lenin developed the idea of uniting not only the workers, but the nation. Ho Chi Minh used this ideology creatively, adapting it to Vietnam. Our movement thus became a national liberation movement as well as a workers' movement and part of the international movement. There were those who did not understand and thought it was wrong, even in our Party, and who went on talking about the need for international revolution only. They thought a national movement could not be proletarian, but as they lived longer they understood that it was right. The combination of the workers' struggle with the national liberation movement was developed first, and most creatively, in Vietnam."

"What about China?" I ask. "Would you say that it developed later there?" Van Tao is rather stern at this point, however, and says that we are not discussing China, but Vietnam.

"The proletariat started out with patriotism, love of country. Ho Chi Minh pointed out that the workers start with that. They had been robbed of their country and were also being exploited by capitalism and imperialism. The peasants could not have the same consciousness as the workers but they too were well aware of having their country taken from them. So patriotic consciousness preceded proletarian. To save the country we had to follow Marxist-Leninist ideology; there was none other suitable. Ho Chi Minh said, 'Only socialism and communism can completely free the people of oppressed nations,' and he was right. We may ask why the workers were able to lead the peasants when their own class was so new, and why the peasants followed them. It was because the workers could meet the needs of the peasants, hence the size of the resistance. The peasants set up many soviets with workers' help, especially in Nghê An and Ha Tinh provinces. Since the reunification of the country this area is now one province, called Ha Tinh.

"Workers led the revolution and workers and peasants were its main force. In the national revolution against imperialism the petty bourgeoisie, the national bourgeoisie—all patriotic persons and even some landlords—were involved. In our country, however, the workers were the leaders, whereas in some other countries the national revolution was shared by workers and bourgeoisie. In Vietnam the national bourgeoisie was incapable of leading the struggle, although it wanted to. Indeed, in 1927 a National Party led by the bourgeoisie was formed and gave rise to a peasant insurrection, but it failed because its line was wrong. This movement came to grief in February 1930, and in the very same month the Workers' Party was founded. After that the peasants followed the Workers' Party.

"In 1930 our party's aim was to carry out a bourgeois revolution, including an agrarian revolution, in order to overthrow the French imperialists and the feudal rulers, to gain complete independence, and to lead Vietnam straight toward socialism and communism while skipping the capitalist stage. In 1951 we began to call this the 'national democratic revolution.' 'National' meant driving out the foreigners, while 'democratic' meant giving the land to the peasants. The national and the democratic revolutions were combined, but it was necessary for us to complete the national revolution before we could complete the democratic.

"Thus, our August revolution of 1945 had the slogan of national liberation, but we did not move on to full-scale land reform until 1953 when we had achieved decisive superiority over the colonialists. Immediately after the August revolution, in October 1945, we did confiscate the lands of treach-

erous landlords who sided with the returning French colonialists, and gave these lands to the tenants who had worked them. But we left the patriotic landlords temporarily in charge of their lands, although we never hid the fact that democracy and socialism were our ultimate goals. As interim measures we merely reduced the patriotic landlords' rents by 25 to 50 percent and taxed them on behalf of the nation. In this way we attacked the power of the colonial regime while also persuading the landlords to help in the national front for liberation. The patriotic landlords knew that they must follow us, for only the workers and peasants could drive out the colonialists.

"In 1953, when we had gained ascendance over the French armies, we began the full democratic land reform; we completed it in 1957. During this period all lands were taken from the landlords and distributed to individual cultivators wherever we held power; we were thus able to complete the national democratic revolution throughout North Vietnam while also distributing considerable land in South Vietnam before the French departed. However, we could never have made the democratic revolution without making the national revolution first; it was a tactical decision to stress national liberation first.

"When the national democratic revolution was completed in North Vietnam in 1957, it was seen to be necessary to go straight on to the socialist revolution. This involved collectivization of the land, which began in 1959; the organization of handicraft workers in cooperatives; and the redemption of private businesses by the state.

"Ho Chi Minh's greatness was his insight that socialism could triumph in a backward country, but that it must first be preceded by a national democratic revolution. Lenin had already said that socialism would win in some backward countries, but not everyone believed him. They thought it could happen only in industrial societies. But in 1930 our Indochinese Communist Party had already stated in its pro-

gram that socialism was possible in Indochina. Now we have it, and we see that our line was correct. The decision was right though the path was difficult.

"Some of our friends thought we could not advance to socialism in the north while fighting U.S. imperialism in the south. They thought the destruction would be too great. Yet in fact, we couldn't have fought successfully or helped the south to struggle without a socialist revolution. It was that which allowed our industry to develop so rapidly. In 1955 we had only 85 factories in North Vietnam but now we have more than 1,000. The wartime development of our agriculture was also unprecedented. Before the war our productivity was less than three tons of paddy per hectare per year, but during the war it went up to five or even seven tons in many areas. Two thousand coops now produce more than five tons per year, and the average in the north is now more than four tons per year.

"I want to stress the conditions that are essential for a socialist revolution. First, we must have *a strong party of the working class,* which follows the path of Marxism-Leninism. This party is based on the viewpoint of the working class, not that of the bourgeoisie, not that of revisionism, and not that of the peasantry. It sounds easy, but the greatness of Vietnam becomes evident in light of the difficulties experienced in the international movement, in the communist movements of other countries.

"The party must have a united leadership. We have never had a split inside our party. This was partly because Ho Chi Minh himself trained our cadres and gave them a correct ideology. Self-criticism and mutual criticism are essential for progress and for helping one another. Criticism must include both reason and love (which we sometimes translate as 'sentiment'); it must not be destructive. Individuals' consciousness varies, so we must be creative with them. Much discussion is necessary to develop consciousness. After that, the minority must follow the majority. The minority can keep its own

opinion, but it must act in accordance with the decisions of the majority. The outcome will show who is right, but meanwhile the majority must not reject the minority. I want to repeat that reason and love are necessary—love is a tradition in Vietnam. Ho Chi Minh taught that Marxism-Leninism is a fight to bring love, not hate, and that it is not fighting for fighting's sake. The fight must go on only against the enemy; there must be reason and love among our friends. But even our captured enemies we must treat humanely, with generosity. In our ancient history, even when we fought with bows and arrows, we cared for the troops who surrendered. In 1967, when we had the Congress of Heroes and Fighters, President Ho Chi Minh's final words were, 'When you fight, don't forget each other, and when you win, don't forget each other.'

"When the delegation of the Communist Party of Japan came to pay tribute to Ho Chi Minh after the construction of his mausoleum, they said that the Vietnamese had deep hatred for their enemies, but warm hearts, love, and fidelity towards their friends. Our First Secretary, Lê Duân, said recently, 'If we see a woman drawing a cart in harness and are not moved, we are not socialists.'[1] He added that an intelligent woman is one with a tradition of full feeling towards the country; she must transmit this love to her children so that they will have it too. When Lê Duân was in prison under the French, he questioned literally hundreds of his comrades, and all of them said they had had gentle, kindhearted mothers who had given them abundant feelings. That is why Ho Chi Minh said, 'The heroic mother of Vietnam has given birth to heroic sons and girls.' Heroism includes both a fighting spirit and love.

"Second, we must have *a firm alliance between the peasants and workers.* This again is easy to understand but hard to apply. Peasants are 80 percent of the people of Vietnam. Workers in the north are still fewer than 10 percent, and were only 3 percent before. The aim of the worker-peasant alliance

is to ensure that the peasants follow proletarian leadership, and to maintain the success of the working-class line. In every period we must meet the peasants' needs. In the Soviet Union, for example, the land was not given individually to the peasants; it was collectivized right away. In Vietnam we had to distribute the land individually because that was the peasants' deepest wish. They were even allowed to sell it if they liked. But after some time the peasants realized from experience that they couldn't carry on alone. They had to cooperate. They maintained their private lands for only two years after the land reform, and began cooperation in 1959. The workers cannot lead the revolution unless they understand the special feelings and aspirations of the peasants.

"Third, we must learn *how to unite the whole people.* This is indispensable; we even declared it in the founding of our party. Our party was aware of a special Vietnamese tradition of solidarity and unity, and so it brought about a close combination between the nation and the proletariat, and between the proletariat and the anticolonial struggle. This is hard to carry out and depends on concrete situations. The first need is to free the nation and bring happiness to the people. Ho Chi Minh said we could do that only through socialism and communism. In every period we have to see to it that the working class will benefit the nation. In 1954, when the Vietnamese were still very poor, Ho Chi Minh said that if we obtained national independence without happiness and freedom, it would be meaningless. Even the bourgeoisie and the patriotic landlords want the country to be free and happy. So the sole aim of the party must be to liberate the nation, and then the working class—this is happiness and freedom.

"In the unity of the whole people there is love. Love is also included in the fighting. When they destroyed the feudal regime, the working class declared that the landlords could live and enjoy life like other workers. The children of the landlords were provided with jobs and professions. After the

reform of the national bourgeoisie, they too were allowed to direct small factories and other enterprises.

"One foreign scientist asked us, 'Isn't it true that the more the revolution succeeds, the smaller the front becomes?' The answer is no, on the contrary, the bigger the front becomes. For example, we have had three fronts, the Vietminh (Vietnam Independence League), founded in 1941; the Liên Viet (Vietnam National Union Association), founded in 1946; and the South Vietnam National Front for Liberation, founded in 1960. In their respective areas, these fronts got bigger all the time. In the course of the revolution people lose only exploitation, but they gain patriotism and freedom.

"The fourth point is that we must have *international solidarity*. We must strengthen the solidarity among the socialist countries, and between ourselves and the communist movements in all the five continents, while drawing lessons from them. We must develop our armed forces to fight all oppressors, and we must consolidate our defense.

"Fifth, to carry through the revolution we must have *a strong and solid government led by the proletarian class*. In the democratic national front, the government represents both the working class and the peasantry, but under socialism it is a government solely of the working class. That is, we now have a dictatorship of the proletariat.[2] We have had it since 1954 in North Vietnam and are now extending it to the south since the country became united. In the south the national democratic revolution was accomplished during the war against the U.S. imperialists and after the liberation of 1975. During the war, the liberated regions were under the leadership of our party with its base in North Vietnam. In the cities we had to carry out the national democratic revolution after the war, in 1975.

"Now the whole country is moving toward socialism. This is a festival for everyone, which celebrates the twenty years during which we developed socialism in the north. In the north we must push up the building of socialism, and in the south we must carry out the reforms necessary for moving to socialism. The building of socialism is more important than the reforms.

"Ours is a country of small production. The big factories in the south are not enough for building socialism. We must have big and heavy industry. Our greatest concern now is for developing industry and agriculture, for increased production is essential for socialist construction. We want to develop a modern agricultural and industrial base in twenty years. This was President Ho Chi Minh's dearest wish when he passed away.

"After thirty years of war we are still very poor, and we have lost many people. But we are proud of our people. During the war we had no starvation or epidemics. As everyone knows, hunger and epidemics are common in wars—but not in Vietnam. Our medical services and our education developed strongly. We were able to advance scientific research on behalf of the whole world, for example, in treating tuberculosis, in performing liver sections, and in new kinds of blood transfusions. We also learned how to cure and prevent leprosy and drug addiction. In education and science we had unprecedented growth.

"Today we have a brighter and more splendid future than ever before. Our inherited wealth is our patriotism, solidarity, love, curiosity, unity, fidelity, identity, and courage. Our very precious treasures are Marxism-Leninism and the party of the proletariat. One of our problems is how to combine ideology and national tradition. If we don't combine them creatively we shall fall into the rut of narrow national-mindedness. Yet if we don't promote tradition either, it's not enough. Martin Bernal, the British historian, visited us in 1972. He said, 'It seems to me that in Vietnam there are two apparent contradictions, but you have somehow turned them into unities. One is that the Workers' Party promotes patriotism to the highest degree, yet it also promotes international unity. The other is that the party has waged a very large campaign in the countryside, and workers are less than 10 percent of the population, yet the party follows a proletarian line.' Well, we agree with these remarks, and they point to the reasons for our success.

"To Huu is our most famous living poet and is also the secretary of the central committee of our party. He said once that the struggle of the 30 million Vietnamese was also that of the 3 billion then in the world. He is right—we are struggling not only for ourselves, but for humankind."

Professor Van Tao's lecture moved me very much: he spoke with such passion and intensity and had gone to such great trouble for a single listener. Khanh, too, worked very seriously and with deep concentration in interpreting his words, while Hoan, Duyên, and the two Liêns wrote busily. I was, and am, puzzled by the Vietnamese communists' firm belief that the working class led their revolution and that they now have a dictatorship of the proletariat; and Professor Van Tao's explanation did not remove my difficulties, although it did confirm my impression of the Leninist orthodoxy of the party position. I did not feel able, however, to challenge this obviously central tenet so early in my visit.

Instead, in the intermission I asked Professor Van Tao about educational progress in Vietnam. Before the revolution of 1945, he told me, an estimated 95 percent of the people were illiterate. Only 47,000 children were in schools. Today more than 10 million are in schools catering for children aged seven to sixteen. More than 6 million of them are in the north; more than 4 million, in the south. Vietnam now has thirty-seven universities. School and university classes normally contain about 30 to 40 students; because of the shortage of buildings the schools run two six-hour shifts per day. The south is still more backward than the north; some southern classes may contain 100 or even 200 students. Women make up 30 to 40 percent of the admissions in universities each year, and 50 percent in elementary and high schools. Until this year girls were required to achieve only fourteen out of thirty points on their university examination papers, while boys must gain fifteen points. This year, however, women have been recognized as roughly equal in competence with men, so the grading is now equal. The Vietnamese are proud of the fact that in a recent international competition in mathematics, in which Austria previously held the lead, the first two prizes were won by Vietnamese women, while a Vietnamese man also won recognition.

When the lecture ended there was time for only one final question. I asked Van Tao, "What do you consider the main contribution of President Ho Chi Minh to communist theory and practice?" I had brought this question from India, partly at the request of friends. I had thought that the answer might have to do with military strategy or with some special gift for uniting the workers and peasants. After a moment's thought Van Tao replied, "Undoubtedly, it was the combination of reason and love." For me this was the morning's central message.

3

A Revolutionary Museum

November 11. Hanoi's Revolutionary or National Museum is situated next to the Museum of Archaeology and History in the old French Customs House. Dao Phiêu, the middle-aged director, radiates warmth and intelligence. Under his and Khanh's guidance, the afternoon of my first day in Hanoi turns into an exploration of pity and terror, of heroism and love.

The museum was founded in 1959. It depicts the Vietnamese struggles against French, Japanese, and United States' imperialism in the context of the nation's age-old fight for independence from foreign invaders. Four million foreigners have visited it, including "many heads and vice-heads of states." Portable exhibitions are taken to other cities, especially to Saigon (now Ho Chi Minh City) and other parts of south Vietnam since the liberation of the south in April 1975. About a million south Vietnamese have seen these exhibitions or have visited the museum since the country was reunified in June 1976.

The first hall sets the stage with maps and pictures of Vietnam's beauties and resources and with portraits and possessions of warriors through history. There is a mammoth bronze war drum of about 2400 B.C., intricately decorated with battle scenes. Much later, we see huge wooden pylons with iron tips left over from a naval battle against Mongol invaders from China in 1288. The stakes were driven into the mouth of the Bach Dang river in Ha Long Bay, north of Haiphong, and the Mongol fleet which had sailed up the river was destroyed when 100 of its junks broke up on the stakes as they tried to leave at low tide. There are letters written by Nguyen Trai, a famous scholar and general who aided the aristocrat and future king, Lê Loi, to repel Ming invaders in 1427 after a ten-year war. And there are books, calendars, portraits, and novels of other great national scholars, such as Nguyen Du (1765–1820), a poet who criticized the decadent feudal society of the late eighteenth century and depicted the sufferings and social convulsions of the poor around the time of the Tayson peasant rebellion of 1771–1789. His master-piece, *Kieu,* a 3,254-line verse novel, was and is a favorite with both peasants and scholars, for it epitomizes the growing popular opposition to the oppression of the poor and of women that marked the period. It tells the story of a beautiful and talented young woman, doomed to fifteen years of tribulation by the cupidity of a mandarin. Transgressing orthodox Confucian ethics, it satirizes the corrupt court and the misery of arranged marriage, glorifies a rebel leader similar to the heroes of the Tayson rebellion, and justifies romantic adultery. It also defends the motives and purity of women forced into prostitution by an unjust society.

We pass to a hall showing early struggles against the French colonialists and instances of their oppression. A French proclamation of the late nineteenth century is framed here. It sets out regulations regarding prostitution, a vice that increased greatly during French rule and during the United States occupation, and that is only now finally being eradicated since the departure of United States troops and the liberation of Saigon. Portraits depict feudal resistance leaders of the late nineteenth century such as Phan Dinh Phùng of Nghê Tinh province and Hoang Hoa Tham of Ha Bac, who led the thirty-year peasant war of Yen Thê in that province; both leaders deeply influenced Ho Chi Minh. Here are pictures and specimens of stocks and head frames in which the French authorities imprisoned patriotic rebels and beat them, sometimes to death. There are portraits of martyrs from 1886 to 1930: women tortured and killed for trying to poison troops of the French army, groups of prisoners executed in 1908 for resistance against taxes, and seventy-two "bourgeois leaders," headed by the nationalist hero Nguyen Thai Hoc, who were executed in 1930 after an uprising that failed. The whole exhibit is an illustration of Van Tao's lecture of this morning, as, of course, my hosts meant it to be.[1]

The hall commemorating the early history of the Vietnam Communist Party contains a photograph of the ship on which Ho Chi Minh first sailed to France as a galley hand in 1911. Born as Nguyen Sinh Cung in 1890 in Namlieu village of Nghê An province in North Vietnam, Ho called himself Van Ba on the ship, and in France and England lived as Nguyen Ai Quoc, the name he retained until the 1930s; evidently he was early suspected of political activism by the French authorities. In France and England, where he traveled in order to study the European working class and the history of colonialism, Ho worked as a snow sweeper, furnace stoker, cook, draftsman, and photography worker. There is a picture of the upper room in Paris where Ho retouched photographs in 1920-1923, a French calling card inscribed "Nguyen Ai Quoc," and a photograph of Ho among his French comrades at the founding of the French Communist Party in 1920. There are pictures of Lenin and of the October Revolution, which more than any other single event determined the course of Ho Chi Minh's life. Newsprint, documents, and photographs record his founding of the Group of Vietnamese Patriots living in France in 1921; their newspaper *Le Paria* which he started in Paris in 1922; Ho's book, written in France, *Le Procès de la Colonisation Française,* and an early document, *Vindication of the People of Annam.*

In December 1924, at the request of the Fifth Congress of the Communist International, Ho moved to China with a mandate to guide revolutionary movements throughout Southeast Asia. In Canton he joined a group of Vietnamese patriots and communists exiled for staging strikes and demonstrations againt French rule in Vietnam. There he founded the Vietnam Revolutionary Youth League, the first Indochinese communist front. He brought out its journal, *Youth,* and wrote *The Road of Revolution,* a training manual for young revolutionaries. These documents, shown here, were circulated illegally in Vietnam. Three regional Communist parties, offshoots of the Youth League, were founded in Vietnam in 1929: the Indochinese Communist Party of Ho Chi Minh in North Vietnam, the Tan Viet Communist League in the central region and the Annamese Communist Party in the south. After they had contended for influence for a year, in 1930 the Communist International sent Ho Chi Minh to Hong Kong, where he succeeded in amalgamating them into the Vietnam Communist Party, which soon became the Communist Party of Indochina. The museum displays its request, in English, for admission to the Communist International and its founding proclamation. The goals inscribed there are:

1. Overthrowing the French imperialists and the feudalists, making Virtnam wholly independent;

2. Setting up a worker-peasant-soldier government;

3. Organizing a worker-peasant army;

4. Confiscating all big enterprises (industrial, transport, banking, etc.) belonging to the French imperialists and handing them over to the worker-peasant-soldier government;

5. Confiscating all lands belonging to the imperialists, turning them into public property, and distributing them to poor peasants;

6. Promulgating an eight-hour working day;

7. Cancelling all public debts and poll taxes and exempting poor people from all taxes;

8. Developing industry and agriculture;

9. Giving all democratic rights to the masses;

10. Establishing equality between men and women;

11. Establishing "worker-peasant style" relationships.

It was these goals that the early communists termed a "bourgeois revolution for democratic rights" and later, in 1951, a "national democratic revolution"; with the liberation of the south in 1975 they have at last been accomplished throughout Vietnam.

Dao Phiêu, the museum director, tells me that 1930–1935 was "the most difficult period of the revolution." In the face of strikes and demonstrations for national independence and of the formation of peasant soviets in Nghê Tinh province, the French instituted a "white terror," killing or imprisoning tens of thousands of communists and their supporters. We enter a room displaying torture instruments used by the French against the patriots in Paulo Condor and other jails: racks, pincers, awls to pierce the brain, and other mechanisms of horror. The French had already condemned Ho Chi Minh to death in his absence in 1929, and from June 1930 to the spring of 1933 the British imprisoned him in Hong Kong. There is a photograph of Loseby, the British lawyer engaged by the International Red Relief Association, who successfully defended him, and of the black clothes and spectacles in which Loseby disguised him after his release so that he might escape deportation by the French. Here, too, are photographs of an international communist meeting in Moscow in 1933 which Ho attended while studying at the Lenin School for high-ranking cadres of the Communist Party of the Soviet Union, and of the Seventh Congress of 1935.

The latter was attended by a famous Vietnamese woman delegate, Nguyen Thi Minh Khai. The first Vietnamese woman to train in the Soviet Union, Minh Khai later married the alternate delegate, Lê Hong Phong. On her return to Vietnam, Minh Khai became the secretary of the Communist Party, but was arrested by the French and executed after torture in Paulo Condor prison on Con Son Island in 1941. Her grave remains on this island, where so many thousands of patriots later died under both the French and the United

States puppets' regimes. There are photographs of this brave woman and a collection of her possessions while in prison, including a sweater knit for her by other prisoners and a pillow embroidered with the message, "Revolution is a Way of Life." Minh Khai left this poem inscribed with her own blood on the walls of her cell:

A rosy-cheeked woman, here I am fighting side by side
    with you men!
On my shoulders weighs the hatred that is common to us.
The prison is my school, its mates my friends,
The sword is my child, the gun my husband.

Khanh and my other hosts have referred several times to Minh Khai as a model for Vietnamese women. She came from Quang Tri but served as a zonal leader in Cochin China. Her speech to the Seventh Congress in Moscow was the first extended statement on the wretched plight of women in Indochina. Minh Khai's sister, Minh Giang, the first wife of General Vo Nguyen Giap, died in prison with her infant in 1943. Minh Khai's husband, Lê Hong Phong, was also murdered by the French. He was beaten to death after torture in Paulo Condor prison, and is buried there. Khanh tells me that the daughter of Hong Phong and Minh Khai, Hong Minh, is a well-known engineer ("just your age—about fifty"), and that she, too, has a daughter Khanh's age who is proud to be the grandchild of these famous patriots.

Following the policy of the Seventh International Communist Congress of 1935, the Indochinese Communist Party temporarily discarded its program of immediate independence and land reform, and formed the Indochinese Democratic Front against the fascist movements of Germany, Italy, and Japan. With a Popular Front government in France from 1936, and with modified aims for democratic freedoms in Vietnam, the party could carry on legal as well as secret activities. In Ho Chi Minh's absence abroad, Lê Hong Phong directed its campaigns and its publication of books and documents, now exhibited in the museum. A photograph shows the antifascist demonstration of 25,000 people in Hanoi on May Day, 1936.

With the Japanese invasion and takeover of Indochina in 1940–1941, the Communist Party entered the modern period of guerrilla warfare against invaders and their puppet rulers. Until their coup of March 9, 1945, the Japanese governed Vietnam through a Vichy French collaborationist regime. Ho Chi Minh, General Giap, and other leaders returned with their forces from Hunan, where they had undergone guerrilla training during the short period of the Chinese Democratic Front. Ho settled in a cave in the mountains of Pac Bo about a mile from the Chinese border beside a river which he renamed the Lenin. From there he trained cadres in Marxism-Leninism and directed what he termed "the revolution for national salvation." Displayed in the museum are photographs and a model of Ho's cave and the Lenin River; the worn suit, small rattan suitcase, pump, grindstone, and dishes he used; the poems and documents he wrote; and a copy of the engraving of Marx that he carved on the walls of his cave.

Having returned on February 8, 1941, Ho convened the Eighth Congress of the Indochinese Communist Party in May. On October 13, 1940, the Bac Son insurrection forces were organized into the first Vietnamese guerrilla unit; later on, this unit grew into three platoons of the National Salvation Army. As a result of the Eighth Congress the Vietminh or Vietnam Independence League was formed as a broad front uniting worker, peasant, youth, women's, old people's, overseas Vietnamese, and other associations. We see a copy of its program, a *History of Vietnam* written by Ho Chi Minh in 1942, Vietminh posters, and a photograph of General Giap's first official platoon of thirty-four fighters, including three women, formed on December 22, 1944.

The exhibits in Room 3 close with the famine of late 1944–1945. Shortly before they withdrew in defeat, the Japanese retaliated by burning rice stocks and running trainloads of paddy into the sea. They had already compelled many peasants to grow jute for export instead of rice. These dislocations coupled with bad harvests created a famine in which two million Vietnamese died, especially in north and central Vietnam. Gazing at a wall of photos of corpses and of hideously emaciated people, I recall the Bengal famine of 1943 in which up to three million died as a result of the war between Britain and Japan and the failure to organize distribution on the part of both British and Indian leaders. What untold miseries colonial peoples have suffered! How shielded we in the West have been from news of their suffering! Although I knew this history in outline before I came, I can scarcely believe the tale of agony and courage before my eyes. To their everlasting credit, the Vietminh were now so organized that in March 1945 they were able to mobilize thousands to seize and distribute rice stocks, thus saving other millions from starvation. Throughout the country the people rose in support of the Vietminh, and following the Japanese surrender of August 1945 they created the Democratic Republic of Vietnam.

Room 4 takes us through the founding of the republic on September 2, 1945, followed at once by the reinvasion of Vietnam by 200,000 Chinese troops of Chiang Kai Shek, by 50,000 Gurkha troops from British India, and, soon after, by French armies in full force.[2] The 1946–1954 war against the French colonial invaders ensued.

It is fascinating to see the material relics of this conflict. There is a model of the people's attack, in the August 1945 insurrection, on the French governor's palace, a building now used as a government reception center. There is a microphone through which Ho Chi Minh read the Declaration of Independence on September 2, 1945, in Ba Dinh Square in Hanoi— now the site of his mausoleum and of the new National Assembly building. Photographs show the last struggles against the Japanese, the first elected National Assembly of Vietnam of March 1946, and war scenes of anti-French battles and of French planes shot down. There are exhibits of weapons stolen from the French, 70 percent of which were supplied by the United States from 1953 on, and of country swords, spikes, and booby traps used against the French troops by Vietnamese villagers. Models show the 1950 Vietminh campaign on the Chinese border and the Second Congress of the Vietnam Communist Party, convened in a forest in February 1951. At this conference the party's name was changed to the Vietnam Workers' Party, with Ho Chi Minh as secretary. There are bicycles whose riders transported food to the troops up to 300 kilometers, but I am told that this is nothing; by the time of the United States war a single rider could make journeys of 700 kilometers. Finally, there is the saga of Dien Bien Phu: photos of its planning by the War Bureau, including Ho and Giap; a large model of the battle scene; and pictures of the surrender of the French General De Castries with 16,000 troops. Here are Eisenhower's and Churchill's messages of admiration and condolence to the French Commander Navarre; but here are also a flag with thousands of French workers' signatures, and the image of a dove, inscribed with the names of hundreds of French women, congratulating the Vietnamese on their victory. The scene closes with the signing of the Geneva Accords of July 21, 1954.

In the hall outside, these exhibits end with a massive guillotine symbolizing French domination and terror. Hundreds of such guillotines were set up in the "white terror" of the 1930s and in the war against the Vietminh, and tens of thousands of patriots were murdered.

Three rooms of the museum document the Vietnamese struggle against United States imperialism. As I go through them accompanied by the quiet, almost whispered comments of Dao Phiêu and Khanh, I recall the same events as seen from the United States and Canada in 1961–1975. I feel curiosity, rage, terror, and, finally, sorrowing pity. Toward the end I am weeping; Khanh's voice falters too, and she takes my hand.

The display begins in 1944 with documents revealing Roosevelt's support of the French return to Vietnam and of

United States schemes and intelligence activities during the subsequent war against the French. Dated within three days after the Japanese surrender, there are United States, British, and Chiang Kai Shek embassies' requests to the government in Hanoi to set up military bases in Vietnam. Photographs depict the first American weapons supplied to the French in 1950 and the subsequent visit of Vice-President Richard M. Nixon in support of French troops in Vietnam. Here are photographs of the first United States military "advisers" to the puppet government of Bao Dai in Saigon, eight years before the American public became aware of the presence of United States military personnel in Vietnam. Here are the familiar photographs of Saigon troops herding South Viet-namese villagers into concentration camps under Ngô Dinh Diém's regime of 1956–1963, and of their hideous torture of captives. And here are models of the "tiger cages" used by the Diem government from its earliest days to imprison opponents of the regime.

From President Kennedy's "special war" period of 1960–1964 come photographs of United States military bases and planes, of United States officers in charge of military operations, of peasant concentration camps or "strategic hamlets" built under the Taylor-Staley plan, of defoliation and hut burning, and of massacres of villagers.

Room 6 depicts President Johnson's and General West-moreland's open war of 1965–1968, with photos of the first contingent of United States marines landing at Da Nang on March 6, 1965. There follow photographs and specimens of bombs dropped on both North and South Vietnam—ordinary bombs, scatter bombs, many-points bombs, orange bombs, napalm bombs, "mother" bombs, steel-pellet antipersonnel bombs, and bombs specially designed to destroy underground air raid shelters. There are photographs of B-52s raining bombs, of the results of carpet bombing, of bombed schools, bombed hospitals, and bombed children, and of the total destruction on March 16, 1968, of Song Sang village in

Quang Ninh province, where 500 civilians were killed. From 1967 comes a long saga of bombs dropped on churches, pagodas, streets, dikes, and children. There is a 3,000-pound bomb which failed to explode on Long Bien beach, and an instrument to detect human traffic in jungles in order to prevent troop movement from north to south Vietnam. For relief, I turn to photos of captured United States airmen— 472 of them taken alive in this period, decently housed and fed, and finally returned to their country.

In Room 7, President Nixon's "Vietnamization" program of 1968-1973 introduces photographs of the conscription of small boys in Saigon, of public executions, and of United States troops carrying the severed heads of Vietnamese and Cambodian patriots. Many dozens of photos of captured pilots are shown from this period. Last come President Nixon's bombing of North Vietnam on December 18 to 30, 1972, in which 100,000 tons of ordnance were dropped in twelve days and nights of incessant air raids, Hanoi alone receiving 40,000 tons. Here I see pictures of Kham Thieu street in Hanoi, totally destroyed; of the Bach Mai Children's Hospital, seriously damaged, with sixteen killed, on December 22, 1972; of huge bomb craters full of water, photographed in many regions; and of examples of the tens of thousands of meters of dikes that were destroyed. Here are United States ships sailing into the attack on Haiphong harbor, and their blockade of the Red River and of the sea. The exhibit ends with the ceremonial furling of the United States flag in Saigon on March 15, 1973, and the last United States troops withdrawing by plane on the twenty-ninth of that .same month.

In the corridor outside this hall there is another symbol, which Khanh calls "U.S. civilization in the twentieth century." It is an iron box, about seven feet square and four feet high, into which up to twenty prisoners would be locked and placed in the tropical sun. United States and Saigon troops tapped on its walls continuously until the inmates lost consciousness, and sometimes shot into it, as the many bullet holes bear witness. A large number of such boxes were used to torture and kill patriots, especially in Da Nang and Quang Tri provinces. This one is preserved for posterity.

A new room of the museum recalls civilian resistance against United States aggression. Here are several kinds of iron-spiked booby traps which were placed in pits under light bamboo frames camouflaged with leaves. Here are photographs of the execution on October 15, 1964, of young Nguyen Van Troi, who tried to assassinate United States Secretary of Defense Robert McNamara. Immediately before his execution he spoke calmly and eloquently to the assembled reporters: "You are journalists and so you must be well informed about what is happening. It is the Americans who have committed aggression on our country, it is they who have been killing our people with planes and bombs. . . . I have never acted against the will of my people. It is against the Americans that I have taken action." He refused priestly absolution, saying, "I have committed no sin; it is the Americans who have sinned," and he would not have his eyes covered before execution: "Let me look on our beloved land." When the first volley of shots hit him he cried, "Long live Vietnam!"[3]

In this room, also, are pictures of the popular movement to free the student leader Nguyen Khanh, who was executed on August 25, 1964. Here are monks burning themselves to death in protest against the American and Saigon troops' atrocities. And here are Saigon troops of Unit 787 deserting en masse to the People's Army. Exhibits of July 28, 1970, show the summit conference of Vietnamese, Laotian, and Cambodian governments and their decision to coordinate their struggles against the United States invasions of all three countries.

The afternoon wears on. Exhausted and wrung out, we decide to terminate our visit although many other exhibits remain. A walk down a long corridor shows us glimpses of the 1973-1975 war in South Vietnam between Thieu's Saigon troops and the combined forces of the Provisional Revolutionary Government and of North Vietnam. It ends with scenes of the liberation of Saigon, the triumphal entry of the patriotic forces on April 30, 1975, and the departure by helicopter of the United States embassy staff. In a room devoted to the Paris negotiations and the Provisional Revolutionary Government, Khanh points out Madame Binh, then foreign minister of the PRG and now minister of education in reunified Vietnam.

Last, we look into a large hall of pictures and souvenirs from Vietnam's supporters throughout the world. I am too tired to examine them, but Khanh leads me to three objects she knows will please me: a shopping bag made by Another Mother for Peace in the United States embroidered, "War is not good for children and other living things," a glass case containing samples of all the antiwar buttons from the United States and Canada, and, from 1959, an old knapsack of Fidel's.

Over tea in the reception room I write in Dao Phiêu's visitors' book. Soviet, Japanese, Chinese, West and East German, Hungarian, French, Dutch, British, Canadian, United States, and probably many other nationalities of visitors have left messages there in 1976. I try to tell Dao Phiêu and Khanh something of what it was like to live in the United States during the war. With distress, I explain how the continual, daily scenes of massacre on television seemed to harden people to crime and suffering, and tempted one to despair. "We did not want this war," I said, "it was forced on us. It is a terrible thing to have been associated with such policies, against one's will." Dao Phiêu's kind eyes rest on me. "Do not grieve," he says. "It is over now. And after all, we won—and you won, too." He wrings my hand and asks me to return.

This evening I have a "welcome dinner" at the hotel with Thê, Hoan, and Khanh. It is splendid, and would have happened last night but for the uncertainty of my arrival. We eat dainty dishes of chicken, beef, pork, fish sauce, rice, and vegetables, and drink three kinds of wine. The central feature is frogs' legs, deep fried on sticks. The Vietnamese love them, but although the piece I take is tender, I can't eat the rest—cultural prejudice is too strong and I am like a Brahman faced with beef. My hosts laugh and try many strategems to get me to taste "a bite of chicken."

When possible, Vietnamese like to cook at home. Vô Thi Thê cooks every day; Khanh is often too busy, but cooks when she has time. This week her mother-in-law, who lives with her, cooks, and her husband helps with the baby.

We talk of Canada and mutual acquaintances. Vô Thi Thê expresses the great appreciation of Vietnamese women for Women Strike for Peace in the United States, and for Voice of Women and Canadian Aid to Vietnam Civilians in Canada, the last of which will soon dispatch its forty-sixth shipment of medical supplies to Vietnam. I ask what in particular supporters of Vietnam should be doing now in Canada, and am told they should (a) press the United States government for the reparations for war damage that it promised in the Paris Agreements of 1973 but has not fulfilled, (b) try to obtain Canadian visas (at present held up by the government) for a new delegation of Vietnamese women to visit Canada, and (c) try to obtain money for reconstruction, including financial aid from the government of Canada.

I ask my hosts about the other countries of Southeast Asia. Their relations with both Laos and Kampuchea (Cambodia) are cordial, they stress, and visits are frequent. The newly formed Air Vietnam runs bimonthly flights to Phnom Penh, and biweekly to Vientiane. Vietnam is attempting to set up fruitful economic cooperation and trade with the Association of South East Asian Nations (Thailand, the Philippines, Malaysia, Singapore, and Indonesia), although it does not endorse their military agreements or their furtherance of United States policies in the region. The coup in Thailand on October 6, 1976, is dangerous to Vietnam, but they do not think the United States would ever again attack Vietnam from Thailand; their past defeat was too serious. Nevertheless, Vietnam must maintain its army and navy in top condition. Young men and women in the forces are now engaged in reconstruction, but all youth still receive military training.

The United States, they tell me, is still engaged in subversion and tries to "sow chaos" in south Vietnam. During the elections to the National Assembly in April 1976, bombs were exploded and others discovered in south Vietnam, and there have been other underground activities. Vô Thi Thê thinks some of the materials were supplied from the United States in small boats and is afraid that the United States government may use Vietnamese refugees to the United States as "henchmen."

I ask Vô Thi Thê about her relatives in south Vietnam, in whom I became interested when she told us something of her personal story at the 1971 women's conference in Vancouver. A learned Chinese scholar, Thê's father refused service under the French colonialists and lived at home on his lands near Hue in central Vietnam. Vô Thi Thê's whole family was nationalist, and as a professor of literature at Hue university she joined the Women's Union for National Salvation and took part with her students in the August revolution. Later, in the war against the French invaders, two of her brothers were killed while fighting in the revolutionary army, and her father died as a result of torture by the French. Vô Thi Thê left Hue in 1950 to work for the Women's Union in Hanoi. For twenty-five years she did not see her mother, and after the bombing and strafing of Hue by the Americans in 1968 she did not hear from her and feared that she was dead. Soon after the liberation of south Vietnam in 1975, however, Vô Thi Thê went south to rediscover her family. Hue was virtually destroyed, but to her great joy she found her indomitable old mother and many other relatives still living.

I try to guide the conversation to India. I explain that I am troubled by the increasing repression carried on by the government of Indira Gandhi, especially since the Emergency was instituted on June 26, 1975. I refer to the suppression of elections, free speech, strikes, and freedom of the press and of assembly; the silencing of opposition parties and dissident members of Mrs. Gandhi's own Congress Party; the further lowering of peasants' and workers' living standards; and, above all, the arrest and imprisonment, often without trial, of tens of thousands of political prisoners over the past decade, the massacre of hundreds of revolutionaries and the torture of thousands.

I say I am especially distressed because the Soviet Union, which has given valuable aid to Vietnam, aids and unequivocally upholds the Gandhi government and supplies most of its military equipment. I am also disappointed in the Vietnamese government's verbal support of the Gandhi regime.[4] I can understand that Vietnam might appreciate Indira Gandhi's seeming opposition to the United States on several issues, but I do not think this opposition reduces American exploitation of India; indeed, United States penetration of the Indian economy has grown during the period of the Emergency. In any case, Gandhi's foreign policies do not excuse the fascistic types of terror going on within the country.

From their cautious responses, it is clear that my hosts are either unable or unwilling to comment freely on India or perhaps on any other foreign country. Vô Thi Thê says only that India needs a "new society," and that it is a pity the communist movement there is so weak and divided. Before its revolution, she says, Vietnam had all the features I have described for India.

I have brought a letter of greetings and congratulations to the Vietnamese patriots from Balan, aged twenty-six, a communist Harijan or "untouchable" agricultural laborer of Kilvenmani in Thanjavur district, south India. In that village, which is two miles from where I last worked in Thanjavur, landlords and their thugs burned to death forty-four Harijan men, women, and children in a political battle on Christmas Eve, 1968.[5] Balan was imprisoned for one year on a charge (which he says was groundless) of conspiring in the previous murder of a henchman of the leading landlord, and seven of his friends and relatives received sentences of one year to life. None of the landlords, however, was punished for incinerating Balan's mother, grandmother, and younger brother, for riddling his father with buckshot, or for slaughtering other friends and relatives in his hamlet. My friends receive this story with horror and accept the letter gratefully.

They ask me about the tribal people of India. I tell them there are about 90 million and that they are exploited by traders, moneylenders, and landlords from the dominant Hindu society and have been robbed or cheated of much of their ancestral land. Many thousands of them have taken part in nationalist or Marxist-Leninist uprisings in recent years in eastern India, West Bengal, Bihar, Orissa and Andhra Pradesh. In Vietnam, I am told, there are sixty such ethnic minorities who were similarly oppressed by lowland Vietnamese before the revolution and who played a leading role in it. Now they have a large measure of autonomy as well as education and publications in their own languages. Every effort is being made to develop their cultures and their contribution to political and economic life, and minority women play an important part in the Women's Union.

Top left: "Big" and "Little" Liên. *Top right:* Liên senior and Hoan outside the Hotel of the Restoration of the Sword. *Bottom:* President Ho Chi Minh's mausoleum in Ba Dinh Square.

Top: A dyke near Hanoi. *Bottom left:* Residents of Camp No. 1 for Permanent Invalids. *Bottom right:* Staff of the camp, with the director, Lê Ngoc Thanh, third from left.

4

"We Know Why
We Are Crippled"

North Vietnam has fifteen camps for people permanently injured in the resistance wars against French and United States imperialism. These camps contain those classified as "more than 70 percent injured," so that they cannot function in normal society. The government's policy is that any of the wounded who can so function are rehabilitated as quickly as possible and put into normal jobs alongside healthy people. Many of the permanent invalids in the camps have been brought from villages, battlefields, and prisons in the south during or since the war.

Camp No. 1 lies in Thuan Thanh district of Ha Bac province about sixty kilometers north of Hanoi. I set off there by car at 8:30 A.M. with Khanh, Liên senior, and Quyên on November 12, accompanied by a government official who works on social problems in the Ministry for Invalids. Our companion's leg was broken in the war but has now healed. Camp No. 1, he tells me, contains 350 people including staff. It was built in 1965 and specializes in dorsal paralysis, including "military and semi-military casualties." (I learn later that "semi-military" usually refers to the victims of torture.) The inmates are people who have lost one, two, or three limbs, whose hips are full of shrapnel, or whose spines are paralyzed. Many of them cannot pass water naturally. They are people of whom our guide says, "The wicked enemy took away most of their bodies." Many have received medals from the state or have been commended as "heroic fighters who killed U.S. aggressors." The government encourages healthy people like us to visit them "so that they will feel encouraged."

I am rather dreading this visit. I do not know how I will react when confronted with seriously injured people. Will I be afraid, tongue-tied, or guilty? It turns out that I need not worry.

As we pull up outside the large modern buildings about a hundred people are waiting in wheel chairs, on crutches, or in white staff uniforms, and rush to greet us. The director and senior staff shake hands with us and ask me to photograph everybody and be photographed with them. On all sides are laughter and greetings, with exclamations because I am from Canada and not (as is more usual) the Soviet Union or Eastern Europe. A young woman, both of whose arms have been amputated above the elbow, guides me and smiles reassuringly. These are the more fortunate patients who can move about and help the others. Outside the main building another crowd of invalids is assembled. Two little girls who are not injured, in short pretty dresses, step forward excitedly to present me a bouquet.

Lê Ngoc Thanh, the director, is an alert, intelligent man of about forty with a military bearing. He lost a leg in the war but with a prosthetic limb his limp is hardly noticeable. He leads us briskly along with a group of about twenty delegates from the staff and patients to an upstairs hall where a lavish midmorning snack of lemonade, tea, peanuts, bananas, biscuits, and wrapped sweets is spread on a long table. (Vietnam makes the most delicious toffees; I have to struggle not to eat too many every time I go through what I have come to regard as the "tea ceremony" that opens and ends each visit.)

Having thanked me and my family for supporting Vietnam, Lê Ngoc Thanh says: "We Vietnamese know who is our enemy and who is our friend. Be assured, we never confuse them. In our camp you will see people who received injuries because they were determined to fight. They fought because, as President Ho Chi Minh said and as all of us know, 'Nothing is more precious than independence and freedom.' You will find that despite their heavy wounds, our heroic fighters are optimistic. Whenever possible they take part in production and handicrafts. They are glad to do whatever work they can, for in spite of the heavy bombing and destruction they and all of us here have received attention and care from our party and government. So we invalid fighters are grateful and satisfied, for we know why we are crippled and we know that it was worthwhile.

"In the just war of our nation we have received sympathy and support from all countries. Today especially we remember those women of Canada who, for the sake of humanity and justice, were tireless in our cause. We consider such women a bright example of the people of Canada, of love and discipline. We want to send through you our greetings and thanks for their solidarity, their friendship and understanding. And let me now wish health and happiness to all of us here present! May you be joyful and have success in Vietnam! We hail you—only next time we hope you won't come alone, for we would like to see more of you."

I begin to thank Lê Ngoc Thanh but tears prevent me. Through my mind flash the signs we carried in the late 1960s and early 1970s in the United States and Canada: "Don't Kill Asians in My Name," "The World Mourns for Vietnam," and "Vietnam, America's Shame." I feel inexpressibly thankful that the war which often seemed endless is really won, but I am overwhelmed by the sight of these brave, gentle people with their bright smiles and poor, crippled bodies. My hosts understand and gather around, to comfort me! Khanh says that she too often weeps in Camp No. 1 although she comes here often, but that the members are only glad because they know we care. I am given a souvenir, a graceful ornament of cranes and lotuses in horn and tortoiseshell, engraved with the camp's name. Khanh and I unload the sweets and biscuits we have brought, and our procession goes to tour the camp.

The workshop is a light, modern hall with tables to which tools are attached, a lecture stand, and a blackboard. About fifty men and women, mostly young, are learning to assemble and repair transistor radios and microphones. Foreign visitors must be somewhat of a novelty, for there is a tumultuous welcome. Their eager faces gladden me; it is easy to talk to them. I tell them a little about Canada and how in the peace movement we tried to teach about *them* in our classrooms. Now, in theirs, I have nothing to say except my thanks. They applaud and reach out as I leave to take my hand.

The buildings where less mobile patients sit or lie house four beds to a room. The light, airy rooms open on to a sunny verandah and are plain but comfortable; each patient has a bed, a chair, a small table, a locker, and various personal possessions around him. Khanh murmurs that the accommodations, sanitary and modern, are very good. "Actually they are better than those we live in in Hanoi," she says. In several rooms, at midday, nurses sit talking to the patients. On the verandahs, staff members help some to walk with crutches or to exercise, and wheelchair patients sit wrapped in blankets in the winter sunshine, reading or talking.

I see so many patients that my impressions blur, but afterwards a few remain vividly. In one room two young women sit dressed at tables beside their beds, folding envelopes rapidly. One is propped up, for she can sit but cannot control her legs or walk; the other is incontinent. Both are guerrilla fighters from South Vietnam. Khanh and I try to ask them their circumstances but they are shy and, laughing, hide their faces. Both of them are under twenty-four. They cannot attend the workshop and cannot gum the envelopes but have attained a lightning speed at folding them. "We like to be working," one of them says.

In another room are men suffering from head and neck wounds, all of them dumb. An older man lies rigid; only his lips can move. He was injured in the war against the French and has lain here or in similar camps for twenty-five years. His eyes greet me as I stroke his hand. Across from him is a younger man whose tongue and throat were damaged in the recent war. He, too, cannot sit up; he writhes, apparently in agony. Beyond him lies a boy, perhaps in his teens, whose tongue was cut out during torture by the Saigon forces. He lies quite still with staring eyes; I do not think that he is conscious.

In a third room is Châu, aged twenty-nine, who was in Bien Hoa prison in the south for seven years. There, he says, they had very little food. Although wounded when captured, he was beaten until a neck injury paralyzed him. In addition he was given electric torture to the genitals and his hands were squeezed and twisted in machines so that today they resemble those of a crippled child. As I go on my rounds I notice that the hands and sometimes the feet of many other men are in this state as a result of paralysis either of their spines or of the limbs themselves. Khanh asks me the English word to describe shrunken limbs, and I tell her it is "atrophied." She writes it down for use with future foreign guests. I ask Châu whether he ever saw or experienced torture by Americans. "They never laid a hand on us," he says, "but they would sit there and watch and give orders, and sometimes smoke." Châu comes from a village northwest of Saigon that fell within the area of the Provisional Revolutionary Government. He was released in the exchange of prisoners after the Paris Agreements were signed in February 1973 and was sent home to "the revolutionary side." He was brought here in 1974 to receive suitable care throughout his life. Behind him lies a man immobilized in the fighting in south Vietnam; the two talk together although they cannot see each other.

In the same room Ngoc, aged thirty, has had bad luck. He came through the war in the north unscathed but was paralyzed by a bomb dropped from a B-52 in Tay Ninh province

on March 19, 1973, a month after the agreement to end the
bombing had been signed in Paris by the United States
government. As a result of his paralysis, Ngoc's feet have
atrophied and he cannot easily hold things, for his hands are
crippled. He can hold mine, however, and he greets me
warmly.

My last room contains Nhieû, Tuu, Can, and Luan, all
victims of torture in Paulo Condor prison. A nurse sits
chatting with them and there's a feeling of great warmth,
even of gaiety, in this room. Tuu, who is thirty-two, was in
prison from 1968-1973. Like Châu he was beaten to a state
of paralysis; his hands and feet have the familiar infantile
shapes. He is more interested in me than in that, however,
and as I sit on his bed he asks my origins, work, family
circumstances, and what my life is like. Can and Luan, who
are similarly paralyzed, try to lean forward to hear Khanh's
translation.

Nhieû is the head of this group; each room whose members
can communicate elects a representative to take part in
discussions of the camp's organization and program. Nhieû
was in Paulo Condor from 1970-1973. He lost his left hand
in prison; it was cut off after torture. His legs, too, seem to
be paralyzed, or perhaps he has lost one or both; I cannot see
them as he sits on the floor beside his bed. With his right
hand Nhieû is painting in water colors on a sheet attached to
a clipboard on his bed. Above the bed the walls are covered
with paintings stuck on with scotch tape. Today he is painting a portrait of Tuu. I'm attracted by a picture of a moun-
tainside with a waterfall, and soldiers with knapsacks silhou-
etted against the sky. "Could that be the Ho Chi Minh
Trail?" I ask. "Yes!—it is—but you must understand, there
were many Ho Chi Minh Trails. This is just one of them."
Nhieû motions to the nurse to take down the picture, writes
my name and the occasion of my visit on it, and gives it to
me. Tears choke me again; I shall keep it all my life. I want to
give him something but don't know what or how. My pen is

the only object available. Khanh hands it to the nurse. She will give it to Nhieû later, when we are gone; everyone knows it is for him but it might be impolite, thinks Khanh, to present it when I have no gifts for everyone.

In addition to the members' rooms the main camp has a large reception hall, kitchens, and a communal dining room. Everything, including the latrines, is spotless, and on the verandah wall beside our lunchroom is a long row of enamel bowls of water with towels beside them for hand washing.

We return to a sumptuous lunch of boiled rice with tiny beans, frog meat and lemon chicken, papaya, oranges, and tea, shared again with patients and delegates from the staff. Lê Ngoc Thanh explains a little about the camp's activities and structure. He tells me that he himself and about half the staff and patients are members of the Communist Party. If I heard correctly, this is a very high proportion, for in all of Vietnam there are reported to be only 1.5 million party members, perhaps 6 percent of the adults.[1] Party members are in charge of the camp and are divided into forty branches; I am not sure whether a branch takes care of a section of the camp or of particular activities. A governing council of seven, plus the director and vice-director, are periodically elected by all the members of the camp out of a large number of candidates who may be proposed and seconded by anyone. The election is by secret ballot. The director is ultimately responsible for the finances and day-to-day running of the camp but cannot make major decisions without consulting the council and cannot change the camp's policies without appeal to "the authorities" (presumably the government), to whom the director, vice-director, and council periodically report and give advice.

The council's tasks are to investigate and supervise the procurement and dispensing of food, medicines, and services; to "see who works well and who does not"; and, once a week, to receive grievances and suggestions from the inmates. The council also settles family and personal problems and is responsible for finding suitable work for the members. In addition to the work I have seen, there are classes in sewing and other crafts.

I ask about the criteria for electing the director, vice-director, and council. Lê Ngoc Thanh thinks for a moment and then answers carefully. "The first condition," he says, "is faithfulness to the party cause, which in our case mainly means service to our members. Second, we must have organizing and leadership ability. Third, we must command the faith and confidence of the whole camp. And fourth, we must have international solidarity and proletarian consciousness." This reply is so compact that I think it must be a standard set of qualities which he and other party members have rehearsed many times, but it is clear from his manner that he takes them seriously. Lê Ngoc Thanh has been elected director of the camp for the past ten years.

I ask whether there is criticism and self-criticism within the camp. "Yes, indeed," he replies, "our nurses, doctors, and auxiliary staff hold these sessions every morning, which help them in their work."

"Do some of the patients become depressed?" I ask. "Do some of them require psychiatric treatment?" When Khanh translates this question Lê Ngoc Thanh at first looks nonplussed. She adds some explanation, then turns and tells me that the hospital does not have psychiatrists in the sense that she thinks I mean. Meanwhile Lê Ngoc Thanh has thought out his answer.

"Morale is certainly our most important problem," he says, "but of course it is all built on the liberation of Vietnam. As I mentioned, we know why we are crippled; it is our service to our fatherland. But we must talk to and encourage everyone every day; the party doctors and nurses, the party members and the heads of rooms all do this. Everyone here has a place; he is encouraged to do his best and is reminded of his duty to the people and of their love and care for him. It is mainly a question of love, and of firmness." Across the table my eyes meet those of the young woman whose arms are amputated above the elbow. She nods and smiles serenely, and I know that these are not just words.

Our time is up. We go out into the sunshine, where patients are again gathering in wheelchairs or on crutches. They are pleased to be photographed and want photos with our group from Hanoi, which they ask me to mail to them. Suddenly we are surrounded by children and by other, un-injured adults whom I have not seen before. These are the invalids' families, says Khanh; as many as possible live on the premises. There are schools and crèches for the children. Some cultivate the camp's extensive orchards and gardens, cook, or do other work. When the relatives of an invalid live far away the state pays for regular visits, for it is important for families to be together and help each other. We walk past a row of small houses with tiled roofs; in the yards laundry is hanging on lines. A long procession, with some bearing gifts of fruit from the camp's orchards, takes us to the car. There are more speeches, handshakes, goodbyes, and injunctions to come back another year. As in the museum yesterday I find that I do not want to leave. I would be glad to return to Camp No. 1.

As I write these notes in Vancouver in January 1977, I remember that there are other wounded. The Vietnamese Communists do not have a monopoly on suffering. There are Veterans' Hospitals in the United States, and, no doubt, somewhere in south Vietnam there are camps for the per-manently injured Saigon troops. Yet their circumstances are different. I do not think that any of them had their hands crushed through torture, their limbs deliberately severed, or their tongues cut out. On the other hand, the Communists are immeasurably more fortunate. They need never think, as United States Secretary of State Cyrus Vance said on tele-vision yesterday, "In retrospect, Vietnam was a mistake." They know why they are crippled.

5

Agriculture and Handicrafts

November 12. On the way back to Hanoi through Ha Bac province, men and women are harvesting paddy with sickles like those used in India. The ripe plants are much yellower than those in Thanjavur, perhaps because of the colder weather. (The temperature now, in November, is around 14°C in the daytime compared with about 30°C in Thanjavur.) Liên has worked many summers in agricultural cooperatives with her students, and like other members of the Women's Union she is still required to spend one month a year in the countryside, living and working among the peasants. She enjoys country life and is eager to answer my questions, the more so as Khanh is exhausted from seven hours of continuous interpreting at the invalids' camp.

The Red River delta, Liên tells me, has been experiencing a "green revolution" technically similar to that in Thanjavur, the effects of which I have been studying this past year. In both regions the last ten years have seen the introduction of hybrid seeds of both tall and short varieties, transplanting of the seedlings in rows along a string, and the use of chemical fertilizers, pesticides, and some tractors. Liên tells me that India is considered ahead of Vietnam in rice cultivation, and will soon build an experimental paddy station not far from Hanoi. This interests me, for Vietnam's paddy yield already compares favorably with that of India. In 1975–1976, north

Vietnam's unhusked paddy yield averaged 2.2 tons per crop-hectare.[1] In Tamilnadu, a south Indian state where paddy is the main cereal, the yield was 1.9 tons per crop-hectare in 1970–1971, but in India as a whole it was only 1.7 tons.[2] Perhaps a more meaningful comparison is that between Thanjavur district of Tamilnadu, known as the "rice bowl" of south India because of the fertile Kaveri delta, and the Red River delta. Thanjavur's average paddy yield was 3.1 tons per crop-hectare in 1975–1976.[3] Liên does not know the exact yield per crop-hectare in the Red River delta as a whole, but knows that most cooperatives are producing from 3 to 5 tons per hectare in each crop. Moreover, most of the paddy land in the Red River delta now grows two or even three crops a year, whereas in Thanjavur only 33 percent of it is double-cropped. Thai Binh province, in the heart of the Red River delta, thus achieved 7 tons per hectare per year in 1974 and has topped that since, whereas Thanjavur in the heart of the Kaveri delta produced only 4.1 tons per annual hectare in 1975–1976. Moreover, the difference between these two areas is not traditional, for both were producing roughly 1 ton or less per crop-hectare in the late 1940s, and had less than one-fifth of the area under double cropping. It appears, therefore, that although hybrid seeds, chemical fertilizers, and pesticides may be more advanced, or more plentiful, in the specially selected green revolution districts of India, Vietnam more than makes up for this through planned irrigation, cooperative labor, and the larger extent of double and triple cropping that these permit. Liên is not satisfied, however, and tells me that there are places in Japan where several times the Vietnamese yield is being produced.

The cut paddy is first stooked in the field to dry and then carried to the threshing floor in two bundles, or two containers, hanging from a shoulder pole. Liên says that nowadays, since the small plots have been amalgamated into large fields and wide paths built through them, the peasants sometimes use carts or light trucks to save labor. Formerly, some peasants carried head-loads of paddy or straw as in India, but today this labor is regarded as unnecessary and too heavy. In many coops the paddy is still threshed by beating with sticks, as in Thanjavur, but in some, small threshing machines made in Vietnam are now used—an innovation that has not yet arrived in Thanjavur.

As we drive along we run over a lot of straw laid out on the roadway. At first I think this is paddy in the husk which has been laid on the road so that cars and buses will thresh it as they go by—a modern labor-saving device adopted in the last decade by Thanjavur farmers whose fields lie by the roadside. But Liên says this is not so; it is already threshed, and is lying on the road to dry. As in Thanjavur, the harvest is a month late this year because of drought in the southwest monsoon of July and August, and the farmers are anxious to finish before the second rains fall in late November.

Like my friends in the Women's Union, the peasant women wear black pajamas, white or colored blouses, padded cotton jackets, and light conical hats made of reeds from the forest; peasant men wear shallower reed hats or army helmets. Most of the women present a rather odd appearance, for they wear black or white flannel cloths tied under their hats around their faces; some, especially the young ones, leave only a slit for their eyes. Liên says these cloths are worn all year to protect their complexions from the sun or the cold. Like Indian women, Vietnamese women prefer their skin to be pale and soft. Whereas in India landlord and rich peasant women ensure this by staying in the shade and leaving agriculture to the poorer tenants and laborers, in Vietnam all rural women work on the land and protect themselves by day so as to arrive beautiful in the evening.

The peasants we meet on the roadsides wear rough but neat, clean clothes. In contrast to India, none of them are ragged and all of them look well nourished. In spite of the chilly weather some go barefoot; others wear leather or rubber sandals or shoes. In addition to the cattle there are many well fed water buffaloes grazing in the meadows or the harvested fields. In both India and Vietnam crows often ride on their backs, but here the boys who take care of them are also often seen riding them, a sight I have not met in Thanjavur where the buffaloes may be less tame and are certainly less sturdy. Buffaloes are used for drawing plows and carts, but Liên says their milk yield is poor. In any case, apart from babies whose mothers cannot nurse them, no one drinks much milk in Vietnam. Protein comes mainly from beef, chickens, and especially pigs, of which every cooperative has a large number.

In Thanjavur, also, there is a shortage of milk; agricultural laborers, especially Harijans, can hardly ever afford it and do not customarily use it except for motherless babies. But in Thanjavur most people also seldom see meat, fish, or eggs. The Harijan agricultural laborers, in particular, rely for their protein almost entirely on the village's carrion beef or on rats caught in the paddy fields or in their homes.

Children in Vietnam are able to graze the cattle and do other farm jobs because the overcrowded schools run two six-hour shifts a day.

Liên tells me that each agricultural cooperative is run by an elected committee under a director. The Communist Party is prominent, its members being recruited from the more "advanced" peasants. Party members are responsible for explaining policies and ideology to the peasants (which Liên and Khanh call "expounding the line"), setting a good example in work and conduct, propagating production targets, and serving as a two-way communication link between the government and the rural people. The cooperative keeps part of its produce to feed the members and sells the rest to the government. How much is sold depends on the yield and the kinds of crops. The food is resold by the government at fixed prices in state-run stores. There is some evening out of wealth by the government between more and less fertile cooperatives, although my friends do not know the details. In addition, during the war each province of north Vietnam "adopted" a sister province in the south and undertook to supply its fighters and when necessary its liberated zones with food. During the war, therefore, a great deal of food was carried south, some of which now stays in the north. Liên says there is felt to be no shortage of food in Vietnam, although the government is currently obliged to import about 1.2 million tons of rice, mainly from China, and some 150,000 tons of wheat from the Soviet Union. It is hoped that the country will be able to end food imports within five years. In 1975 north Vietnam's total paddy production was 4,360,000 tons.

The money that the coop receives from food sales is spent on chemical fertilizers, tools, machinery, improved seeds, construction materials, and raw materials for the craft shops each coop runs. Part of the money also goes as wages to the peasants, who are paid in both cash and kind. Wages vary somewhat, although not much, according to the type of work done and the coop's prosperity. There is no distinction in wages based on sex. During the wars against both the French and the American invaders, more men than women went as fighters and women took over much of the work traditionally done by men, even ditch digging and plowing. Some of the more arduous tasks traditionally done by women, such as transplanting, also command higher wages.

Again I silently contrast all this with Thanjavur, where transplanting is classified by the government as "light work" and commands a wage only half as much as that paid to men for carting or plowing. Even worse, in Thanjavur the statutory daily wages for both men and women, even when fully paid, mean little because of extreme underemployment. Women, whose participation in the labor force has declined and is now only about 11 percent, seldom work more than 90 days a year, and men usually between 90 and 140. In Vietnam every able-bodied adult under fifty-five works an eight-hour day, five days a week, either in the fields or in craft shops.

Liên says transplanting methods have greatly improved in recent years. Part of her job was to teach the peasants to space seedlings evenly in rows marked by strings and to hold them in a particular way in the left palm so that it took less time and energy to plant them. Khanh says that sometimes the string would be broken by a bomb while the women were planting! Both friends confirm that women indeed carried rifles to the fields and sometimes shot down bombers.

Each peasant house in a cooperative is surrounded by a private garden of 0.05 acres. The family may use this as they please. Most keep a pig, chickens, and pigeons, and also vegetables, bananas, and a fruit tree. The produce from this plot belongs entirely to the family and is often sold by the women in a market in some nearby town, to a private store or restaurant, or to passersby on a city pavement. Liên says that women usually take charge of the private plot and handle the money from its produce, and are very keen and economical about its use. Private sums derived from the sale of family produce augment the peasants' wages and may be used to buy clothing or household items or saved in a bank account.

Beside the road are many gravel mounds and brick kilns; a great deal of road mending and house construction is going on. The clusters of tiled or thatched houses resemble those of middle or rich peasants in India. Occasionally, we pass a small village temple. Liên says that some older peasants still worship the gods but that "the young do not have much religion, for they have grown up through the war and they know that their comrades, not heaven, will help them." The village temples, as well as the bigger temples and pagodas and the monasteries, formerly owned much land, but this was confiscated in 1955 and now they are maintained by voluntary contributions. Priests and monks are also permitted to cultivate land for their own livelihood along with others.

I notice that many large blocks of fields are completely surrounded by long lines of casuarina trees. They protect the crops from cyclones, afford shade, and are used for fuel and green manure and to provide poles for house building. As in Thanjavur, banyan and other trees have been planted by the government along the roadsides.

The road to Hanoi, like those in the city, is swept completely free of refuse. Liên says that before the revolution of 1945 people spat, urinated, or defecated in gardens or by the roadside, left garbage in streets and gutters, and drew drinking water from the ponds and channels. All this is now prohibited; indeed, throughout my visit I do not see a single person spit or even a child urinate in public. By law, each house in the countryside must now be provided with a well, a bathroom, and a latrine. The latrine is built with two compartments side by side. Each is used for six months and then nailed shut for the rest of the year. The decayed matter is then removed and processed to fertilize the fields. The Vietnamese seem, in fact, as debris-conscious as the Chinese: every speck of human, animal, and vegetable refuse is collected for use in cultivation.

Most villagers, says Liên, are actually better housed now than the people in Hanoi. Both Liên and Khanh live in one-room apartments and share their kitchens and bathrooms with other families. They hasten to tell me, however, that they are not complaining. As things are, they pay only 1 percent of their salaries as house rent, like all other city people. They know that everyone lives similarly and they expect that now that the war is over their circumstances will gradually improve. Outside Hanoi, we see a large block of sizable modern flats going up to house urban workers.

So far I have not seen any dogs in Vietnam. Liên tells me that they had to be destroyed during the war against the French lest they reveal the movements of the fighters. Since the end of the United States war a few have been reimported to north Vietnam from the Soviet Union and China, but it is necessary to obtain a permit to keep one. Cats and rabbits are popular as household pets.

As we draw close to Hanoi I see that the city is really beautiful with its tree lined avenues, ancient pagodas, several lakes and parks, and recreation grounds for children. Hanoi and Ho Chi Minh City still have trams as well as buses. We enter the city by Hang Ngang and Hang Dao streets, both bazaars containing busy family stores. These stores sell flowers, clothing, leather goods, suitcases, spectacles, baskets, furniture, toys, food, and many other items: apparently a great many consumer goods are marketed privately. As Liên has told me, peasant women sit on the sidewalks with trays and baskets of fruit and vegetables. Hang Ngang street also contains the state-owned Dong-Xuan department store, the largest in north Vietnam, which, according to Khanh, sells "everything." People shop as they please in either the state or the private stores; prices are sometimes lower in one, sometimes in the other. Most everyday items are available when needed, Khanh says, but sometimes, for example, one may see many suitcases in the stores, and sometimes none at all. I have the impression that everyone here is very poor by Western standards but that no one is destitute and no one is hungry. The contrast with Indian cities is acute, for here after thirty years of war no one begs and no one can who can work is unemployed. Everyone, moreover, has free education, medical care, and other social services. My friends, highly educated, cosmopolitan, and cultured, are materially less well endowed than the working-class people I know in England or Canada, even perhaps than most on welfare. Their dwellings are tiny and crowded, their clothes well worn and few, their personal possessions very meager. Yet they do not *seem* poor, for when all are poor, there is in a sense no poverty but only "shortages" which will be made up for by further cooperative effort. The effect on me, after the palatial homes and hotels and the vast, atrocious slums of Madras and Calcutta, is a tremendous lightening of the spirit, for I feel that everyone here has just enough, and is cheerful with it, and that my own convenience is not bought with others' woe.

It is not very late, so Khanh and Liên take me on a walk to a government exhibition of handicrafts for export. We first view the exhibition and then repair to a store containing the same kinds of goods reserved for purchase by tourists and foreign delegates, where I buy some Christmas presents with United States travelers' checks. There is a great range of objects in silk, cotton, rattan, rush, bamboo, tortoiseshell, horn, wood, lac, ivory, bone, and pottery—bedspreads, carpets, furniture, art objects, jewelry, and bric-à-brac. The Vietnamese are engaged in an export drive to obtain foreign currency to buy machinery for industrialization. Although their main exports of consumer goods go at present to the Soviet Union and Eastern Europe, they wish to export widely to capitalist countries as well. Trade delegations have already visited Hanoi from West Germany, France, Japan, and the Scandinavian countries, and facilities for export to Canada will be set up by the Canadian peace movement early in 1977. Some of the handicrafts are very beautiful; many resemble those in handicraft stores throughout India and, no doubt, the whole of Asia. There are some special features such as paintings of Ho Chi Minh's house and the stream where he fished, and of his cave in the mountains beside the Lenin River. Khanh and Liên are very proud of the handicrafts, which they say have improved remarkably in the last three years. Embroidery, rather similar to that done in Catholic convents in India, is also being developed. I too admire the goods, but am sad to see cheap Vietnamese labor used to produce luxury goods for the wealthy in Western and Eastern industrial states. At the same time I do not see how Vietnam is to obtain the capital and technology necessary for industrialization without this trade, especially given the exchange rates of all the industrial nations. And I am glad that the work is being done in decent, sanitary surroundings by people who are well fed and who work a forty-hour week.

Vietnam does not yet have many tourists, but it is hoped that their numbers will increase. Khanh points out a government tourist bureau. At present it chiefly handles visitors and official delegations from the Soviet Union and Eastern

Europe, but tourist groups from France, Scandinavia, and West Germany are fairly common and Canadian groups may soon be welcomed. I do not think, however, that tourists will ever be allowed to run rampant over Vietnam. At present they are subject to a number of restrictions. Most guests, for example, may bring in only black and white photographic film; colored film has to be left in storage at the airport. When I want to take photographs I must ask my hosts' permission, not always given. This morning, for example, Khanh and Liên asked me not to photograph my hotel until they had consulted Hoan. She in turn sought permission from the hotel manager, who gave it. In general, photographs of "enterprises" (factories, cooperatives, party buildings, hotels, etc.) may be taken only with the consent of their directors, for the everyday control of industrial and cultural units is highly decentralized. Street scenes, pagodas, parks, and historical monuments are permissible, but individuals should not be photographed without their permission, and there is an objection (with which I agree) to singling out children as objects of curiosity or admiration on the part of tourists. It is of course forbidden to photograph airports, docks, or other places of military significance.

As we stroll home in the twilight we see a well fed cow with heavy udders tethered to a lamp post in front of a small hotel, eating fodder from a basket on the pavement. It will soon be milked, says Liên, and the milk used by the hotel or sold to passersby. There are quite a number of such cows in Hanoi, although these are not allowed to roam the streets. A homey touch in a well ordered society.

6

Women in Revolution

After dinner on November 12 I received my second lecture from Professor Lê Thi of the Institute of Philosophy at the University of Hanoi. It was on "The Women's Movement in the Three Revolutions," that is, the revolutions in science and technology, in social organization, and in the creation of socialist men and women. Lê Thi, the sister of Duyên, was a delegate to the conference held by Canadians and Americans to celebrate the end of the war and the Vietnamese victory in Vancouver, B.C., in June 1975. Aged about forty, she is an expert in her subject and an animated lecturer.

Mme. Lê Thi Xuyên, a vice-president of the Women's Union, met me with my hosts on the morning of November 13 for a final lecture on the Women's Union, its history, organization, and present programs. An older leader who has served the women's movement since its founding, Mme. Xuyên impressed me deeply by her knowledge and moral stature. Her modesty and warmth made learning from her a happy experience. Watching the interactions among these women, I began to see how values, skills, and knowledge are passed on from old to young. The older women or those longer in the movement make serious demands and set high standards. They show great dignity, assurance, and firmness, but also tact and kindness. The younger women show loving respect, a growing self-confidence through the mastery of

75

tasks, and eagerness to serve and to achieve. At all the lectures and interviews I attended, Hoan, the two Liêns, and Duyên sat with me and took notes while Khanh translated. Later, they drew on these notes as a basis for discussions as we drove or walked about the countryside. Our talks were often animated but always carried on with calmness and gentle manners, which seem to be the hallmarks of the Vietnamese Communists I have met.

As we parted, after the usual messages of goodwill and gratitude to the Canadian and United States peace movements, Lê Thi Xuyên laid her hand on my shoulder. "The U.S. imperialists are now accusing Vietnam of preparing to invade Thailand," she said. "Please tell people that this is untrue."

As these two lectures were complementary and were augmented by reading and observation, I shall try to summarize what I learned and concluded about women in Vietnam.[1]

History of Vietnamese Women

The Vietnamese trace their civilization to a Bronze Age culture which flourished in irrigated river valleys of north and central Vietnam in the first millennium B.C. Lê Thi said that its legends suggest a high degree of parity between men and women in the village communes, and matrilineal kinship among at least some of the tribes, especially those of the mountains. Patriarchy was established by the Chinese conquest of Vietnam during the first millennium A.D., but women as well as men maintained a tradition of fighting in rebellions to expel the invaders. Among the heroines of this period were the famous Trung sisters, aristocratic Boadiceas who expelled the Chinese at the head of a popular army in 40-43 A.D. after a Chinese governor had executed the husband of one of them. In 248 A.D. Trieu Thi Trinh, a peasant

woman, led another rebellion after taking a pledge still popular in Vietnam today: "I will not resign myself to the usual
lot of women who bow their heads and become mere
concubines."[2]

These women and many like them committed suicide
rather than submit to conquest. Lê Thi believes that in spite
of the Confucian ethic of feudal subordination of women,
introduced by the Chinese, the tribal component in Vietnamese culture and the need to fight invaders or to take the
husband's place while he was fighting kept alive an older
tradition of female independence and self-assertion. For
2,000 years women responded to such proverbs as "When the
enemy comes, even the women should fight."

But in feudal society women had no appreciable rights in
law. As in India and in other precapitalist agrarian states,
they were always under the legal guardianship and authority
of father, brother, husband, or son. The French prolonged
their servitude: according to a decree of October 3, 1883, in
Cochin China, for example, "The woman is represented by
her husband in all affairs concerning her."

Upper-class women were secluded in their homes, and
peasant women, too, although obliged to work out of doors,
had no place in councils, government, or law courts. Women's
marriages were arranged by their fathers and entailed the
payment of a brideprice by the husband and his family which
gave them authority over the wife's person, children, and
services. Child marriage was common and widow marriage
frowned on. Divorce was rare and was usually on the initia-
tive of the husband, for a woman's family was normally
either unable or unwilling to return the wealth that had been
paid for her. Children belonged to the patrilineal line and
were forfeited by the mother if she was divorced or fled from
her husband. As in India, widows who remarried were despised. Polygyny and concubinage were common, but un-
faithful wives and unmarried or widowed women who be-

came pregnant were severely punished. Often they were obliged to abort or kill their infants, while illegitimate children who did survive were treated with ignominy.

Within the patrilineal extended family the mother-in-law had informal authority over the daughter-in-law. She and her son often beat or otherwise ill-treated the girl. Boys were, of course, preferred to girls; Vietnam's feudal rulers maintained the Chinese view that "One hundred women are not worth a single testicle." Female education was rare. Lê Thi thought that 99 percent of Vietnamese women remained illiterate during French rule and that only three girls' schools, all at the primary level, were established for the daughters of rich families. Bergman reports that schools began to be opened to the daughters of wealthier families in 1919 and that in the following decade 8 percent of all Vietnamese females became literate, roughly the same proportion as the number of prostitutes. In 1924, 3 percent of girls aged five to fourteen and 6 percent of boys were in school.[3]

Most women were poor peasants, oppressed both by male relatives and by landlords. Their conditions were atrocious. They were often forced to rise at 3 A.M. and labor until sundown. Sometimes a poor peasant woman would draw the cart or the plow when her husband could not afford to buy an ox. Women received bare subsistence, and could be raped or beaten by their landlords. For the same kind of work, they were paid three-quarters of the wages of men.

The French added still heavier burdens typical of colonialism. Women were recruited, often by force, into plantations, mines, and factories. Between 1917 and 1945, 16 percent of the 280,000 workers on three large rubber plantations were officially reported to have died; more died unreported. By 1945, 60 percent of the plantation workers were women. Factory hands worked a fifteen-hour day, seven days a week. The women sometimes gave birth on the factory floor, afraid to lose their jobs if they reported sick. In the 1940s, 30 percent of the Vietnamese women who died, died in childbirth, and the infant mortality rate was between 30 and 40 percent. Women factory workers in the 1930s were paid one-fifth the wages of men, sometimes less. In famine years women sold themselves, or were sold, into slavery or concubinage for a few pounds of rice. Women workers who protested against their conditions were placed in head stocks, jailed, tortured, or executed. French administrators admitted that there were "three prisons for every school."[4]

In the 1920s a middle-class movement arose for the liberation of women. It focused first on education, and later on political rights for women, and attacked the traditional rules regarding arranged marriages, female chastity, and occupational restrictions. My friends in Hanoi spoke disparagingly of this movement. Lê Thi Xuyên said that its demands for "freedom" were to relax and play, that it led young women into debauchery through its belief in sexual freedom, and that it even held beauty contests! It seems likely that there were differences over policy in this early movement. Nhu Man, the editor of the Hue Women's Labor-Study Association, for example, wrote articles in praise of socialism and of political organization for equal rights, as well as attacking the Confucian ideal of chastity.[5] It is clear, however, that this bourgeois movement for women's rights remained weak and scattered and that it failed to focus on the class oppression of women peasants and workers. In the 1930s, the most progressive women from middle-class, scholars', and landlords' families entered the Communist Women's Union.

Rise of the Women's Union

The Women's Union of Vietnam was founded on October 20, 1930, eight months after the formation of the Communist Party. Today it has a membership of eight million throughout the country and so must include at least half the women in Vietnam. About half a million of the members belong to the Communist Party. Most, although not all, women professional workers, youth organizers, political and trade union leaders, directors of enterprises, and members of the Communist Party are active in the union, and small groups of women in Hanoi and in each of the thirty-eight provincial capitals work full time for it. The union has brought the women of Vietnam successfully through the revolutionary wars of the last three decades, has revolutionized their position in society and in the family, and has trained them to become fully participating members of a modern nation.

It was Ho Chi Minh, above all, who recognized that a Women's Union closely associated with the Communist Party but having its own goals and structure was essential for the salvation of women in Vietnam. Ho showed a special concern for women throughout his career. My hosts told me there is a mystery about him: no one seems to know "whether he ever loved"; certainly he did not marry. But as Khanh put it, "We know that he loved all women and made them his special care." Ho often reminded his countrymen that "Women make up half of society. If women are not liberated, society is not free." In classes and public meetings Ho made women sit at the front and often asked why more of them were not present.

Ho Chi Minh and his early associates saw that peasant and working-class women labored under the combined burdens of feudalism, through exploitation by traditional landlords, and of colonialism, through unjust laws and taxes, lack of education and political representation, imprisonment, forced labor, and the horrifying conditions imposed by French capitalists in plantations, factories, and mines. In addition, all women of every class suffered the injustices of feudal family life and of male domination throughout the society. They decided that of these, the first two were the most significant, for without ending landlordism and colonialism neither women nor men

could be free. They also decided that women would necessarily be liberated to a considerable extent in the very process
of destroying landlordism and colonialism. The Communist
Party therefore taught that the landlords, colonialists, and
comprador Vietnamese, rather than men in general, were the
main enemies of women. At the same time a secondary
"inner struggle" against all forms of sexual inequality and
male contempt for women must go on in the revolutionary
ranks. Vietnamese women communists are very firm about
these priorities and completely oppose those feminists
(whom they regard as bourgeois) who claim that men in
general are the main exploiters and oppressors of women.
They point out that the oppression of women is not class
oppression, but cuts across the oppression of class and nation
while being reinforced by them. It must be tackled indepen-
dently, but never to the detriment of class and national
struggles.

Some of the most famous leaders of the Women's Union
were personal disciples of Ho Chi Minh. Minh Khai, who
founded the union and was executed by the French,
was trained by Ho in China in the late 1930s. Ly Thi Phuong
went at the age of sixteen for instruction by Ho Chi Minh in
Hong Kong and was arrested along with him but released for
lack of evidence. Noiy Thi Trung, a woman still active in the
union, came from the Tay minority, the largest group in
Vietnam. Trung learned to read and write and studied politics
and history every day with Ho in his cave by the Lenin River.

As a result of such efforts in the early 1940s the party
recruited a large number of women among the minorities,
who were numerous in the mountain provinces where guerrilla warfare began. Today, women of the minorities form a
special branch of the union and are prominent in framing its
policies. From its foundation in 1930, the equality of men
and women was written into the constitution of the Communist Party, as it was later into the constitution of Vietnam
and the proclamations of the first National Assembly of

1945. The Women's Union changed its name in different periods along with that of the Communist Party according to the policies of the times. In 1930-1935 it was the Women's Alliance; it became the Democratic League of Women in the popular front period of 1936-1939. From 1941-1946, in the struggle against the Japanese, it was the Women's Union for National Salvation; it spread throughout the country and its numbers greatly increased. After the August revolution of 1945 it became the Vietnam Women's Union, the present title. In 1960, with the organization of the South Vietnam National Liberation Front against the United States invaders and the Saigon regime, the union in the south became known as the South Vietnam Women's Union for Liberation. The northern and southern branches were reunited as the Vietnam Women's Union in June 1976 with the reunification of Vietnam. Lê Thi Xuyên stressed that through all these changes of name the personnel and organization, both in north and south, were continuous and united.

In 1930-1935 the Communist Party and the Women's Alliance operated clandestinely in the face of extreme terror by the French authorities. Meetings took place at night, in darkness. Members hid their faces, used aliases, and arrived and left one by one. Each member knew the identity of only two others so that under torture she would have little to reveal. Moving quietly among the people, the Alliance organized hundreds of strikes and demonstrations around such demands as "Reduce Wages and Interest Rates!," "Equal Pay for Equal Work!," "No Dangerous Work for Women!," "Two Months Fully Paid Maternity Leave!," "Down With Forced Marriages!," and "Abolish the Habit of Holding Women in Contempt!" At the same time, in Nghê An and Ha Tinh provinces (now Nghê Tinh) peasants armed themselves, formed soviets, and drove out the landlords and their functionaries. Under the party's and the union's aegis they distributed lands for the first time to women and admitted women to public meetings and political education classes.

The Nghê Tinh soviets fell under French bombs and shells but in many areas the party and the union had won the peasants' hearts. Wherever they organized, union members were required to practice the "Three Togethers": eating, living, and working among the peasants and the city workers. The mobilization of workers, peasants, and the city poor was the key to revolutionary struggle. From them in each period new cadres were drawn who helped shape the union's line. Said Lê Thi Xuyên, "The union must be a gentle mother, close to and understanding women, knowing all their hopes and troubles. It must study their capacities and find ways to solve their problems. If we have merit in our work we are rewarded and set an example for others. We become greater through overcoming the people's miseries."

Rich women were especially oppressed by the men of their families, and their children "spoiled and debauched" by colonial culture. Confined and disrespected in their homes, many of these women, whose families owned land or businesses, also left their comforts for life in the forest. Some later brought kinsmen and kinswomen to the revolutionary side.

The period of the Popular Front government in France was the only one in which the party and the Women's Union could organize openly. The union expanded its membership, formed reading groups to spread its literature, led strikes and demonstrations involving thousands, and in some regions gained certain basic rights: small wage increases for women, a ten-minute break to nurse babies, a factory medical center, a stoppage of corporal punishment of women and of crippling taxes imposed on women traders. Five thousand women attended the May Day rally in 1938 in Hanoi and heard Women's Union speakers voice their demands for democratic rights and for freedom from family oppression.[6]

Even in the Popular Front period, membership of the Communist Party remained secret, although the Women's Union, the trade unions, and the Youth Front became open.

"Our followers did not know who were members and who not, or even that there was a party," said Lê Thi Xuyên. She justified this on the grounds that the party won people's trust by deeds, not by explaining its structure. The people followed because of the quality of organization and because of such tangible benefits as rooms to hold meetings and ink and pens for classes. When terror returned in the 1940s under the Japanese and Vichy French regime, "the cadres were able to minimize their losses and thus preserve the people. When we had reverses through indiscretion we learned lessons from them and tried to do better next time."

During the struggles against Japanese imperialism of 1941–1945 and later against the French invaders in 1945–1954, the Women's Alliance again went underground and formed part of the Vietminh or Front for National Salvation. Women mobilized demonstrations against high taxes, against the Japanese confiscation of rice, against their policy of forcing the Vietnamese to grow jute, and against the press-ganging of men into the Japanese and later the French occupation armies. Association members bought and transported weapons, opened inns and restaurants to finance the movement, carried messages among the revolutionaries, and agitated among the enemy soldiers. In many cases women forced into prostitution by the French, and later by the United States invaders, engaged in sabotage on behalf of the Women's Union or served as spies.

During the 1940s, the Communist Party and the Women's Union gradually built nationwide structures. The union formed groups led by party members in every village, district town, and provincial capital under the organization of its national central committee. Hanoi, Haiphong, and Saigon, the only large cities, had their own organizations comparable to provinces; Hue and Da Nang were important provincial centers. Leadership and authority from the national through the provincial and city to the district and village hierarchies were maintained throughout the whole period, even during the United States occupation of the south. Lê Thi Xuyên mentioned that after the "temporary" division of the country in 1954 and the repression unleashed by Ngô Dinh Diêm, many party and women's organizers were able to remain in hiding in the south, although some, like Vô Thi Thê, were regrouped to the north. Once the liberation war began in the south in 1960, communications and aid flowed constantly from north to south in spite of the dangers and obstacles. Women traveling south from north Vietnam often took two months to reach their destination; some took six months to return. "Strict disguise was essential, and cadres had to have an indomitable spirit." In the south in the face of the propaganda and terror of the puppet regime and the United States forces, the "Three Togethers" became more than ever mandatory in order to gain the people's confidence and to hide the cadres.

Throughout, women members of the trade unions and the Youth Union (composed of people aged fifteen to thirty) also belonged to the Women's Union. Men and women organized together in the trade and youth unions and both sexes provided their leadership, but the leaders of these organizations consulted with the Women's Union about the special problems of women and female youth.

Women's achievements reached their height during the war against the United States invaders. No task was too unfamiliar, dangerous, or arduous for women volunteers: constructing roads and bridges in forest zones near the border between the north and south, carrying ammunition to the front, making and planting spikes for ambushes, shooting down planes with rifles and antiaircraft guns, infiltrating and organizing villages under enemy control, smuggling mines into enemy encampments, and carrying on guerrilla and regular warfare. Many tens of thousands of women were captured by the enemy and put to torture, often later to be executed or to die of their injuries.[7] In the liberated zones and in north Vietnam women carried on the less spectacular tasks of production, care, and healing that kept the war going and raised the next generation. With most able-bodied men in the forces, women performed extraordinary feats in irrigation, agriculture, construction, industry, medicine, education, and child care, frequently under bombing raids and in some areas in underground tunnels. The hardest contribution of hundreds of thousands of older women was to have some or all of their children and grandchildren killed in action, and to discipline their grief into still greater efforts to serve the nation and expel the enemy. In south Vietnam, women organized clandestine trade unions, even in Saigon where all trade unions and public gatherings of nonfamily groups were illegal. In 1970, such efforts culminated in a general strike of 700,000 workers demanding higher wages and peace negotiations. Many smaller strikes paralyzed particular industries and hastened the day of victory.

7

Vietnamese Women Today

In north Vietnam since 1945, and in those areas of the south that were liberated some years ago, women's lives have been revolutionized beyond all comparison with their traditional roles. Lê Thi and Lê Thi Xuyên highlighted in particular the modern rights and contributions of women in the family, the economy, and the political and administrative spheres.

Women in the Family

Throughout their history, the Vietnamese communists have seen the family as a focal unit to be both protected and revolutionized. The first constitution of independent Vietnam of November 1945 declared the equality of men and women in all fields. In the north during and after the liberation from the French invasion of 1945–1954, these rights were established in a series of laws, while at the same time the needs of women and children were met by welfare provisions relating to maternity, health care, nurseries, and kindergartens. As early as 1945 women received the right to vote and to stand for elections to the National Assembly, the People's Councils, and the executive committees. In 1950, a Law on Marriage and the Family guaranteed the equality of husband and wife, full juridical power of the married woman, the right of widowers, widows, and children to divide the ancestral property, the right of illegitimate, abandoned, or adopted children to seek out their natural parents, and the right of persons of eighteen and upwards to marry without parental consent. In 1959 a new Law on Marriage and the Family confirmed and expanded these provisions. Since the liberation of the south in 1975, these laws relating to women have been extended throughout Vietnam.

While explaining the provisions of the modern law, Lê Thi and my other friends gave me some sidelights on how it works in practice.

Love marriages, they told me, are now in fact as well as in theory normal in Vietnam, and parental consent is not required. Although the legal age of marriage is now eighteen for women and twenty-one for men, a girl who becomes pregnant before eighteen will be encouraged by the union to marry ("and," says Khanh, "severely criticized!"). And although divorce is permitted at the request of either or both parties, it can take place only after the Women's Union and the People's Court have counseled the couple, have tried to save the marriage, and have established that the differences are irremediable. Many women who have made unhappy arranged marriages were divorced soon after the revolution, but today divorce is rare.

Monogamy, premarital chastity, and fidelity in marriage are highly valued for both men and women in modern Vietnam. The 1959 ban on polygyny, which was formerly prevalent, made great changes in family life, although polygynous marriages contracted before the revolution are honored if all parties wish it. Prostitution and concubinage are forbidden and, thanks to the union's vigilance, are said no longer to exist in the north. In the south, the rehabilitation of 500,000 prostitutes is an urgent priority. In the north rape is now said to be unheard of, whereas it was once common on the part of landlords and of the French, Japanese, and (in the south) the United States invaders. In the family ideology propounded by the government, the Communist Party, and the Women's Union, not only premarital sexual relations and adultery, but also all forms of lewd or "loose" behavior appear to be severely frowned on. The ideal is a period of courtship followed by monogamous marriage in which the couple permanently and lovingly serve one another, their children, their parents, and their society in equal partnership. Men and women mingle freely in their work and social life, but they appear to do so mainly in groups and, as far as I could see, with a kind of gentle comradeship. The union has protected women from the abuses so often prevalent in wartime and has maintained high standards of conduct while introducing women into public life in a democratic, industrializing society.

It may be that being middle aged and listening often to older women leaders, I received a rather one-sided impression of relations between the sexes in Vietnam. Margaret Randall reports, for example, that a young woman Communist in north Vietnam told her that although it was customary, and expected, that everyone would marry, illegitimate births are not exactly rare and even when both are single the parents do not always marry. If the couple have different ideas about life they may decide to separate even though they love each other and the woman is pregnant. This young woman thought there was nothing wrong with such behavior, but said that some people looked down on it.[1] It seems likely, moreover, that "aberrant" marriage customs are still found among some of the ethnic minorities and the peasants of the north. Polygyny, for example, does not appear to have entirely gone out of practice, for Lê Thi Xuyên mentioned it as one of the abuses against which the union occasionally still has to struggle. What is perhaps most important is that the children of unmarried parents, who were once despised or even killed, today receive the full protection of the law and, as far as can be managed, equal treatment with other children.

The Women's Union is primarily responsible for settling

family disputes. In small quarrels they remonstrate with the parties. In big ones, union leaders select a "reconciliation group" of three to five local men and women who are respected by the people, to arbitrate the dispute. If the union or the committee is unable to effect arbitration, the case goes to the People's Court. Most disputes are settled locally and require the court's ratification only in cases of divorce or division of property. It seems that women are especially encouraged to appeal to the union against a family member who infringes modern law through "feudal" behavior. Wives whose husbands beat them or try to marry a second wife, or whose mothers-in-law ill treat them, were mentioned as examples.

The families of wounded and dead fighters are a special responsibility of the Women's Union. Lê Thi Xuyên stressed that "the spiritual life of these families is in our care, especially when they are ill or sorrowing." Union members take turns in helping such families with household chores, feeding their cattle, tending the children and cooking if the mother falls ill or if she gives birth while her husband is away or is wounded, and helping the children with their schoolwork. Special days are set aside to honor dead and wounded fighters and meet their wives and mothers, ask after their health, and explain the party's and the state's policies towards them. Union members pay visits to such families on all holidays and festivals "to encourage them."

Women in the Workforce

What is the position of working women today, and what are the Women's Union's goals? The Vietnamese believe that women can become equal to men without playing identical roles with them in all spheres of activity. They also believe that equality can be attained without any weakening of the family as the main residential unit and focus for love, sexual relations, and daily cooperation. These views interested me, for they contrast with beliefs prevalent in the women's liberation movements of Western Europe and North America, that equality of the sexes must involve occupational androgyny, complete sexual freedom, and eventually, the disappearance of the family.

Vietnamese woman leaders hold that women's reproductive capacity, the average differences in physique between men and women, and the differences in their history, make it more appropriate for *some* activities to be done by women, while at the same time the *majority* of roles and occupations are fully opened to both sexes. This belief reflects back into child training. As Phan Minh Hien, a south Vietnamese delegate to Vancouver, said in 1971, "A good man is loyal to his wife, and a good woman is a good housewife. We educate women to take care of the family as well as other things. Double responsibility for the family as well as the organization is our slogan. If the wife is busy with work in the community the husband must take care of the children, but generally the responsibility rests with women. We think that boys and girls should be valued equally; however, we think that little boys should act like little boys, and little girls like little girls. I bought some toys for my children, and I bought a ball for the boy and a doll for the girl."[2]

This statement by an older woman might be considered old fashioned by at least some younger Vietnamese, and I am sure that Vietnamese girls play with balls! Nevertheless, even young women agreed that motherhood is a special and central responsibility for women and that certain tasks and attitudes are more easily learned by women than by men. Lê Thi pointed out, for example, that in 1950 Ho Chi Minh remarked that the emancipation of women did not mean, "Today I sweep the floor, tomorrow you," but rather a general standard of equality in culture and politics. She said that it is not intrinsically important for men to wash the dishes, but that it *is* essential to have day-care centers, kindergartens, hospitals, canteens, and welfare measures to reduce the domestic work of women, free them for work outside the home, and give them leisure to enjoy education and take part in politics and culture. She added, however, that the modern standards of equality and comradeship do require men to help their wives to the extent that the woman is not left with an unjust burden of home care and outside work. Many men in Hanoi, for example, do all the family's marketing and heavier chores.

Women's Union leaders expect that for a long time to come, perhaps indefinitely, women will do most of the child care and will be prominent in light industry (especially food industries and textiles) and medicine. Women are actually prohibited by law from working underground in mines or in other heavy work judged dangerous or detrimental to their health—a reaction against the murderous conditions imposed on women and children in mines and plantations by the French. Women are not, however, prevented from volunteering for dangerous work in wartime or work issuing from the war. Many women, for example, volunteered along with men to remove bombs and mines during the restoration of agricultural and forest lands, and some were killed.

Quite apart from ideology, thirty years of warfare necessarily affected the sexual division of labor. In north Vietnam, although both men and women went south to the front, more men than women left their homes. As in most modern wars, women took over their jobs. The census of North Vietnam of 1972 found women to be 65 percent of agricultural workers. They continued to do their traditional tasks of transplanting, weeding, assisting with the harvest, growing vegetables, and tending poultry, but also learned to plow, fertilize the fields, dig irrigation ditches, and breed pigs, cattle, and buffaloes. Women have, however, virtually given up plowing, digging, and other very heavy agricultural work since the war ended and men began to come home. The fact that in 1972 women formed the majority of workers in light industry, trade, medical work, and education may also have been at least partly a reflection of wartime conditions.

In spite of some continuation of a sexual division of labor, it must be emphasized that the participation of Vietnamese women in all major fields is truly remarkable by comparison, for example, with both India and Canada, two other countries with which I am familiar.[3] In north Vietnam almost all able-bodied women work outside the home, whereas in Canada the participation rate for women over fourteen was 36 percent and in India 20 percent in 1969. Women were 35 percent of all government officials and civil servants in north Vietnam in 1972, 17 percent in Canada in 1969, and 16 percent in India. Vietnamese women were 65 percent of those in agriculture and livestock care and 25 percent in forestry. Roughly corresponding figures for women in India were 13 percent of independent cultivators, 34 percent of agricultural laborers, and 19 percent in forestry, livestock care, plantation labor, fishing, hunting, and allied activities. In Canada the proportions of women in these occupations were too low to be listed separately, but women were only 6 percent of all "laborers and unskilled workers." In Vietnam, women were 31 percent of those in communications and transport, whereas they were only 3 percent in India, but were 53 percent in Canada, probably mainly as telephone operators. Vietnamese women were 63 percent of those in light industry and 25 percent in heavy industry; women were 9 percent of all factory workers in India in 1969 and 21 percent of those in cottage industries, while they were 15 percent of all craft and "production process" workers in Canada. In Vietnam, women were 59 percent of all those in trade and sales, whereas they were 37 percent in Canada (where they predominate as salespersons in stores) and only 6 percent in India. Thirty-five percent of civil engineers in Vietnam were women, but only 1.2 percent in India; 0.3 percent of engineers in Canada were women in 1961. Vietnamese women are 19 percent of scientists, and 36 percent of those in "culture and the arts," 65 percent of medical workers, and 54 percent of educators. Comparable figures are not available to me for Canada, but women are 18 percent of all "professional and technical personnel," while in India women are 16 percent in "other services," which presumably include science, culture and the arts, and the professions.

The different structures of the three economies, of course, make these comparisons only partly meaningful. Thirty-four percent of all Canadian women workers, for example, are clerical workers, 22 percent service and recreation workers, 18 percent professional and technical, 12 percent in crafts and industries, and fewer than 1 percent in agriculture and unskilled labor. By contrast, 83 percent of working women in India are in agriculture, and probably a similar percentage in Vietnam. Nevertheless, the contrasts are sufficiently gross to reveal the much greater participation of Vietnamese women in almost all fields of the economy, including those requiring professional training.

Women's Wages and Incomes

Incomes and wages in Vietnam, although very low by Western standards, do not differ according to the sex of the worker. Such discrimination is, of course, commonplace both in Canada and in India. Equal pay for equal work, and equal chances of promotion for men and women, are normal in Vietnam. In agricultural cooperatives all adults receive a basic payment in rice and money, which is increased for unusually heavy or skilled work. As examples, I was told that sowing and transplanting, done by women, and ditch digging (traditionally masculine) rank as "heavy" or "skilled" occupations and command higher wages. In south India, by contrast, women's work of transplanting paddy and weeding the paddy fields, although back-breaking, is usually paid only half or less of the average wage for male agricultural labor.

In India and Canada, a majority of women are financially dependent on men for a large part of their lives, but in Vietnam, both men and women are financially independent. They receive pensions in old age and sickness and, in the case of women, three months' fully paid maternity leave. Much of the housework and part of the childcare is done by older women, who live on pensions after the age of fifty-five and who can thus free younger women for work outside the home.

Women in Politics and Government

Similar contrasts appear in women's participation in government, politics, and management. Women are 26 percent of the Vietnamese National Assembly, elected in 1976; they were 16.9 percent of the North Vietnamese National Assembly in 1971, when 4 women were also vice-ministers in the government. Of the 132 women elected in 1976, 18 are from ethnic minorities (comparable to India's "tribals" and to Canada's Native People), 45 are political cadres, 8 are from the armed forces, 21 are workers, 31 peasants, 22 intellectuals, 4 craft workers, and 23 Women's Union cadres, while 12 are women elected by the people as "national heroines" in war or production, and 37 are youth. By contrast, women formed only 9 percent of India's upper house of Parliament and 4 percent of the lower house in 1976. In Canada, although women received the vote in 1918, only 1 percent of federal and provincial politicians elected between then and 1970 were women. Canada had only one woman member of Parliament, or 0.4 percent of the total, in 1969, and only four women senators out of 102. In north Vietnam in 1971, two-thirds of the members of village administration committees were women, and out of 5,000 villages, 4,300 had women as village heads. In the liberated areas of south Vietnam in 1971, 75 percent of the members of village committees were women, and in both north and south, women were largely represented in district, provincial, and regional councils. In 1976, women were directors or vice-directors of 3,580, or more than 40 percent, of the agricultural cooperatives in north Vietnam, and women headed 13,783 rural production units. In India women are seldom elected to other than the single seat reserved for them on village (*panchayat*) committees, and are never, to my knowledge, elected as presidents of village committees or appointed by the government as village headmen. In Canada, women fill only 2 percent of all "managerial" roles.

In spite of their great advances, it is still apparently too early for women to play a fully equal role in the highest political and governmental councils in Vietnam. Although about half the members of the Communist Party are women, there were only 142 women among the 1,008 delegates to the Fourth Party Congress in December 1976, and only seven women were elected to a Central Committee of 133 members and alternate members.[4] Two of these Central Committee members are the president of the Women's Union and the former president of the Women's Union for Liberation in south Vietnam; the latter became vice-president of the union after the reunification of Vietnam. In the Women's Union report on the Fourth Party Congress no women are mentioned as having been elected to the seventeen-member Political Bureau or the nine-member Secretariat. Only one woman, Mme. Nguyen Thi Binh, the former foreign minister of south Vietnam's Provisional Revolutionary Government, is a member of the thirty-six-member Government Council of Ministers elected by the National Assembly in July 1976. It seems clear that at present, women leaders in Vietnam regard raising the educational, cultural, and political level of all women, and the leadership capacities of women of middle rank, as more urgent priorities than struggling to place a small number of women in the highest centers of power. As more and more women attain the highest qualifications, however, there would seem to be no bar to the selection of women for the top governmental positions.

Tasks of the Women's Union

Lê Thi Xuyên said she saw six kinds of tasks for the Women's Union today:

1. Educating women in scientific knowledge and "exemplary values."

2. Mobilizing them in production.

3. Inspiring and organizing them to create a new, socialist type of family.

4. Preparing them for the proper care of healthy living conditions.

5. Developing and consolidating the organization of the union.

6. Developing the union's international relations.

While I do not know the precise structure of the union, it is clear that a small number of women, perhaps several thousand, work full time at these tasks at the national, provincial, and district levels, and that a much larger number use their spare time to conduct classes, give demonstrations, and "make propaganda" (i.e., disseminate knowledge and values) in the towns and villages.

(1) *Education:* The union's education of women goes on side by side with that in the schools and colleges and is much concerned with "describing and showing exemplary characters." This is done through personal example and by means of books and magazines printed by the union press and written by its members, articles about women in the newspapers, films and programs on radio and television, and public and private meetings.

The values stressed by Lê Thi Xuyên include, above all, patriotism and hatred of imperialist aggression. Women, she said, must learn to understand and love national independence and socialism, recognizing that without these they have nothing, but with them they can achieve equality and emancipation.

Second, she stressed hard work to improve production and build the country, and third, "the spirit of collective mastery," which allows women to see that where once, individually, they were slaves, now together they can be free. "Women must try to equal men in skills, knowledge, and self-command, while remembering that being a mother is their special and lofty responsibility."

Women, of course, have had to be thoroughly acquainted with military training, which continues among both male and female youth. From 1930 to 1936 they used swords and sticks in guerrilla actions against the French in Nghê Tinh. Fighting became more widespread under the Japanese, and almost universal in the anti-French and anti-United States wars. Books and stories about Vietnamese heroines from the distant past form a storehouse of values for the woman fighter.

At the same time, women are urged to throw off the subordination of the past and take part as fully as possible in scientific education, medical care and research, and in "helping to manage state affairs at every level." Through broadcasts, meetings, and articles, the Women's Union also educates men "to see the capacities and heroism of women, to enhance their worth and dignity, and not to denigrate them."

(2) *Production:* Mobilizing women for production especially involves spreading improved agricultural methods. While each rural cooperative has a group of experts in engineering, construction, social welfare, and medicine, and an elected managerial staff, leaders of the union hold technical classes for women. The classes include teaching women to transplant paddy seedlings in rows; to grow green manure; to select and soak seedlings by modern methods; to mix chemical fertilizers so as to correct the balance of various soils; to

improve animal hygiene and the breeding of cattle, pigs, and poultry; and to weave, cook, and sew. Monthly meetings of women are held in each production team to discuss their problems, explain new government policies, hear grievances and give advice. Women are taught to practice economy with money and food, not to use all their wages on the first of the month, and especially "not to eat everything at harvest time and not to spend too much on marriages and festivals." They are not forbidden to buy jewelry but are discouraged from prizing it too much and from vying with one another.

(3) *The Family:* In spite of the momentous changes that have already occurred in Vietnamese families, the union is not yet satisfied and is currently carrying on a special drive to promote socialist family life. Lê Thi Xuyên said that there is still a great deal to be done to "eliminate feudal customs." What the union most wants are "real sentiment and love between husband and wife, with democratic discussion and mutual respect, in their work together and in rearing their children." My friends admitted that some men still try to dominate their wives and that men must be urged to do more of the heavy work around the house and garden; some young men do this, but not enough. It occurred to me that marital problems might have come more to the forefront with the end of the war and the return of men to their homes, and I asked whether many couples were finding themselves incompatible after years of separation. "No," they said with some surprise, "that's not the problem—we are only too glad to be together again," but they acknowledged that men and women, especially men, must adjust their roles now that families are being reunited. The Women's Union has a large part to play by holding meetings of parents and of men and women teachers in villages and explaining to them the proper family norms, but the trade unions must also step in to reeducate the men. "Is there a Men's Union? Do you need one?" I asked them. The women laughed ruefully and said there is not, but that they sometimes feel the men need one

in order to reeducate themselves, while some of the men joke that they need one, for self-defense.

Another problem is lack of cooperation and amity among city families who occupy rooms in a collective block and share a kitchen and bathroom. My hosts (who live in similar circumstances) want to see all such families educated to be "civilized, orderly, and clean."

Peasant families, they told me, have two particular weaknesses that they would like to see eradicated. One is "superstition," by which they said they meant horoscopes, palmistry, and belief in ghosts and in magic. As an anthropologist my impulse was to say, "Why worry?" but I realized that for Marxists belief in omens is a particular sign of failure, for it suggests that fate and not humans control the future. The Vietnamese communists have, moreover, waged decades of ideological struggle against such modern religious movements as the Hoa Hao and the Cao Dai, which relied much on omens and prophecies.

The other weakness relates to birth control. The 1975 census of Vietnam surprised the government by revealing a population of 48.8 million, an increase of more than 50 percent since 1945. Although the overall density is only 383 per square mile, the government wishes to curtail further increase as fast as possible. The ideal, as in China and India, is two children per family, and the union is in charge of distributing birth control devices and disseminating propaganda. Union members give out condoms free of charge to married couples and try to persuade women with two children to have intrauterine devices fitted. A woman who undergoes the insertion is given the same cash bonus she would receive if she had a baby.

The idea of compulsion in family planning is, however, abhorrent to members of the union; my friends were horrified to hear of forced sterilizations under the Emergency in India. The sterilization of men is rare in Vietnam; it is usually done for heads of cooperatives or other enterprises who already have two children and want to be sure they will set a good example and have no more. Tubal ligation for women, my hosts thought, is either a rare surgical procedure carried out in certain illnesses or is not practiced at all. Above all, they explained that birth control is designed to make individual women's lives happier, healthier, and more leisurely, quite as much as to benefit the nation. Peasant families, however, still tend to prefer four children to two, and it is expected to be several years before most of them meet the norm.

Among the minor problems of family life are the tendency of some women to try to dominate their daughters-in-law, and of some families to prefer boys to girls. But these "feudal" features are disappearing with collectivization, for once land is owned and managed communally, elders lose their right to dictate to juniors, and boys are no longer valued as heirs of the patrimony.

(4) *Improving Living Conditions:* If one contrasts Vietnam with India, or with what Vietnam is said to have been like before the revolution, it is clear that a vast educational program has gone on in relation to hygiene, health care, and personal habits. I have already mentioned the universality of latrines in town and countryside; the absence of garbage in the streets and of spitting, urination, and defecation in public; and the campaign to collect all waste for fertilizer. All of these changes have required patient, kindly instruction and explanation over many years, much of which has been done by the Women's Union. Lê Thi Xuyên also referred to regular liaison work between the union and the schools, law courts, trade unions, and hospitals so as to preserve the health and make happier the lives of women. As a result of the union's pressure to fulfill the needs of working women, a number of laws and customs have come into being which give them special protection. One such law is the prohibition against women working underground in mines and in similarly dangerous places. Peasant women who are pregnant or menstru-

ating are exempt from tasks which require them to stand in cold water (such as paddy transplanting) or to walk far from home; instead they are given lighter, more convenient tasks close to home. Pregnant women have the right to two free medical examinations and to free hospital treatment during childbirth, whereas they once had only the care of a local midwife untrained in modern hygiene, as in much of India today. As a result of the union's efforts, day-care centers and kindergartens have been established in virtually every village in the north and are increasing in numbers in the cities. For a year after a birth, working women are allowed two half-hour breaks a day to nurse their babies; those with twins have two one-hour breaks. Members of the union hold classes to teach women to care for their own health through cleanliness during menstruation and after a birth, to carry out first aid in emergencies, and to observe rules of hygiene in cookery and daily living. As the society moves toward socialism, they must constantly report back women's reactions to their changing circumstances, so that new legislation may, if necessary, be formed to further their protection and liberation.

(5) *Organizing the Women's Union:* The union's fifth main task is to develop its own organization and train its members. Most women in government are members of the union and received at least part of their training from it, and most highly placed women executives are members of the union's central committee. The union has its own constitution, officers, statutes, finances, cadre training schools, special advisory relations with the ministries of health and education, and legal ties to all other governing bodies. Its members must learn the main laws and programs of the state as well as the statutes and policies of the union, and in addition to their special skills must learn how to organize meetings, hold discussion groups, and carry out educational work. Officers of the union, like other intellectuals, must

spend one month a year in a village, living, eating, and working with the peasants.

(6) *The Union's International Relations:* The union's foreign policy, says Lê Thi Xuyên, is "to strengthen solidarity with women in other countries, to take part in movements for peace, social progress, and democracy throughout the world, and to educate Vietnamese women about the spirit of internationalism." She adds, "We believe that winning our own national independence was a contribution to world independence and peace." The union's main ties, she explains, must be with the socialist countries, especially in Laos and Cambodia, but it must try to strengthen solidarity with women in every country.

During the war the union sent delegations of women (often with male interpreters) to countries throughout the world to explain their liberation struggle and mobilize support. Visits to Canada were especially valued as offering opportunities to meet American women's groups; it was at two such large conferences that I first met Lê Thi and Vô Thi Thê. In the middle of my visit to Hanoi, Duyên, one of my hosts, hurried off to a conference in Portugal. The sixteen members of the union's international affairs branch speak more than a dozen languages between them and write and translate articles on women for the union's foreign language publications, in addition to receiving delegates from countries throughout the world. Its foreign relations seem to me to be among the union's most important mandates, for it is through them that Vietnamese women's rich experience can be transmitted to other lands.

8

A Hanoi Textile Mill

The March 8th Factory in Hanoi was founded in 1960 on Vietnamese Women's Day, the anniversary of the Women's Union. The buildings were completed in 1965. The workers lent sums from their earnings to pay for them, as did women from outside the mill.

The factory contains 6,000 workers and officers and is probably the biggest textile mill—certainly one of the best—in north Vietnam. Fifty-five hundred of the personnel are manual workers, of whom 76 percent (and 75 percent of the total personnel) are women.

When Khanh, Liên, and I arrive at 2 P.M. on November 13, one of the three eight-hour shifts is ending and hundreds of people on bicycles are pouring out of the gateway. We are met by Mrs. Hoa, a vice-director of the factory, and by a trade union leader who is vice-president of the women workers. The former is about sixty, thin and worn, but eager, active, and precise; the latter is in her early fifties—a plump, warm person with an impulsive manner. Unlike most women I have met, these two go barefoot in their office building, although they put on sandals to cross the yard and to enter the workshops. As always, tea and toffees punctuate our meeting, which opens with a kind speech of welcome.

Women are almost, although not quite, as prominent in the factory's leadership as among its workers. About half the board of directors and the heads and vice-heads of departments are women. Three hundred and five of the workers, or 5 percent, have completed their technical training at the secondary level; another 103 have passed the first, or university level. Seventy percent of these advanced workers are women.

A few months after the factory opened in 1965, the government had to evacuate the personnel and machinery to avoid "the Johnson war." Women workers alone removed 3,000 tons of equipment to five scattered places outside Hanoi. United States planes bombed the factory buildings; there are still big holes in the ceilings.

Despite the war, the mill has overfulfilled its targets every year, and as a result has received the Third Order of Production among all factories in north Vietnam, and the First Order of Emulation among all factories concerned with light industry. (There are also First and Second Orders of Production, but, as the vice-director says smiling, "We haven't achieved them yet.") I do not know what the production targets have been, but winning these honors has clearly cost enormous effort.

Continuing her recital of exploits, Mrs. Hoa tells me that three women workers have won individual Third Order of Production awards for "fighting while working"—that is, they shot down a United States pilotless plane during working hours on March 13, 1968. The factory's kindergarten has received the Third Order of Production rank for excellent child care, and the kitchen a "recommendation paper" (certificate of merit?) from the state. Thirteen women hold President Ho Chi Minh badges for acts of outstanding bravery or merit. The award of "emulation fighters" has been granted to individual workers 1,880 times, 1,385 of them to women, and whole production groups have received the acclaim of "socialist production groups" 234 times for excellence in every field. With pride, the women tell me that on ninety-four of these occasions the group was composed entirely of women, while seventy-nine times about half its members were women. In 1971, the mill won the first prize in a competition among factories throughout the north, and twenty-four of its workers obtained the title of "skilled workers." In 1976 these skilled workers hope in turn to win a competition among skilled workers in factories throughout north Vietnam.

I cannot help smiling at this torrent of honors and badges, which reminds me of Girl Guide days, and wondering what it really means to the workers. After an hour of conversation there enters one worker, Châu, aged thirty-five, to whom the honors do mean much. She has been declared an "emulation fighter" many times, and is introduced as a model worker. She is also an executive member of the Hanoi branch of the Women's Union. She started work when the mill opened in 1965 and helped to evacuate and later to replace the machinery. Smiling brightly, Châu says that her achievements are really nothing; the highest honor in the mill goes to a woman named Cu Thi Hâu, who has been elected a Heroine of Production. Châu has two daughters. Her four-year-old attends a kindergarten near her home; the nine-year-old is also a prize winner, Mrs. Hoa tells me, and stands first in her class.

The factory itself has two kindergartens, each with attached day-nurseries and each containing about 500 children. Infants under the age of two go home with their mothers after the eight-hour shift; the mothers enjoy two half-hour breaks per shift to nurse them. Children over two may stay in the kindergarten throughout the five days and nights of the work week if their parents wish. Parents may choose whether to leave their children in a kindergarten in either the factory or the residential neighborhood, or with an older relative at home. Most people prefer the kindergarten because children learn cooperation and lessons and are prepared for the elementary school at five. Each kindergarten has isolation rooms for sick children; the factory also has rest rooms for workers who are indisposed. The vice-secretary tells me that these welfare measures proved essential in wartime to maintain health and production, but that they are needed anyway, since most mothers like their children near them, even more so when the child is ill. For more serious conditions, the factory has a hospital with seventy beds—twenty for child-birth, twenty for sick children, and thirty for medical or surgical cases.

I have been curious about the social origins of the women I have met so far. In *Community and Revolution in Modern Vietnam,* Alexander B. Woodside notes that only 16 percent of the Communist Party members of north Vietnam were of worker origin in 1968.[1] I know that a substantial number of the Hanoi leaders of the Women's Union are the daughters of professors, bureaucrats, or landlord-scholars, some of whom boycotted service with the French. The Hanoi leaders' poise, articulateness, dignity, and delicacy of manners suggest upper-class background, although they are quick to point out that the "proletarian viewpoint," and not social origins, is what counts. In this factory, however, the authorities are almost entirely of worker origin.

The structure is as follows. The director, a man, was appointed by the Ministry of Light Industries. He was for-merly a thread-maker in another mill, and is a member of the Communist Party. Under him are three appointed women vice-directors. Mrs. Hoa, our host, headed the canteen before her promotion. Mrs. Hao and Mrs. Lau, the two other vice-directors, were respectively a clerk in the mill's counting house and a production worker. A fourth woman who was formerly a vice-director has been promoted and is now a member of the central committee of the Women's Union.

Under the vice-directors are the heads and vice-heads of the eleven cabinets. They are (1) overall planning and admini-stration, (2) technical problems, (3) finance, (4) building con-struction and civil engineering, (5) furnishing of materials and equipment, (6) health care of staff, workers, and children,

(7) canteen, (8) education of workers and kindergarten children, (9) cultural events, (10) technical training of workers, and (11) workers' politics.

The mill is spatially and technically divided into eight sections, each with a head elected by the workers. All workers belong to a trade union which has a branch in each section and is itself a branch of the National Trade Union of Weavers. This mill's trade union has an executive committee of nineteen workers elected by the workers at large. Its job, I am told, is to express the opinions of workers to the management and to mobilize workers to fulfill the production targets and programs of the state. It can modify the way in which the factory is run and the work carried out, but cannot change the targets.

My companions do not answer my question about the cash size of wages, I think perhaps because they feel the amounts would seem too small to a Westerner. Instead they tell me that wages are low but prices are also low and welfare facilities are free. The minimum wage in this factory is adequate to maintain two adults, and the differentials are small. The mill's director earns three times the wage of the highest paid workers. There are five grades of pay among the workers, the highest being twice that of the lowest; thus, the differential in the mill as a whole is one of six times from top to bottom. Workers undergo examinations before promotion to a higher grade, in which both their production and their discipline are considered. There is equal pay for equal work between men and women; and heavier work, whether by men or women, commands higher pay.

Most workers live in government housing, the rest in private homes. Workers pay 1 percent of their incomes as rent; so do Khanh and Liên, both of whom live in government apartments. The quality of housing in Hanoi does not vary much, I am told, but as one's wage rises, so usually does one's accommodation.

Wages in all institutions are coordinated by the government across the country. If, however, a factory exceeds its target, it receives a bonus which is distributed to particular workers whose productivity (measured as piece work) is exceptional. The size of bonuses and the number of workers receiving them seems to.be quite small. Châu is a fifth (the highest) grade worker and also receives a bonus for excellent production. When I ask if all fifth grade workers get bonuses, everyone laughs and says no, indeed, what a thought!

My head is full of questions about this prize winning. Does it produce harmony and satisfaction among the workers, or does it breed backbiting, competitive individualism, and apple polishing? Is it really necessary to boost production, or could the same material result be achieved through moral incentives and cooperative determination among the workers? What is the philosophy of Vietnam regarding material incentives and where do they stand in the recent controversy about this between China and the Soviet Union? I cannot ask all these questions now, but when I do question whether this system brings out the best in people, there is a chorus of affirmation. Everyone present insists that those who work hardest *should* receive more, and that people enjoy emulation in serving the country and take pride in receiving and according its honors. Two well known sayings of Ho Chi Minh are mentioned: "More work means more pay, less work means less pay, no work means no pay," and "To engage in emulation means to love one's country; anyone who loves his country must be engaged in emulation."

Although the struggle for honors, prizes, and bonuses looks like competition to a Westerner, my friends do seem to see it rather as emulation—trying to improve by imitating the best in others or, perhaps, competing in service and virtue and obtaining just rewards. And although I fail to inquire closely, I learn that at least some of the awards are made to people recommended or elected by their peers. In particular, "heroes" and "heroines," whether in battle or in production, are elected by the people, and my friends are as astonished to know that heroes are not elected in North America as I am to learn that they are in Vietnam.

The state buys the mill's products and sells them in state-owned stores. It is impossible for any enterprise to sell privately to another.

We cross the courtyard to one of the main buildings of the factory; Châu excuses herself, saying she can't spend any more time away from her work.

One of the buildings in the courtyard bears in enormous letters the message, "ALL FOR PRODUCTION, ALL FOR SOCIALIST CONSTRUCTION." It is the current national slogan, adopted after the war and the reunification of Vietnam. Hearing my hosts discuss it, I do not feel it is "materialistic" or "economist." Their strenuous determination to rebuild their country and provide decently for everyone seems to me a sacred intention after all they have endured. Above the main workshop another huge slogan reads, "President Ho Chi Minh lives forever in our cause." And this too, it seems to me, is not idolatry or "personality cult": Ho Chi Minh represented all that is noblest in the Vietnamese revolution and set the standards for its future. Elsewhere, all over the country, one sees signs inscribed with his last injunction: "Our mountains, our rivers, our people will always be; the American invaders defeated, we will rebuild our land ten times more beautiful."

The front veranda of the workshop we enter is adorned with a banner welcoming the Fourth Congress of the Workers' Party, which takes place on December 10 to 20. The last congress was in 1960. None could be held during wartime, although congresses should normally be scheduled every five years. Banners welcome the congress at intervals along the streets all over Hanoi, and every factory, cooperative, and other workplace is holding meetings to discuss its objectives. Provincial congresses of lower level delegates meet next week to debate the main issues before the central congress. Below the banner, lists of production targets for the mill's sections, and of actual production, are posted. There is also a long list of workers who have exceeded their individual targets for this year, together with the amounts of their targets and of their actual production.

On a blackboard on the veranda, in neat handwriting in white chalk, are some criticisms by trade union leaders of unnamed workers:

1. High heels are dangerous in work and are better discarded for flat heels.

2. Lateness is a discredit to the mill; workers should be prompt.

3. Shifts should be changed promptly and in an orderly way.

4. Bare feet are dangerous—shoes should be worn.

On the walls of the passage from the veranda into the workshop are items assembled by workers for the party congress, including photographs of Ho Chi Minh and other leaders, and several news articles. Half a dozen handwritten articles and poems by workers express their thoughts on the party congress and their experiences in work.

The workshop we enter is very large, the noise of machinery deafening. Hundreds of looms are at work with one worker to each row of four. The workers, mostly women, are in white uniforms, and many wear masks to protect them against the cotton fluff. Others find their masks uncomfortable and discard them. Fluff seems to be everywhere—on the rafters, around the bomb holes in the high, dark ceiling, in the air, and on the machinery. As they tend their looms the workers keep collecting and discarding the fluff into bins. The product of the looms is bales of unbleached cotton cloth. People grin at us as we walk through, and the section leader comes up to shake hands. It is impossible to talk because of the din, and I want to get out quickly before my eardrums split.

We pass through two other, quieter workshops, one in which thread is being transferred from large rollers to small spools, with women at work removing the spools and joining the snapped threads, and another in which coarse cotton and fluff are processed on to the rollers. Thick fluff on the roof and walls and in the air resembles a snowfall. A small group of women and one workman, some in masks, sit chatting in the corridor during a break; they stand up politely as we pass.

The machinery in this factory came from China in 1960. The vice-director says the workers soon get used to it, but the trade union leader says it causes headaches across the top of the head, and echoes in one's brain for hours after the shift is over. Research is being done on how to reduce the noise. The management does its best by providing ear plugs, but, as in the case of the masks, many workers discard them, so their discomfort from the noise is evidently not incapacitating. Although of course I cannot penetrate the real feelings of the workers or perceive any conflicts between workers and management, my general impression is of early Victorian machinery and buildings, made as tolerable as possible by a concerned management drawn from the working class. In contrast to factory conditions in many Third World countries, the workers' load is lightened by limited working hours, above-subsistence wages, free health care and cultural events, the knowledge that their efforts are valued and are justly rewarded, and above all, the prevailing fervent sense of cooperation in national development and in spiritual joy in defending and freeing the country.

As we leave, a group of Hungarian labor experts is being met and is entering the office building. Liên offers to introduce me, but I don't want to interrupt their schedule.

As on all my visits, it is hard to say goodbye. Each of our hosts makes me a little speech in the courtyard, telling me that their machines and conditions are poor because of the war, but that they will strive to improve them, and sending their greetings to the Canadian working class. They hug me and my union friends, and wave as we drive away.

Liên, who is my age and who seems to be losing her shyness about her English, talks to me very thoughtfully during our drives. Today she tells me about her recent visit to Ho Chi Minh City, where part of her family lives whom she had not seen since 1954. She is distressed by the lack of care for the country that some of them show, and by the effect of the United States occupation, which she thinks has produced hedonism, hooliganism, and immorality that will take years to eradicate. "In general, you know, our women are pure," she says. "We value that—it is part of our tradition. So we are very shocked when we go down there and see women, even our own relatives, who have no care for their modesty." She is especially anguished by the half million prostitutes in south Vietnam, the half million drug addicts, and the more than 1 million people who suffer from venereal disease, all of whom must be cured and rehabilitated.

"Vietnam had never before witnessed the depths of depravity introduced by the U.S. invaders"—and she asks me whether rape is common in North America. I tell her I am sorry to say it is, and is increasing. "We thought it must be so," she says, "but it is not part of our tradition, and it horrifies us." I tell her it is not really part of *our* tradition, but may be increasing with the breakdown of our civilization.

Liên was in Hanoi during Nixon's Christmas bombing of 1972, from December 18 to 30. It was atrocious, she says; you never knew whether you would live to see the morning. It was her worst experience of the war. Liên lives beside a lake, and one night saw a house completely lifted off the shore; it exploded in midair. Each family had an air raid shelter, but adults often stayed out to try to shoot down planes, and sometimes succeeded.

Liên often mentions the "low level" of housing and culture in Vietnam and the need to improve conditions rapidly. I agree with her, yet to my eyes, in spite of the grievous war, most of what I have seen is more prosperous than most of India. I am, of course, living in a comparatively beautiful and comfortable part of Hanoi, somewhat similar to middle-class residential streets in New Delhi. Even so, throughout the city the houses and shops look tidy and clean, if crude. The streets are washed down from water trucks every day ("Don't you wash your streets daily in Canada?"); there are trees and plants everywhere; all the city children have access to parks, playgrounds, and children's palaces; most workers' housing is tiled; clothing is plain but neat and not ragged, and most people wear shoes. Liên and Khanh say they think everyone eats *some* meat, fish, or eggs with their rice and vegetables on most days.

My hosts' care and politeness, indeed their loving kindness, are remarkable and remind me of the hospitality I have so often received in India. Every day brings small, unsought attentions: green tea for my rest hours, a strainer to strain it, a sweater for a chilly morning, a foray across town to get my broken briefcase mended. . . . When I thank them they say, "It is our duty," "It is an honor," "It is a pleasure."

This evening my friends bring films to the hotel to entertain me. One is *To Pave the Way,* a color film of a group of young men and women from north Vietnam cutting their way through jungle in the Truong Son mountain range to build a road and bridges for convoys of food and military equipment to pass to the south in the recent war. This route was one of many "Ho Chi Minh Trails" built with extraordinary courage as lifelines from north to south. The young volunteers brave snakes, wild animals, dangerous precipices, and bombing raids by Phantom jets and B-52s. They befriend the tribal people, and there is a charming girl-boy romance. Men and women work together to set dynamite charges, cut away granite with picks and drills, carry sacks of earth and gravel, shift boulders, and operate antiaircraft guns. In the evenings they sing and dance with the mountain dwellers, paint pictures, or write letters home. The film, shot while the work was in progress, portrays so much feeling for natural beauty, so much intelligence, dedication, tenderness, and heroism in the face of evil, that I am deeply moved and, for the hundredth time here, think, "This is a truly loving and heroic people." Hoan and Little Liên sit on either side of me, softly commenting in the darkness and occasionally holding my hands.

A second film documents the victory celebrations in Hanoi of May 1975 that marked the triumphal end of the revolutionary war in South Vietnam. After the ten years of almost unimaginable suffering and cruelty of the war in Vietnam, and the near despair I experienced while living in North America, it is inspiring to see Lê Duân, Pham Van Dong, General Giap, and other leaders greeting delegates from countries throughout the world as they pour from their planes in the Hanoi airport, embracing and kissing them with joy. Very moving, too, are the colorful, magnificently organized parades and dances of many thousands of soldiers, sailors, airmen and women, youth, children, peasants, mountain folk, and workers from both south and north in Ba Dinh Square, where Ho Chi Minh first read Vietnam's declaration of independence on September 2, 1945. His mausoleum now stands on that site, facing, across the square, the new National Assembly building of what is now the reunified Socialist Republic of all of Vietnam.

On the balcony of the mausoleum as the march passed stood the leaders of both north and south Vietnam together with those of other, allied communist nations including the Soviet Union and China—I think the most recent time that these two countries' representatives have stood together on a ceremonial occasion in Vietnam. As I watch the documentary I think of the enmity between them, grown deeper since 1975, and of the current instability in China. But I feel that the Vietnamese, with their "combination of reason and sentiment," will surely keep alive the ideals of their own revolution, and I hope they will be able to help draw ever more of humanity into a common fold.

9

Death and Spiritual Life

Hoan, Liên senior, and Khanh take me at nine this morning, Sunday, November 14, to visit the mausoleum of President Ho Chi Minh in Ba Dinh Square. The embalmed body is housed in a graceful, raised square building surrounded by columns and approached by steps. It is built, reportedly with Soviet technical and economic aid,[1] with delicately colored stones and marble brought from every province in Vietnam.

When we arrive, about three thousand people are waiting to get in. The line stretches four deep halfway around the square and is protected by police, very smart in red and blue uniforms with gold braid and white gloves. As I am a foreigner we are ushered to the front. We move in with the silent crowd, up a staircase and corridors of marble and polished stone to the central chamber. The president's body lies in state on a silk covered catafalque surmounted by a wooden canopy, and is flanked by four young police who stand on guard. We file slowly around the body and out by a back door into the wintry sunshine of a pleasant memorial garden.

Ho Chi Minh's face is serene in death, his hands lightly folded over the coverlet. The people gaze on him reverently. Some are weeping silently, and a young soldier is shaken with sobs which he tries to control. I think of a memorial meeting that left-wing faculty and students held for Ho Chi Minh at Simon Fraser University in Burnaby, British Columbia, after his death in 1969, and the many times we carried his photograph in antiwar demonstrations in North America, and I am glad to have made this pilgrimage.

Khanh says that between 1000 and 5000 people have been seen lining up outside the mausoleum ever since it was opened in 1975. She herself waited a day and a night the first time and has been back often since. Liên met Ho Chi Minh frequently in the 1960s, as it was her duty to take him educational documents; she says he was always kind and often humorous.

Although they do not believe in supernatural forces or in an afterlife, the Vietnamese communists' attitude to Ho Chi Minh seems to me religious in the special sense in which Julian Huxley and others have used this word.[2] His life, and by extension his person, possessions, and sayings and the anecdotes of his actions are preserved and treated ceremonially, and are sacred in that they inspire awe and reverence (although not, of course, in any sense that they are believed to hold supernatural or magical powers). As in the traditions of Christ or of the Buddha, his memory evokes lofty, sublime feelings of dedication to the cause he lived for, a desire to observe the ethics he propounded, pride in and solidarity with the community of those faithful to his message, and a wish to engage in ceremonial acts of veneration towards the symbols of his life. As with Christ and the Buddha, moreover, it is his reasonableness, his self-sacrifice, and above all his altruistic love for humankind that most endear him to his followers.

All this seems appropriate to me, for I think that some recognition of the sacred (or what Liên and Khanh often call "the spiritual life") and some need to ceremonialize it are probably universal in human beings regardless of their existential beliefs. Just as religions in general may celebrate what is sublime, banal, or even vicious, so may particular cults of national leaders. The Vietnamese are fortunate to have had a leader with a keen ethical sense, a broad, universal consciousness, an intelligent, logical, and organizing mind, a poetic imagination, extraordinary courage and dedication, and, evidently, a loving heart.

I do not mean to suggest that the Vietnamese are not Marxist-Leninists as well as patriots. It seems to me that certain key ideals and themes, partly nationalist and anti-imperialist, partly class-based, and partly universal, are all sacred to them, and that the "cult" of Ho Chi Minh is one element in this larger ideological and "religious" system. Among these themes are beliefs in a socialist future for Vietnam, in a classless world communist society for humanity, and in a view of history which sees Vietnam's long resistance to tyranny as contributing to the gradual emancipation of all humankind.

If a sympathetic observer from another culture, or with a different philosophical outlook, examines the acts, statements, and history of the Vietnamese communists, he or she may find contradictions and inconsistencies. One example might be the Vietnamese belief that their proletariat led the revolution and that the present state is a "dictatorship of the proletariat," whereas in fact fewer than one-fifth of the ruling party are workers, while intellectuals of middle- or upper-class origin play the most prominent roles in government, and peasants rather than workers supplied the majority of revolutionary fighters.[3] Similar inconsistencies can no doubt be found in every society, perhaps the more so to the extent that its ideology is close knit. This does not necessarily reflect on the truthfulness of either the observed or the observer. What is significant for the twentieth century is that the Vietnamese communists did organize their experience, values, and goals around a particular point of view or vision that was as truthful and coherent as they could make it, and lived out this vision so effectively that they were able to rid their people of foreign oppression and the cruelest forms of material want, to unify them, and to inspire them once more with faith, hope, and love. During their long struggle the *ideal* of proletarian leadership leading to a "dictatorship of the proletariat" has, moreover, had great symbolic significance. For the Vietnamese, proletarian values or a "proletarian line" are a kind of shorthand expression for a complex of values and institutions involving such qualities as a scientific outlook, freedom from superstition, knowledge of modern industry and technology, flexible willingness to change and improve society for the sake of the general welfare, discipline and punctuality in work and struggle, egalitarianism, and, above all, cooperative effort.

The Vietnamese have thus developed a complex variant of Marxism-Leninism, shot through with national, regional, and even former tribal imageries, but unified around certain themes and persons having universal significance. It is noteworthy that in spite of the impersonality of dialectical materialism as a philosophical system, the outstanding Marxist-Leninist revolutions of this century have all focused similarly around national themes and heroes who became, in the special sense used above, "sacred" in the eyes of the people. I am doubtful whether these revolutions could have been carried out without such "sacred" figures, any more than they could have been without those "very precious treasures," Marxism-Leninism and the leadership of the vanguard party.

A Catholic church, newly rebuilt since the bombing, stands a few yards from the mausoleum in Ba Dinh Square. I ask to see inside, but although it is Sunday and although Catholics, like Buddhists and other religious devotees, may worship freely in Vietnam, this church turns out to be locked.

Sunday (a holiday in Vietnam) being evidently suitable for pondering on national symbols, we drive on to the Historical Museum which adjoins the Revolutionary Museum. As usual, everything is well organized. We are greeted with speeches by a woman vice-director and several subordinates, and refreshed with tea and sweets at the beginning and end of our visit.

This museum was founded under the French but has been much augmented and reorganized since the revolution. Archaeological and physical anthropological research continued during the recent war. Although the exhibits had to be removed to scattered places to avoid the bombing, cataloguing went on and new finds were made in the course of repairing dikes or building irrigation works. As we move through the halls, each devoted to a dynasty or cultural period, the vice-director lectures enthusiastically on the main events. As usual, Khanh translates all her words; and Khanh, Liên, and Hoan, all of whom are well versed in Vietnamese history, add points of their own.

Liên brought her pupils here for history lessons in the late 1940s and the 1950s, and knows the museum well. There is quite a sizable crowd this morning but the halls are so large that we are not disturbed. For someone with as slight a knowledge of Vietnamese history as I have, the periods and exhibits would take years to master, but some highlights can be mentioned here.

As Alexander Woodside points out, "The depth of the Vietnamese people's consciousness of their own history and literature would astonish the far less imaginative nationalists and relic worshippers of North America and Western Europe." He mentions that in 1964, "Hanoi children were shown animated film cartoons which attempted to depict life in the legendary Vietnamese kingdom of Van Lang, a kingdom which was supposed to have come to an end, after being ruled by eighteen glorious sovereigns, in the third century B.C. The purpose of these cartoons was to show that in this kingdom even a heroic child had once managed to defeat a seemingly invincible invader king who 'wore nothing but black, and whose sleeves were too big for him; he scooped up everything; chickens, pigs, geese, all small children, handfuls of bananas and coconuts, and all were stuffed into his two sleeves.' Not every society in the world would have prepared for what turned out to be years of warfare and American bombing by encouraging its children to think of events that had supposedly occurred three thousand years before the invention of national flags and socialist realism."[4]

This poetic imagery and consciousness of national history continually delights the visitor, but it can also bewilder an untutored foreigner. Faced with streams of comment and allusion as we drive about, I have several times asked my friends, "Did this (or that) event in this (or that) temple (bay, cave, or lake) happen under the French or during the U.S. invasion?" and the answer has come back, "No—you remember—it was in 1418-1427 when we were resisting the Ming," or "No, that occurred, you know, in the naval battle of 938." Some of these stellar events are put in chronological order for me today as we pace the museum, or later, this evening, as I delve into *Vietnam: A Historical Sketch* (Hanoi, 1974) that my hosts have provided. This excellent work by a group of Vietnamese scholars should surely be read by anyone with an interest in the country.

Vietnam has been inhabited from very early times; thousands of chipped stone cutters and scrapers and almond-shaped, Chellean hand axes were discovered on Mount Do in Thanh Hoa province in 1960. The earliest known Vietnamese hominids turned up as late as 1965 in a cave in Tan Van village of Lang Son (now part of Cao Lang) province approaching the Chinese border. They resemble *Sinanthropus* or Peking Man and date from the Middle Pleistocene, perhaps 500,000 years ago. Such early men lived in caves near rivers and forests, as did the various groups of *homo sapiens* who appeared later in north and central Vietnam, perhaps about 50,000 B.C. All of this took place long before the Red River delta became fully silted and the deltas and coastal plains took their present shapes towards 3000 B.C. Tools of stone, bone, and horn, and vessels of bamboo, coconut shell, gourds, and calabashes from the Upper Paleolithic resemble many found today in the tribal regions. Polished stone tools as well as pottery derived from bamboo baskets coated with clay to make them watertight developed toward the end of the Old Stone Age millennia of hunting, fishing, and food gathering. The dead were buried sitting, knees raised, in tombs along with their tools and beads. On a cave wall in Hoa Binh (now Ha Song Binh province south of Hanoi) there is a stone relief of a man or god with an animal body, a human head, and horns. The museum copy fascinates all of us, and I think back to the magnificent, mysterious cave paintings of Palaeolithic hunters and animals at Lascaux and Les Eyzies in southern France. French scholars played a part in unearthing and organizing some of these early relics of Vietnam, and some of the best French ethnographers have depicted the cultures of modern Vietnamese tribes.[5] The French thus began the work that is now being carried on by scholars of Vietnam, although, in colonial fashion, French archaeological investigations often led to the plunder of ancient treasures and their exportation to foreign lands.

About 4000 B.C., Neolithic sites arose on the basis of cultivation, especially along the coast in places like Ha Long Bay in Quang Ninh province, north of Haiphong, where I shall go tomorrow. Later Neolithic villages of the Phùng Nguyen culture were built in the open instead of in caves, and were strung along the Red River valley and in the midlands north of it, where legend puts the cradle of the Vietnamese nation. The people, probably mixed Mongoloids from the north and Australo-Negroids from the south, were among the earliest in the world to practice the cultivation of rice in temporary, burnt out forest clearings, and later in submerged fields in the plains, and to domesticate the pig and the buffalo. They shaped smooth reddish pottery with geometrical designs, fashioned bone, shell, and stone jewelry, wove clothing, and built their houses on stilts similar to those of some of the present day ethnic minorities—legend has it, to ward off tigers. The dead were often buried collectively, with implements, ornaments, and pottery, their equal graves suggesting a tribal life without class differences. The best

Phûng Nguyen site was discovered in a village of that name in Phu Thô province south of Hanoi and excavated in 1969.

Since then, Neolithic graves of about 3000 and 2300 B.C. have been found and housed in the museum. The former consists of a coffin containing the skeletons of a woman and child with wooden and clay vessels. The latter, which was discovered by a peasant of Ha Tay province when he was digging irrigation works, contains a male skeleton with vessels, an axe, a spear, and an arrow.

Vietnam's Copper and Bronze Ages began toward the end of the second millennium B.C. French investigators, who discovered advanced artifacts at Dong Son in Than Hoa province, thought they were brought by invaders, possibly from Europe! Vietnamese archaeologists have since found some thirty Bronze Age sites with tens of thousands of artifacts scattered in all parts of present day north Vietnam. They now conclude that although subject to external influences, Vietnam's Bronze Age developed out of the indigenous Neolithic culture, using the plentiful deposits of copper, tin, lead, and zinc in the local soils. They believe that it underwent an evolution of several centuries, culminating in the sophisticated Dong Son creations, and that an advanced and unitary Bronze Age civilization spread throughout north Vietnam and the neighboring Kiangsi province of southeast China. The Champa kingdom of south Vietnam (c. second to fourteenth centuries A.D.) is also believed to have been founded by an indigenous people who had earlier possessed Neolithic and Bronze Age cultures similar to those of the north.

Vietnam's present day scholars ascribe the legendary Hung kings of the Van Lang kingdom in north Vietnam to this Bronze Age period of the early first millennium B.C., whereas legends would put the Hung dynasty as far back as 4000 B.C. The state must, at all events, have arisen out of tribal society sometime during the Bronze Age. Legends recording annual struggles between Son Tinh, the mountain genie, and Thuy

Tinh, the water genie, are thought to symbolize the early state's need to conquer the Red River floods and establish centrally controlled irrigation works.

The museum contains marvelous objects from this period. The best are bronze drums, found widely in Southeast Asia and China but most developed in Vietnam. That from Ngoc Lu in Ha Nam Ninh province is cylindrical, sixty-three centimeters high and seventy-nine centimeters in diameter. In the middle of the upper face is an image of the sun with radiating beams and sixteen concentric rings with imaginative decorations: flocks of deer and aquatic birds, dancing to the sound of clappers. There are houses on stilts and, on a circular swelling below the head, boats and warriors carrying axes, javelins, and arrows. This festival drum echoes two to three kilometers when struck. Another treasure is a covered urn to store rice, three feet high, bearing designs that resemble the Hindu *lingam* and *yoni* (sacred emblems of the male and female sexual organs) and decorated on the lid with a couple in the act of copulation, an obvious fertility motif.

The Van Lang kingdom was conquered by mountain people from what are now Viet Bac and the Chinese Kiangsi province, who merged the hills and plains areas into a new kingdom, Au Lac, about 258 B.C. Its citadel, Co Loa, has been excavated about twenty kilometers from Hanoi, and a model of it appears in the museum. The citadel's massive and complex ramparts and deep moats, the temples or mausolea built to honor its kings and approached by 500 steps, and the thousands of bronze arrowheads discovered early in 1959 suggest a professional army and a relatively complex division of labor. There are paddy fields at the foot of the citadel today, as probably in ancient times. Khanh, who has been there by bus, tells me the peasants who cultivate them in the cooperative there still place flowers on the mausolea to honor the dead kings on a date in mid-March calculated by the lunar calendar. Honoring sacred, dead leaders in mausolea is thus ancient in Vietnam. From a combination of legends and archaeological finds, scholars tentatively conclude that Bronze Age Vietnam had joint peasant communities or communes and also slaves, perhaps war captives, who may have built the mausolea and some of the larger irrigation works.

North Vietnam was conquered from Han China in 111 B.C. and incorporated as a Chinese province until the tenth century A.D. Confucianism, Buddhism, writing, the use of iron, and a feudal political structure came from China during or before this period. For at least part of the period central Vietnam, already called Annam, also came under Chinese rule. Today, the Vietnamese communists recall the period of Chinese dominance mainly in order to celebrate various famous uprisings against it—of the Trung sisters (40-43 A.D.); Trieu Thi Trinh or "Dame Trieu" (248 A.D.); Ly Bon, who founded the Kingdom of Van Xuan (544); Mai Thuc Loan (722); Phùng Hung (791); and Khuc Thua Du (905), whose victory inaugurated the period of independence.

An attempt at reconquest by the Chinese court in 938 was smashed by Ngo Quyên in a famous naval battle on the Bach Dang River in Quang Ninh province, a model of which is shown in the museum. Tradition has it that the Vietnamese drove massive wooden spikes into the bed of the estuary near its mouth. The Chinese ships, which had entered at high tide, were unable to leave as the tide receded, and were destroyed by arrows shot from small Vietnamese craft.

With the expulsion of the Chinese, a series of small Vietnamese kingdoms arose, among them the tenth-century Tien Hoang dynasty which built its capital in the forests of Ninh Binh province, Khanh says because of weakness. We examine a model of this capital with its fortified walls and ornate royal mausoleum, a portrait of Lê Dai Hang, a tenth-century king, and a large vase with dragons on it, which Khanh says "reflect the power of the ruling class" and were used only by feudal dynasties.

In 1009, the stronger Ly dynasty began to reunify north Vietnam, and built its capital on the site of modern Hanoi in

1070. We admire a cast from this period of a ten-foot statue of the Buddha seated on a lotus leaf, carved in 1054-1072 and reflecting the spread of Mahayana Buddhism, and a five-foot copper bell. Remarkable Buddhist temples and pagodas graced the period, and a national literature developed. Although Buddhism became the religion of most of the kings and the commoners, Confucianism provided the moral order of the developing mandarin (scholar) bureaucracy. A famous Temple of Literature was built and was the focus of the first Confucian school and university. The first mandarin competitions took place in 1075 and in 1089 the mandarin hierarchy was strictly organized. Today the Temple of Literature is a "place of culture" where national festivals are held at which people recite their poems and are presented with bouquets of flowers.

The Doi Tran dynasty (1225 to late fourteenth century) consolidated feudal power and unified north and central Vietnam southward to modern Da Nang, where the Hindu Champa kingdom of south Vietnam began. Thang Long or Hanoi continued to be the capital. There was great expansion of irrigation and foreign trade, of cotton, silk and brocade weaving, of brick and tile buildings and earthen statues, of silver, gold, tin, and lead mining, and thus of metal working and jewelry. Shipbuilding, the development of printing from engraved wooden plates, and the growth of craft and trading guilds marked the period. In the museum an elaborate chart with decorated figures outlines the feudal social structure. The ruling class included the king and the royal lineage, the military and civil mandarin families who had access to official examinations, court dignitaries, aristocratic landowners, and the various ranks of Buddhist *bonzes* living on monastic domains. The "popular classes" comprised peasant landowners, merchants, free tenant cultivators, craftsmen, serfs, and domestic slaves drawn from former criminals, insolvent debtors, war captives, and children sold by their parents in famines. The common people were forbidden by law to dress and wear ornaments like the privileged classes, and the slaves could marry people only of their own class. Battles against Mongol invaders under the Tran dynasty are commemorated in the museum by models and weapons. In 1288, as in 938, a Chinese fleet was again trapped with iron-tipped stakes at the mouth of the Bach Dang River; 100 junks were destroyed and 400 captured.

Vietnamese scholars think that a class struggle developed in the thirteenth and fourteenth centuries between the kings, the older military and landed nobility, and the Buddhist clergy with their vast domains on the one hand, and the new class of peasant owners allied with serfs and slaves and led by Confucian scholars on the other. By this time a proportion of the mandarins were being recruited from the independent peasants. These Confucian scholars thought that people were primarily social beings bound by social obligations. Instead of proclaiming the unreality of the world and directing people's minds to supraterrestrial hopes, they taught the paramount need to "serve the king, honor one's parents, remain loyal to one's spouse until death, manage one's family affairs, participate in the administration of one's country, contribute to safeguarding the peace of the world . . . [and] educate oneself so as to be able to assume all these tasks. This should be the fundamental pre-occupation of all men from the Emperor, Son of Heaven, down to the humblest commoner."[6] It is noteworthy that except for the reference to the Emperor, these duties are paramount for Vietnamese communists today. The scholars attacked both Buddhist beliefs and profligate royal donations of land and labor to pagodas and *bonzes*. As the contemporary historian Lê Van Huu wrote in 1243:

> The first Lê king, hardly two years after his accession to the throne, at a time when the ancestral temples of the dynasty had not yet been consolidated, had already had eight pagodas built in the Thieu Duc district, and many others restored in different provinces; Lê kept more than one thousand *bonzes* in the capital;

much wealth and labor had thus been wasted! These riches had not fallen from the sky, that labor had not been supplied by the gods; to do such things was to suck the blood and sweat of the people![7]

Buddhism, Confucianism, and Taoism continued side by side, however, even among public officers, and competitions in all three doctrines were held under the Tran dynasty, but by the late fourteenth century Confucianism predominated.

The Hindu kingdom of Champa in the south, which emerged in the second century A.D., was several times annexed by the Chinese in the first thousand years of its history; it was then briefly conquered by the Cambodians in the twelfth century and by the Vietnamese and later the Mongols in the thirteenth. By 1390 Champa had been absorbed into Vietnam, although Vietnamese settlement and development of the south became prominent only after the Lê dynasty's final conquest of the region in 1471.

Chinese troops of the Ming dynasty occupied Vietnam in 1407. They were driven out in 1427 in famous battles led by Lê Loi, a landowner opposed to the great landed nobility, and Nguyen Trai, a Confucian scholar. The former founded the popular Lê dynasty, which expropriated the large estates of the Ming and their Vietnamese collaborators, distributed their rents (but not the persons of the peasants) among the mandarinate, abolished serfdom, and regulated the periodic redistribution of communal rice fields among all villagers according to their varied ranks.

Lê Loi was the hero to whom a mythical tortoise presented the sword that has given its name to my hotel and to Hanoi's famous lake. In the museum a massive, lifelike, and magnificently sculptured tortoise sustains the gravestone of Lê Loi. Another immense and famous sculpture of the period is of the Buddha in the form of a woman seated upon a lotus. It is backed by a screen carved with hundreds of hands each with an eye set in its palm. This is the "Buddha with a thousand eyes and thousand hands," a figure of mercy who grants charity and gifts.

It was Nguyen Trai, Confucian scholar, military strategist, political adviser, geographer, humanist, and poet, who persuaded Lê Loi to protect 100,000 captured enemy soldiers from the people's vengeance and restore them to China, establishing the tradition of mercy to war prisoners that has prevailed in modern times. Nguyen Trai is beloved by the Vietnamese communists for his compassion, his reliance on the common people, and the uprightness and integrity of his interpretation of Confucian ethics. Unfortunately, the envy of lesser men drove him into exile, and in 1442 he was falsely incriminated and executed.

In 1483 the Hong Duc code of laws was promulgated; it remained in force until the end of the eighteenth century. The code protected the property of the state and the landlords, ensured the authority of the father, the first wife, and the eldest son, and fixed the rules of marriage and mourning. Ten capital crimes were listed, including rebellion and neglect of filial duties. The communists regard these provisions as "feudal and Confucian" but also point to certain "progressive" features: women could own their own goods and chattels and could enjoy equal rights with men in inheritance. When there were no sons, the daughters inherited the whole family fortune. A wife could divorce a husband who abandoned her for a certain period. Modern Vietnamese scholars point out that these provisions owed nothing to Chinese influence. They were suppressed in the nineteenth century when a reactionary feudal monarchy was restored.

The Lê dynasty of the fifteenth and early sixteenth centuries saw Vietnam's Golden Age of scholarship and enlightenment. Its chief writer was Nguyen Binh Khiem (1491-1585), a Confucian scholar and poet who advised statesmen from his hermitage. In his time the court and mandarinate had already grown corrupt, usurped the people's lands, and engaged in personal conflict and intrigue. Whereas Nguyen Trai had tried to "stay on" and serve the people by serving the monarchy, Nguyen Binh Khiem felt obliged to "go out" and to serve them by retiring from a predatory government into a simple rural life. The choice between "staying on" and "going out" periodically troubled the Confucian conscience for a millennium. Many of the Vietnamese communists are people whose mandarin families had "gone out," perforce or voluntarily, under French rule, and who have emerged to "stay on" under a more virtuous mandate.

From the mid-sixteenth century, the Lê dynasty became weak and power was divided between two noble families, the Trinh in the north and the Nguyen, with their capital at Hue, in the south. Despite a degenerate and divided government, Vietnam produced a brilliant literature in the seventeenth and eighteenth centuries, of fables, satires, verse novels, and medical research, some of whose prescriptions are in use today. The peasant upheavals and the crises of Confucian government gave rise to freer philosophical speculation and challenges to ancient mores as well as some return to the otherworldliness of Buddhism. It also gave rise to the translation of the Chinese classics into Vietnamese for the benefit of literate commoners and, beginning in the seventeenth century under the influence of French missionaries, the introduction of the Latin script, which facilitated literacy. Some novelists portrayed the inner lives and frustrations of noble women confined in seraglios or abandoned by warrior husbands. The poetess Ho Xuan Huong, a heroine for the modern women's movement, not only portrayed but also attacked and satirized polygyny, arranged marriages, male dominance, and the miseries of unmarried mothers.

Population growth, as well as the peasants' distress from famines and from the rapacity of corrupt rulers and landlords, gave rise to massive peasant revolts in the seventeenth and still more the eighteenth century. These culminated in the famous Tay Son rebellion which began in Binh Dinh

province of south Vietnam in 1771. Weapons and booby
traps used by the rebel army are preserved in the museum,
some of them identical with those used by peasants against
the French and the United States invaders two hundred years
later. The uprising ended with the defeat of the Nguyen and
the Trinh rulers and also of the Lê king, who brought in
reinforcements from China; the reunification of Vietnam;
and the installation of a new king, Nguyen Hue (renamed
King Quang Trung), one of the three mandarin brothers of
Tay Son who led the rebellion. Success was proclaimed in
1789, the year of the French revolution.

The Tay Son rebellion itself had some of the elements of a
democratic revolution. It took place in a period of growing
overseas trade and incipient commodity production and was
carried out by a popular army of peasants, artisans, miners,
and merchants. But Vietnam lacked a cohesive bourgeois
class capable of restructuring the society. In spite of a decade
of popular reforms (the documents of which are preserved in
the museum), the regime fell apart with the death of Quang
Trung.

With French military aid, a prince of the former ruling
household of Hue reconquered the country and established
the Nguyen dynasty, the last feudal regime, with its capital at
Hue, in 1802. Exhibits of costumes and a throne from this
period appear in the museum, together with many other
objects. With growing French interference, the Nguyen governed the country until the French conquest of Da Nang in
1847. Despite half a century of bitter popular resistance the
French conquest of Vietnam was completed in 1897.

After glowing tributes to the Tay Son rebels by our guide
and my three friends, we pass briefly to a hall dedicated to
the Champa kingdom of the fourth to fourteenth centuries, a
brilliant Hindu civilization which flourished south of Da
Nang in south Vietnam. Suddenly all is familiar, yet curiously
new, and we are lost in a world of Hindu gods, snakes, and
warriors springing with wild energy from the quieter har-

mony of the Gupta and perhaps the Tamil traditions. The worship of the Hindu god Shiva predominates, but there are both Hinayana and Mahayana Buddhist relics; Krishna with his flute is also enchantingly represented. The Chams were a vigorous society of sailors, pirates, and rice cultivators who spoke an Indonesian language written in Indian characters, with Sanskrit as their literary medium. About 16,000 of the Cham "minority" remain in south Vietnam. They are matrilineal paddy cultivators and traders plying between the hill peoples and the lowland Vietnamese. The cult of nature spirits is still important to them and, says Khanh, some of them still make sculptures in the Hindu mold.

10

A Hanoi Interview[1]

When I arrived in Hanoi I asked my hosts to arrange an interview on ideological and political questions with some leading member of the Communist Party. On Sunday, November 14, I went with Khanh, Hoan, Duyên, and both Liêns to meet Comrade Hoang Tung, editor of the daily newspaper, *Nhân Dân,* secretary of the Journalists' Union, and member of the Central Committee of the Communist Party. We met in a spacious but simply furnished room in his apartment from 3:00 to 5:45 P.M., with Khanh interpreting.[2]

Aged about fifty, Hoang Tung is handsome and dapper, with a charming, somewhat courtly manner and a sense of fun. When I arrived wearing an Indian sari he greeted me with a broad smile and outstretched hands, led me to a sofa, and said, "Why! You look as if you had just stepped out of a box!"

The previous night I had hurriedly prepared twenty questions, which Hoan translated into Vietnamese and gave to Hoang Tung an hour before the interview. Although he answered all of them, at the end Hoang Tung gave me permission to publish only fifteen of his answers. Five answers, and parts of several others, referring to foreign countries, he declared off the record; they are omitted here.

Hoang Tung's caution was part of a general policy of the Vietnamese communists of not openly criticizing or even freely discussing the policies of friendly states, especially of states within what they still insist on calling "the socialist camp." Although this policy hampered my discussions in Hanoi of several important subjects, I came to appreciate it because it seems essential to their goal of restoring and promoting solidarity in the communist movement throughout the world. On many issues the Vietnamese communists' publicly expressed ideological positions show indirectly where they stand, notably in the controversies of the past fifteen years between China and the Soviet Union. At the same time, their refusal to criticize in public specific internal or foreign policies of these and other socialist countries prevents the exacerbation of conflict between them and leaves the door open to change and rapprochement.

The interview opened with Hoang Tung asking me about a number of Canadian comrades and sending his best wishes. He asked if I had been in Vietnam before. I said no, nor in any socialist country. He then said:

"Actually, we cannot say that Vietnam is a socialist society. At present we cannot even say that it is a just society. I would like to talk about this a little, and so gradually lead into your questions. Vietnam is rather a special case.

"We can divide the world into three categories of countries according to their productive forces. These forces include industrial power, tools, and productivity. The first kind of country has the most developed industry, for example the United States, Canada, Japan and Western Europe."

What about the Soviet Union?

"Well, I'm speaking only of the capitalist countries at present. At most, only about twenty capitalist countries fall into this first category.

"The second kind of state has relatively developed industry, but its agriculture is backward and not mechanized, and there have been no land reforms. India and Brazil would be examples; Spain, yes, though Spain is rather high. Mexico and Argentina are examples. The problem is that they do not have much heavy industry, and they have dependent economies. Then in the third category there are the really backward, predominantly agricultural societies.

"In the nineteenth century, Marx and the Marxists said socialism could develop only in the first category of states, not in the second or third. Yet in fact socialist movements did win revolutions in Russia and Eastern Europe, which then belonged to the second category. In the states of the first category, the proletariat is strong and big, but it is not yet strong enough to overthrow the capitalist class. From 1917 until now, socialist movements have been victorious in, at best, some states of the second category but not the first. The Soviet Union was rather backward at the time of the revolution, but it was very large, and that was why it was able to stand firm and to serve later as a base for other countries in their revolutions. Therefore it is a backbone for the socialist camp, and has helped in the setting up of the socialist system elsewhere. Socialism was thus able to spread from the second category of states to some of the third category. The Soviet Union also had the ability to build up a modern, large-scale industry. Now it is level with the capitalist states which developed in the previous century and so creates a new balance between capitalist and socialist systems; both have modern industry.

"At the same time, the capitalist system grows smaller in scope and is in deeper crisis. So socialism can develop in different kinds of countries; socialist movements have been victorious in backward countries like Angola, Cuba, and Vietnam before the highly developed capitalist states. In Eastern Europe, Czechoslovakia was highly developed, but Rumania, Bulgaria, and Albania were very backward. However, these countries were able to ally against fascism and move to socialism. In Asia, Vietnam, Laos, and Cambodia, also Mongolia and North Korea, were very backward but underwent socialist revolutions."

What about China?

"Well, I would put China in the second category because it is so large. It was not very industrialized, but altogether it had a fair amount of industry. Again in Africa, we have three countries which have recently moved to socialism—Guinea-Bissau, Angola, and Mozambique—which have different levels of development. Cuba was very backward industrially. So the starting point of socialism was in the second category of countries; it moved to some of the third, but has not yet moved to the first category.

"This means we have to decide whether Karl Marx and Engels were right or wrong in their prediction. I think they were right because, true to their theory, socialism could not really be victorious in backward countries except in terms of political line—we cannot call it complete socialism. But if the proletariat took power in the United States or Canada, socialism could quickly be victorious because the material base is laid.

"In Vietnam the working class was able to take power only by allying with other classes and achieving solidarity with them. The working class was able to have this success because it had to fight against international capitalism from France, then from Japan, from France again, and then from the United States, and it took power during terrible wars. This was done not only by overthrowing the feudal regime, but also by overthrowing the invading imperialists and international capital. After taking power, the working class had to return to the point of production and begin to develop heavy industry. That's why what we have is only the beginning of socialism. Industrialization is essential—we must be as industrialized as Canada. The difference is that the capitalists took hundreds of years to industrialize, but under socialism the time is shortened to about twenty-five years. With one socialist country already established which has developed industry and science, it creates favorable conditions for new socialist countries.

"The biggest problem in Vietnam is industrial production.

We have to develop the material base of a modern society. Until we obtain that, we can't have complete socialism—we can only build step by step. Our production is still small scale, and our people's lives are difficult. Only when we have a developed industry can the policies of socialism be realized. The task is new and difficult for us, beginning on the basis of a small-scale agricultural system, not an industrial one. And now I am ready for your questions."

1. *What are the precise reparations demanded by Vietnam from the United States as their due for the ravages of war? How could they best be paid—in money, matériel, or technical assistance?*

"The twenty-first provision of the Paris Agreement contains a fascinating point. Never before did the United States sign such a provision. In the course of negotiation, the United States refused to make amends for its war damage, but Kissinger was eventually forced to include the reparations clause. It is very important that they had to accept such a provision. Everybody understands that it is reparations, but they had to state it another way in order to present it to the U.S. people. Similarly, the U.S. government can't accept the word 'defeat,' but it is a fact. Instead they call it 'withdrawal,' and instead of 'reparations' they accept only the idea of returning for the purpose of reconstruction. We in Vietnam had to settle the same problem with Japan last year. The Japanese refused to accept their defeat of 1945 in Vietnam, but in the international agreement they signed a clause relating to amends for the casualties in Vietnam. In the event, they made amends only to the Saigon puppet regime, but they still have to make amends to us. They are now willing to give us 'aid,' but they don't want it called reparations.

"Kissinger recently said that Vietnam fought Vietnam itself, which means he is trying to abolish Clause 21 on the grounds that it was a civil war. But never has the United States dared to say that Clause 21 is not operative. The talk of prisoners is election propaganda, and meanwhile the

United States is preventing the entry of Vietnam into the United Nations by the use of Madame Veto. So once more they reveal their bad faith before world public opinion. They say, 'If Vietnam's behavior is good, we will reward them,' but they don't call it reparations. But we Vietnamese are very stubborn in asking for amends, and we will do so into another century if necessary. The United States is in debt to Vietnam, and we will ask until they pay their debt, and redeem their promise. We want to show that the United States cannot continue to be stubborn as before.

"The best way to realize Clause 21 is to give some $3.5 billion. Nixon agreed to $7 billion for the whole of Indochina. For Vietnam, that means $3.7 billion including South Vietnam. Like our ancestors, we will continue asking for the debt to be paid every time we meet them—forever. The best way would be for them to give the money outright. Alternatively, equipment is needed for steel, electronics, and other factories. But they are afraid that if they give money or industry, Vietnam will become powerful, so they want to give only things like automobiles, which we can't use."

Did they really offer automobiles?

"Well, that was just my fun, but in the negotiations that kind of thing did come up. The best way would be for the United States to pay in gold! We should say that for fun, anyway, because the United States is not rich in gold. But if they won't give money, they must give equipment."

2. *I have read that Vietnam is willing to accept aid and even foreign private investment from some of the capitalist industrial states. If this is so, can it be done while safeguarding socialist construction?*

"Our main purpose is to rely on ourselves and build our own economy. Second, we rely on support from the socialist countries, and third, on support from international friends like you. No, don't laugh, your gift was small but you have a large heart. We also plan to broaden our trade with the capitalist countries on the principles of mutual respect, mutual interest, and sovereignty. Of course, according to our custom, we will allow foreign investment in our country. For example, the oil companies of Canada can invest here if they wish. This does not affect the socialist character of our construction. It simply means that, at the beginning, we haven't enough money to invest in all fields of our economy. So we would like to sell some raw materials in order to obtain a deposit of capital for building industry. If we had the money, we would extract all our oil ourselves and sell some of that; but we haven't, so we shall allow them to invest here instead. Nevertheless, the extraction of oil will be done mainly by ourselves.

3. *There seem to be several levels of wages in the industries and agricultural cooperatives in Vietnam, and I understand that bonuses are paid to workers who achieve higher production. While I see the justice of this, isn't there a danger that it will undermine cooperation and mutual aid? In general, where do you stand in the controversy between the Soviet Union and China on the question of material incentives?*

"Our productivity is still very low and is mainly handicrafts and agriculture. Our standard of living is still low. Communism has two different stages of development; as Marx said, the first is the lower stage. Because our productive force is low, we cannot realize the principle of 'from each according to his ability, to each according to his needs.' That is an ideal that we eventually aim to achieve—to fulfill our capacity for production, and to meet all the needs of our citizens. In our present conditions, we try to encourage those workers who reach higher production so that production in general is enhanced—it involves a unity of the material and the spiritual factors. At the present stage, people's capabilities are different, so wages must be different in the state. We must use wages to give justice to those who produce more. It is unjust, for example, if a steel worker enjoys only the same income as a peasant. There is a difference between unskilled and skilled labor, and between mechanical and nonmechanical work. There's also a difference between manual labor and brainwork. If we tried to fulfill Marx's ultimate goal now, it would be utopian and reactionary.

"Nevertheless, we must draw lessons from experience; the differences must not be too large. It is wrong if there is a difference of a hundred times between the highest paid and the lowest. At the same time it is wrong if an unskilled worker with lower productivity and a skilled worker with higher productivity are paid the same or with only a little difference. There must be a larger difference.

"Along with the policy of payments according to productivity, we must of course establish common welfare programs—canteens, kindergartens, crèches, pensions, hospitals—all necessary welfare programs in the cultural and economic realms. Socialism involves not only payments for production, but also cultural and spiritual life and welfare.

"On the way to socialism and communism, no country is always right. Each sometimes makes mistakes and must correct them. Nothing is stable—there must be changes, because it is a new path, and we must learn from others' experience as well as from our own, from our work, and from reality. We must always be correcting ourselves. The road from socialism to communism is a rough and uneven way. It isn't all plain sailing."

4. *What is the role of the market in the Vietnamese economy, and of profit making on the part of individual enterprises? What does Comrade Lê Duân mean when he says: "We must attach importance to both use value and exchange value and make a judicious application of the law of value"?*[3]

"In the first stage of socialism there are differences in workers' productivity and in their wages. That is why the market still exists. Only when we achieve communism can we abandon the use of wages and of the market. Even in socialist countries there are two kinds of property ownership, public and private. In socialist countries use value is more important to meet the requirements of the people, whereas in capitalist countries the aim is to make profits, and that is why 'value' is more important to them. But the problem of value remains, even in socialist countries, because value is the measure of management standards. If we don't use it in the enterprises, they will invest more and produce little. In socialist societies there still remain some kinds of goods to be sold on the market, but in order to serve the needs of the people, not in order to make private profits."

5. *Is land reform being carried out in south Vietnam? What are its prospects?*

"In south Vietnam the main problem of land reform has already been solved, because in the course of the revolution against the French colonialists we divided the land and gave it to the peasants. During the second war, the U.S. imperialists were willing for the landlords to take back the land, but because of the peasants' own struggle they could not succeed, and the peasants forced the landlords to give it back. And the other side were afraid that if they didn't allow it, the peasants would support the communists, which was harmful to them. Now there remain only a few big landlords' estates; we will abolish them in the next few months. Collectivization in south Vietnam has not yet started, but we have tested the ground in a few places, and the state will create cooperatives in order to mechanize and do irrigation work. In south Vietnam it is also possible to set up new and larger state farms, as we have much virgin land to cultivate."

6. *Nayan Chanda's article in the* Far Eastern Economic Review *of August 20, 1976 ("Bridging Hanoi's Food Gap"), gives the average paddy yield in north Vietnam in 1975 as 2.18 tons per crop-hectare. This seems rather low by comparison with other estimates I've seen. Is it correct, and what has the yield been like in 1976?*

"The paddy yield in north Vietnam before the revolution was very low. It was only about 1.5 tons per crop-hectare, and at that time we had only one crop per year. Now we try to have two and even three crops. In north Vietnam as a whole, therefore, we now get an average of about 5 tons per hectare per year. In some cooperatives, however—for example, some in Thai Binh province in the Red River delta—we are recording as much as 7 or even 10 tons in a year, and in a few places the yield for 1976 will be 11 tons per hectare per year. In the Mekong Delta in south Vietnam, the overall average is already 3 tons per crop-hectare, or 6 tons per hectare per year where there are two crops taken. This is unprecedented in Vietnam, and it happened because the U.S. puppets experimented with new methods in a limited acreage. You can see up to 4 and even 5 or more tons per hectare per crop in small areas of north Vietnam, but it's true that the 1975 average for all of north Vietnam was 2.2 tons per hectare per crop."

7. *Is rice rationed in Vietnam? If so, what is the adult ration for workers and for peasants?*

"Peasants sell part of their rice yield to the government—20 percent is the highest amount sold by individual coops. The rest is divided among the peasants in the coop according to their production. Everybody in Vietnam receives a basic ration, but those who work harder get more. The basic ration is 13 kilograms per month or 15¼ ounces per day. That's the adult minimum, and then there are different levels above that. Children receive varying amounts according to age. Our peasants get more than the Cubans get, but the Cubans have more fish and eggs. If we had more eggs, butter, and milk we could reduce the rice ration."

8. *Did the U.S. bombing permanently destroy any of the land in Vietnam, so that it cannot be cultivated? How long will it take to restore cultivation in general?*

"Even the worst destroyed regions have been recovered quickly, and some are now ready for cultivation. We are now in the process of returning the peasants to the lands in south Vietnam from which they had been driven off. None of the land will be permanently destroyed. The recovery is happening rather quickly."

9. *Turning to more general political questions, what*

meaning do you attach to the term "revisionism"? Does it exist in the socialist camp?

"Revisionism can happen either in a party in power or in one not in power if it does not follow the principles of scientific socialism. At one time or another any party can fall into this error."

10. *Does the term "social imperialism" mean anything to you, or is it an imaginary concept?*

"I have never seen social imperialism in this world!"

11. *What is your view of the dictatorship of the proletariat? Is it necessary that it be established in every country?*

"We have discussed this question in our party, and have decided it is necessary to set up the dictatorship of the proletariat in all countries. The project of the Fourth Party Congress which is approaching has pointed this out quite clearly. Of course, we have never understood that the dictatorship of the proletariat means the fist. Above all, the dictatorship of the proletariat means the leadership of a certain class. By contrast, the ruling class of a capitalist state has to struggle *against* the people in order to protect itself. So the bourgeois class is very conscious of *its* dictatorship, and has been conscious of it through hundreds of years. The ruling class (in capitalist countries) allows the people the freedom to criticize, but they can't touch the hair on their legs, because the factories belong to the bourgeois class."

12. *Does class struggle continue to exist in socialist societies? If so, how should it be carried out in Vietnam?*

"In socialist countries there is no struggle between classes as there is in capitalist countries. Of course there are always contradictions. They're like the contradictions between husband and wife—you have to struggle through them, but they are not class conflicts. Of course they're bigger! There are conflicts or contradictions between different sections of the people, but they are not antagonistic contradictions."

13. *Is there any difficulty about combining "normal relations between countries with different social systems" and "full support to the anti-imperialist movements in Asia,*

Africa, and Latin America"?[4] *Are there guidelines for combining these two principles?*

"There will be differences in social systems for about a hundred years, we suppose—from 1917 to, say, about 2017—because socialism can't come everywhere at once. At the same time, there is not continual fighting. Peaceful coexistence is possible in some periods. For the socialist countries to have normal relations with the capitalist countries does not mean they will not help the revolutionaries in those countries. Therefore, the establishing of normal relations does not rest on the criterion of whether a country is socialist or not. But there is a limit to this. If a socialist country helps the socialist party in a particular capitalist country to overthrow the government, talk of peaceful coexistence is meaningless. And if it brings troops, it is certainly meaningless."

14. *Is it ever right for a socialist country to bring troops into another country in order to aid revolution there?*

"In some cases, it is right. But we would need a careful discussion of concrete conditions."

15. *How can Vietnam best contribute to solidarity in the world communist movement?*

"The party of the Vietnamese communists has always tried, and will continue to do its best, to restore and enhance solidarity in the world communist movement, on the basis of Marxism-Leninism and proletarian internationalism, and in ways conformable to both reason and sentiment."[5]

Hoang Tung was amused by so many questions, and shortened his later answers as he had to leave for another engagement. At the end he raised both hands and said, "There! I've finished all of them! Do I pass the exam?" I told him he got an "A," and he laughed heartily, then led me by the arm down to our waiting car. After handing me in he bowed, and grinning mischievously said, "Goodbye, Madame Gandhi!" The slight, neat figure stood on the steps and waved us out of sight.

11

Hanoi to Quang Ninh

After saying goodbye to each other, Duyên and I both spent last evening packing, she for a conference in Portugal and I for Quang Ninh and Thai Binh provinces, where I am to spend the next four days.

Little Liên is very concerned about my packing, as she is in charge of my material welfare and the safety of my possessions. This morning at seven she brought my mended briefcase and loaned me an extra suitcase to hold the things I don't want to take to Quang Ninh. Although my hotel room in Hanoi will be kept vacant until I return on Friday, Liên is not easy about leaving things here. Theft is rare, she says, but you can't be certain. We agree, too, that it is not fair to leave items around which might tempt others who are very poor. The extra suitcase is packed and placed in the wardrobe.

Even without it, I have an unfair share of luggage when we reach the car—a large suitcase and briefcase, while Khanh, Hoan, Liên senior, and driver Quyên, who are accompanying me, each carry a tiny bag. I tell Khanh, "I guess I'm a capitalist." She says smiling, tugging my suitcase, "Never mind, it's all right. Your ways are different."

The weather is cold now, down to 11°C, and my hosts wear wool socks, sweaters, and padded jackets over their pajamas. Hoan snuggles into a white wool shawl. Khanh has changed into thick tweed trousers and added a plastic raincoat and a headscarf. With the sudden drop in temperature, she is worred about her four-month-old baby whom she has left with her schoolteacher husband and her mother-in-law. He does not have enough clothes for the winter temperatures, which in December and January can go as low as 1°C. Khanh hopes they will find something warm enough to wrap him in. Although people are much better off since the war, she says, they are still poorly equipped for the winter in Vietnam. Many do not have enough clothes for comfort and convenience, and some do not yet have shoes. Khanh admires my Canadian polyester summer dresses and says the stitching seems stronger than theirs, which often comes undone. (Actually, they are equally bad, but I have reinforced mine by hand.) As we drive out of Hanoi in a chilly drizzle, many passersby on the road do seem poorly dressed in cotton or silk pajamas, light jackets, and sweaters. Even so, I think they are more warmly clad than most people in a Delhi winter.

Khanh is also rather disturbed about leaving her baby because she is nursing him. When she goes away her mother-in-law feeds him cows' milk, bananas, and oranges. I ask if she gets on well with her mother-in-law. She says, "Well, yes, she is actually rather good, rather easy." Hoan tells me that Khanh's mother-in-law is a prominent member of the Women's Union, so she is naturally in accord with its family policies.

As the sun peeps out and we enter the countryside of Haihung province, spirits rise, and my friends are soon laughing and chattering. Quyên turns on the car radio. Children are singing folk songs with catchy rhythms from Hue in a morning program for schools. All four of my companions join in. They tell me the Vietnamese love folk songs and know hundreds of them, and many ordinary people compose them. Hoan, in particular, often hums them as we drive along. She says most mothers sing and rock their babies to sleep.

Liên opens the morning copy of *Nhân Dân* and translates bits for me. After almost incredible feats of engineering and debris removal, the railway from Hanoi to Ho Chi Minh City, destroyed by bombing, is nearly rebuilt. Daily bulletins of its progress are issued in the press and on radio; today, only 200 kilometers remain.[1] At present people go by bus between north and south. This is inconvenient, for unless you have kin there is nowhere to sleep en route. Even so, Khanh, Liên, and Vô Thi Thê have all visited the south since liberation for reunions with their relatives. Khanh and Liên say Ho Chi Minh City was not badly damaged. Khanh went with her mother-in-law, whose family lives there.

The newspaper contains reports of themes to be discussed at the Fourth Party Congress in December, which are being studied in advance in workplaces and political classes and will be debated in the preliminary provincial party congresses that take place this week. From the foreign news section Liên reads about arrests in South Africa, and about the report of an American committee on violence in United States schools and the growing danger to teachers.

Khanh is studying part-time in addition to her union and household work. She will take an examination on Marxism-Leninism soon after my visit and is worried about finding time for review. She receives four consecutive days of study-leave each month. Her present courses last three years, after which she may take more advanced work if she likes. The classes include political economy, economic regions of Vietnam, the history of Vietnamese communism, philosophy, and the history of world communism. Hoan and Liên took these courses some years ago.

I ask about the structures of various institutions in Vietnam. The Women's Union, the Youth Union (aged fifteen to thirty), and each of the separate trade unions (such as journalists, artists, lawyers, and those of each industry) have their own central committees, evidently quite powerful bodies. The central committee of the Women's Union contains 111 members.

Liên is unhappy that I do not belong to a communist

party. Very gently, she suggests that I would be politically more effective if I did. I tell her the Left is fragmented in North America, as in India, and that apart from the Fourth International, with which I have disagreements, most groups seem to approve too uncritically the policies of either the Soviet Union or China, and to be sectarian toward one another. I cannot "go down the line" with either of these countries' policies. I disagree with parties supporting the Soviet Union because of its military aid and economic support for the Gandhi regime in India and because of what seems to me a long history of revisionism and of political repression. I also think the Soviet Union is in some respects imperialist toward Eastern Europe. I think it is a strongly hierarchical society, and I am not happy about its income differentials and the curtailment of civil liberties. On the other hand, I cannot uncritically support China because of various facets of its foreign policy, especially toward Angola and Chile, and its insistence that the Soviet Union is capitalist and that its government is the main enemy of socialism. Liên listens intently, though almost silently. On Soviet (and Vietnamese) support for Indira Gandhi, she says only, "Things are not always quite what they seem," and on China, "We, too, have had some of these difficulties." I realize that although deeply interested, she does not feel free to discuss these countries' policies nor those of communist parties in other nations, so I drop the subject.

At all events, Liên thinks I should study Vietnam as well as India, "because, after all, we have had a certain success." Perhaps I might visit sometime for a longer stay and study Marxism-Leninism here. "In Vietnamese?" I laugh.

"Why not?"

"Well," I say, "I'm a little old for that." Khanh and Liên pounce. "One is never too old!" they cry.

On the road to Haiphong the paddy harvest is nearing its end, though several fields are still being cut with sickles by both men and women. Some are carrying away sheaves slung on shoulder poles for threshing; in other fields light motor trucks are in use. Dotted here and there are bright green seedbeds with spring crop seedlings nearly tall enough for transplanting. In many fields plowing is going on either by tractor or with a wooden plow and a single, hefty bullock. In some the plowing has finished and the fields are already flooded in preparation for transplanting the new seedlings. Many fields contain potatoes, cabbages, and mustard seed. As before, there are heavy trucks and innumerable bicycles on the road. A steamroller is at work on a stretch of new road near Haiphong.

Haiphong, some sixty kilometers southeast of Hanoi, looks surprisingly normal. Although pulverized by United States bombs in 1972, the center of the town today shows few obvious signs of damage. The main streets are rather wide and the buildings modern, and there are squares with gardens. Rows of private stores offer spectacles, furniture, lamps, baskets, food, and clothing. The population is just under one million. We stop while Hoan goes to buy an enormous grapefruit for 1 dong (about U.S. $.20), a good price for the size, she says. In the car, she slices it and hands us pieces. Several small, motorized trucks full of vegetables and grains go by. An old woman in an ancient black skirt and shawl trudges past dragging a cart containing milk drums covered with cloths. She wears boots and has pieces of black flannel tucked into her bonnet to protect her face from the cold. She grins at us, showing black stumps of teeth which, by traditional custom have been filed.

We drive to the harbor and wait for a ferry to take us across one of the wide estuaries of the Red River's branches that lie between here and Ha Long Bay, our destination up the coast to the northeast. The docks are lined with ships from many countries, including China, the Soviet Union, Denmark, France, Norway, Cuba, and East Germany. A crane is unloading a tractor into a Vietnamese ship bound for Ho Chi Minh City.

Broad, flat, raftlike ferries surrounded by low railings, with engine rooms attached to one side, ply continuously across the coastal bays and branches of the river. They carry passengers, bicycles, cars, trucks, and peasants with baskets of fruit, meat, and vegetables. Peasants, mainly women, also sit on the roadsides approaching the ferry stations, selling peanuts, cabbages, potatoes, melons, caged birds, trussed chickens, mats, and baskets. For about twenty minutes we cross a wide, beautiful bay on which dance small, Chinese-style fishing boats with gaily colored sails. The ferry is crowded but there is not much commotion. People quietly stack their cycles and stand chatting near the rails; there are no seats. When we arrive they file off unhurriedly, smiling and stepping back politely to let others descend in turn. About a dozen visiting Russians, Czechs, and Scandinavians are riding with us; I am ushered up to the front along with them to get the best view.

Hoan lets me photograph anything in sight from the ferries, but not Haiphong harbor or the ferry stations from land. In one village while we wait for the ferry I ask to photograph a Communist Party office hung with streamers announcing the Fourth Party Congress. Hoan goes to ask the party official in charge, but is refused. I do not like to ask why, but imagine the Vietnamese still fear sabotage of any of their installations, and that each person in charge of one feels responsible for protecting it from any conceivable damage. After all, they have been at war thirty years, have had endless trouble with spies, infiltrators, and traitors in the Haiphong region, and still experience sabotage and occasional bombing in the south.

As we sail along, Liên tells me how dangerous and arduous was the work of demining Haiphong harbor and the surrounding areas after the United States blockade of 1972. It was accomplished quickly and skillfully but some people lost their lives. I ask her whether it is true that, according to the Paris agreements, help was given by United States Marines.

She says that there was such an agreement and that some marines came, but she has heard that they were unable or too fearful to do the job, removed only two mines, and left thousands more in the harbor and along the coast for the Vietnamese. There is still a great deal of dangerous work to be done demining fields and forests in south Vietnam, and in each province several hundred people have been killed while doing it.

Near one of the ferry stations a small party of men and women troops down the village street. The women carry covered dishes; the men, live chickens hanging by their legs. They are off to a wedding, says Khanh. Although brideprice, expensive gifts, and lavish displays at marriages are forbidden by law, the families hold a small feast. Liên tells me that marriages have to be approved by the local branch of the Communist Party, and that when appropriate, trade union authorities must also give consent. This surprises me, for the law guarantees freedom to choose a spouse. Perhaps the permission refers only to approval to conduct the marriage on a given date, to take a holiday, and to hold a feast.

We reach Ha Long Bay about 1 P.M. It is a beautiful resort town with a long shore road beside which are villas and cottages on the low cliff sides. The ferry terminal has a small, open waiting room with a pretty, Chinese-style roof. Across the road from it is a long, pleasant looking but plain hotel building for trade union workers on vacation. A little further up the road, on a cliff side surrounded by trees and gardens, is the government hotel where we shall stay. Its services are better than the trade union hotel, says Liên; it is reserved for foreign guests and their Vietnamese guides. From the yard just above the garden wall, and from the balcony outside my upstairs room, there are breathtaking views of the ocean between the landscaped bushes and pine trees. Out to sea, strangely shaped black rocks, some pointed, some mushroom shaped, rise up, as do barges with upturned prows and fanshaped sails. In the mist the whole scene looks mysterious and slightly unreal. My hosts are proud of the hotel and tell me they have brought me for rest and pleasure as well as work.

Waiting for us at a tea table on the patio are four women delegates from the Quang Ninh branch of the Women's Union. Their spokeswoman, Mrs. Pham Thi Huong, aged forty-seven, is a member of the union's central committee and a leader of the trade union of coal miners in Quang Ninh province. Mrs. Linh, vice-head of propaganda and education in the provincial Women's Union, comes from Nghê An like Ho Chi Minh. She gives a specially warm greeting to Quyên, our young driver from the province. Miss Tinh, a schoolteacher in her early thirties, is an executive member of the union's provincial committee, and Mrs. Tu is a vice-head of the personnel committee of the union in Quang Ninh. Mrs. Huong, who is secretary of the union in Quang Ninh, has charge of its clerical office. She was formerly a civil engineering worker, and in childhood worked in the mines. Talkative, effusive, and delightful, she hugs and kisses all of us repeatedly and bursts out with lots of news, jumping round like a spaniel. ("She's a *worker*," says Khanh in a smiling aside.) Laughing, and nearly bowled over, my friends calm her down and get us all into chairs so that she can deliver her speech of welcome.

After greeting me warmly, Mrs. Huong tells me Ha Long Bay means "bay of the descending dragon," whereas Thang Long, the old name for Hanoi, means "city of the ascending dragon" (or as Khanh puts it, "fly-up dragon"). Dragons, like people, have done remarkable feats in Quang Ninh, she laughs; in time I may learn all about them. This area is also famous because the bay nearby is the one in which the hero Ngo Quyên defeated the Chinese in the naval battle of 938 A.D. (Khanh mentions hurriedly that I have heard about that, and perhaps we should move on quickly to recent events, and to lunch.)

Mrs. Huong tells me that on August 5, 1964, the first day of the United States attack on the north, the people of Ha Long Bay shot down many aircraft and captured their first American pilot. Like most buildings in Ha Long Bay, both this and the trade union hotel were largely destroyed by bombing. This one is still not fully rebuilt.

All these women led very active lives in the war. Mrs. Tu has been a long-time cadre in the villages of Quang Ninh. Mrs. Linh was formerly a mine worker in a place which "recorded many feats in struggle." Mrs. Huong's engineering factory was split up and evacuated, although many of its workers stayed in Ha Long Bay. Miss Tinh's school, too, was evacuated to the countryside.

We go in to a sumptuous lunch. Wonton soup is followed by Chinese rock cod, frogs' legs, green vegetables and many fruits, with beer and coffee. Mrs. Huong, Hoan, and Khanh accompany me to the dining room. Liên and the rest eat elsewhere, presumably more humbly. The chopsticks come from China and are decorated with delicate figures on lacquered handles.

Apart from us there are only two tourist parties in the hotel, one Soviet and one East German, both comprising about twenty people. The Soviet group, all men, wear gray or black suits, some with capes attached to their collars; they keep their gray cloth caps on at table, probably against the cold. In the East German party are three young women with flowered dresses and shoulder length hair.[2]

A number of young soldiers, no doubt on guard, stand or stroll about the hotel grounds. Young women in white uniforms wait at tables or carry luggage up and down. They all smile brightly, exchange greetings with my hosts, and seem a little breathless, inexperienced, and eager to do well. Workmen are repairing the French window in the dining room and painting the entrance hall and corridors, and one whole wing is being rebuilt after the bombing.

12

Mining in Quang Ninh

"Just now," says Mrs. Huong, "our miners are celebrating forty years of all-out struggle." We have reassembled at tea time on the hotel veranda for a talk on Quang Ninh province, interpreted by Khanh. "Their struggles date from October 12, 1936. We have a miners' festival on that date every year, but we celebrated it specially this year.

"October 12, 1936, marked a real turning point in our fight against the French mine owners. They used every trick you could imagine to oppress and terrorize our workers. They were that much stronger, too, because they were linked up with Emperor Bao Dai, the last of the Nguyen dynasty.

"I think miners were the worst exploited of all our workers. Even skilled miners got only 24 Vietnamese cents a day (about U.S. $0.05 at today's exchange rate). Really starvation wages. Many of us had no houses, and everyone was hungry. Sometimes we couldn't even afford pants to work in. We all looked like skeletons.

"We used to make up poems about our life." Mrs. Huong recites one, but I cannot catch the full translation. One line is

When I hear the workbell I feel that it's a call from hell,

and another,

Cutting coal is worse than going to jail.

154

"I started mine work in 1939 when I was nine—I went to learn with my mother. Of course they didn't give me any wages! I wasn't paid at all until I was thirteen, and then I got only 400 grams (14 ounces) of rice a day. My coal cart was Number 10—how well I remember it! Every morning the boss would call each cart in turn; mine went at four in the morning, and I worked till seven at night. We had to drive that cart thirteen times a day to get our wages. Two of us loaded and unloaded it, and a third one drove it. All by hand shovel—there were no machines in those days. Every day they would measure the coal and give me rice if I'd worked enough.

"Even pregnant women had to work like that, even at seven months. I once saw a cart fall on a woman who was seven months pregnant; she miscarried right there in the mine. They took her to the hospital, but even then she had to pay for her own food.

"Sometimes we worked down tunnels only thirty centimeters wide, just like a prison. If we refused, we got no wages, and if we didn't work enough we had to do overtime to get the money. That meant going at 2 A.M. to earn wages for days we'd already worked. The highest wage was only 6 or 7 dong (U.S. $1.20 to $1.40) a month.

"Well, at last we workers organized ourselves to struggle. The communists encouraged us—they showed us. And October 12, 1936, was the day of our first strike. We had another again in 1939, from November 12 to 24. That was a real triumph, and the bosses had to compromise. What a fight it was! I was nine, and I used to bring drinking water to the pickets—my father, my mother both were there, and I helped them. I would bring them coconut shells and half-grapefruit rinds to drink from. Fruitsellers would give us fruits, to support the struggle. And those workers got no wages for twelve days. But then the bosses ran away!—they were scared, you see, as the strike got bigger and bigger.

"To tell the truth, we drove them away!" At the memory,

Mrs. Huong snorts with excited laughter. "Our folks used mining tools to chase them! And when we caught them, we tied them up with string! Of course the police were sent in to crush us, but we won.

"There were a lot of foreign ships in Haiphong harbor then. British, French, Japanese—the French exported coal to other countries. We put the lot of them out of work because they had no coal! Ten thousand of us, 10,000 miners went on strike. And then they increased everybody's wages by about 3 dongs a month.

"So anyway, let me tell you about the things we have today. Now, the miners' wages are about 100 dongs (U.S. $20.00) a month. That won't seem much to you, but they are rich compared to yesterday. Working conditions have improved a lot. Our government buys equipment from other countries, and we make some ourselves in Vietnam.

"Women's lives are very different. Women aren't allowed to work the stoves today, as they're too hot, and they don't do various other kinds of heavy work. Women have three months' paid leave during childbirth, and free hospital care and health examinations. They have crèches and kindergartens for their children, and half an hour's time out, morning and afternoon, to nurse their babies.

"Altogether we've built about a hundred day-care centers and kindergartens in this province. In Ha Tu mine the workers themselves gave money to start a crèche and kindergarten. They laid the foundation stone in 1961, but then a U.S. plane destroyed the whole thing in 1965. But our folks rebuilt it, and now we have not one but four kindergartens around Ha Tu mine.

"Today our miners work an eight-hour day. During the war we had a slogan, 'Fight and work together.' When the enemy came we fought, and when he went away we worked! My husband and I were both soldiers way back in the war against the French. I was quite a good shot!—in the second rank. My husband's a mine worker, but he went and fought for eleven years against the U.S. invaders in south Vietnam. Now he's home, thank Heaven. A great many women in the mines joined self-defense units in the U.S. war. Some of them got awards as 'heroic units,' in fighting or in work.

"You know Bach Dang River, where Ngô Quyên defeated the Chinese?" (in 938 A.D.!) "Well, there's a women's self-defense unit, the Minh Vuong unit, at Yên Hung on that river. It has forty-two women, all agricultural workers. It's been rewarded as a heroic unit—those women shot down U.S. planes along with men. There's another peasant women's self-defense unit at Lê Chân coop in Yên Thô. They chased and harassed a U.S. plane with short-distance guns until it was shot down by military fighters. By the end, 200 U.S. planes were shot down in Quang Ninh. A self-defense unit on a small island off our coast shot down the last of them.

"Every single worker in Ha Tu mine took part in self-defense. On the very first day of the U.S. air invasion, August 5, 1964, they nabbed a U.S. plane and captured Junior Lieutenant Aberat. He was a prisoner until the war ended and was the first to be released under the Paris agreements.

"We have a lot of minority people in Quang Ninh province. Fourteen nationalities of them. No, we don't call them tribes! —that word has gone. The Tay, Nung, Han, San Diu, and San Chi are among the most important. They are cultivators. They live just like the other Vietnamese but have their own languages. They're about 30 percent of Quang Ninh's people, higher than other provinces because Quang Ninh is mountainous and they live mainly in the hills.

"They played a big part in the war. Every one of them voluntarily joined agricultural cooperatives, and among them they shot down three U.S. aircraft. A woman of the Dzao minority is in the National Assembly—she was elected twice in succession. And many minority women are in our People's Councils. Three are in the secretariat of the Women's Union. Before the revolution our ruling class persecuted them and many people looked down on them, but not today.

"It was the minorities who fed President Ho Chi Minh and defended the revolutionaries in the underground period in the mountains. In fact, the mountains were the base area from which the revolutionaries moved out into the towns, so you can see how essential the minorities have been. Of course, the rulers tried to divide us. Both the French and the feudalists would burn down minorities' houses and blame the Vietminh! They would cut the heads off minority people and blame the Vietminh! But people didn't believe them, and hated them.

"Comrade Thach of the Dzao minority is the head of the provincial district in Quang Ninh; his wife is a cadre of the Women's Union. Thach was trained in politics, economics, and culture by the party—and, of course, in Marxism-Leninism! His wife, Tu Khai Hong, is a Han woman. She worked as a liaison officer running affairs for the party in the 1950s. In 1965 she was made a member of the Executive Standing Committee of the Youth Union. In 1966 she went to study economics and engineering, and then came back to be an engineer here. After some time she returned to her minority area and was chosen as president of the administration of her district. We're proud of such people.

"Another man, a heavy-tractor driver from one of the minorities, was elected a hero because he did his work excellently. He recorded the highest speed in transporting coal, and did it safely."

I ask Mrs. Huong whether all heroes in Quang Ninh have been elected.

"Oh, yes!" she says. "In their efforts to boost production, workers elect people who have achieved a lot, to encourage and honor them. A hero has to be first in work, but he also has to show good, virtuous behavior and think up ways to increase production and encourage others. First, a group of three will nominate somebody, and then if they're lucky he or she will get elected by bigger groups, up and up till they reach the top—till they're elected by about 2,000 workers.

There may be seven elections between the bottom and the top. As people get nearer the top, of course, not everybody knows them, so then their supporters write a paper with their exploits, and people elect whoever seems the best."

Mrs. Huong would like to go on longer, and I to hear her; but Khanh and I are both tired from the long work days and our journey, and dinner time is near. The four Quang Ninh women leave us affectionately until tomorrow.

Khanh and I go for a stroll in the hotel's cliffside garden. Khanh is interested in Canada, my family, and my way of life, and asks several questions. What is my son doing? (Training to be an actor.) How many rooms does our house have? With some shame, I tell her eight.

"Eight rooms for three people!" she says. "That *is* large. We have only one room—my mother-in-law, husband, the baby, and myself."

I tell her that we are favored because my husband inherited money from his father, who was an American businessman. On a small scale, we are capitalists as well as university teachers.

"Capitalists!" she says. "Your father-in-law was a U.S. capitalist! What was his business?" He was first a wholesale dealer in whiskey, I tell her, then manufactured chocolates when prohibition came. Khanh goes off into a shout of laughter. "You mean you made *only chocolates!*" she says. "Did you eat a lot? I'd have been always eating them!" I say that was long ago, before my father-in-law's death in 1935, which was twenty years before I went from England to North America and met my husband. Khanh asks what my own father was, and I tell her: first, a blacksmith, then an agricultural engineer selling and repairing farm machinery in Yorkshire. She ponders all this quietly as we go back to our rooms.

Top: From left to right, Hoan, Mrs. Linh, the author, Liên, Mrs. Tu, Miss Tinh, and Mrs. Huong. *Bottom:* Road mending, Quang Ninh.

Top left: From left to right, Hoan, Khanh, and Liên. *Top right:* Children of Hong Gai, Quang Ninh province. *Bottom left:* Bombed housing in Hong Gai. *Bottom right:* View from the Hotel of Foreign Relations in Quang Ninh.

13

Caves, Wars, and History

The weather in Quang Ninh is now quite cold, with winds and occasional lashing rains. I'm thankful for the sweater Little Liên urged on me before we left Hanoi, and whenever I let her, Hoan wraps her white shawl round my shoulders. My hotel room has a small electric heater around which we occasionally toast our toes. My friends' rooms do not have heaters, so I ask them to share my big room with its two double beds, mosquito nets, and ample blankets. They refuse with laughing amazement—evidently such luxury is not for them. It feels wrong to be so pampered when all around are living a spartan existence, but that is the way Vietnam likes to treat its guests.

Both here and in Hanoi, each morning brings three fried eggs swimming in a dish of melted butter, with firm white bread, fresh fruit, and coffee. My friends breakfast early elsewhere—on humbler fare, I suspect. Lunch and dinner, which I share with two or three companions while on tour, are lavish and superb. Each meal features soup, shrimp or fish, roast pork *and* frogs' legs or chicken, rice and cabbage, bananas, beer, and tea.

My companions meet, I think, either in the evening or the early morning, to plan and evaluate our tour, for they have told me they practice criticism and self-criticism every day.

The road through the garden behind the hotel is being

repaired, mainly by young women. They wear conical hats tied with strings, and with towels tucked into the brim and strings to keep out the cold, completely covering their faces except for the eyes. I ran into one of them around a corner of the building this morning and was thoroughly startled by her strange appearance; her eyes danced, then she ran off with smothered laughter. The women carry baskets of stones in their arms, not on their heads as in India; some have small hand barrows. Some are using pickaxes. Two girls on tall ladders are painting the hotel walls green; from another ladder a young man is cleaning windows.

This morning, November 16, Hoan and Khanh come to chat with me before our day's expedition. Hoan reminisces about the early days of the revolution in 1941 when President Ho Chi Minh and General Giap were training fighters in the mountains of Pac Bo. She names several cadres of the period who later became important, among them Chu Van Tan, now a junior general, and Nguyen Son, a prominent fighter who died in 1956.

The River Claire or Son Lo, a branch of the Red River, was the site of a famous battle won by Vietnamese forces against the French in 1947; three thousand French troops were killed or wounded. Hoan hums a song from the period, and Khanh translates it:

> The river glitters and flows down,
> Bringing silt to our land.
> Have you seen the forest of paper trees
> Of flickering green?
> Have you seen the thick forest of paper trees
> On the banks of the dike?
> At the fork of the river
> Have you seen the young men in peasant dress
> Who pledge to liberate our land from the foreigner
> So that people under the control of the enemy
> May be freed and return to their homes?
> Son Lo River,
> Give our love to our countrymen.

Hoan sang this song when she was young, and Khanh learned it from her mother and sang it while running after the troops.

Around a tree in the hotel garden is built a circular wooden cage containing swings and branches. At present it is occupied by a single monkey which chatters excitedly when we approach. In our off moments Khanh and I amuse ourselves by passing him sticks through the bars, which he examines and sometimes throws out again.

At ten, Liên arrives with our Quang Ninh friends for a pleasure trip. Our destination is a huge cave known as "Hidden Spikes Cave" in a cliff about an hour away by ferry. A man awaits us at the landing stage in a covered launch with a small engine room and seats for about thirty people. We set off up the coast.

Liên tells me that a big steamer-ferry moored in the harbor was the last one to carry out the departing French troops in 1954. We meet a pleasure boat carrying about a hundred workers on holiday, who wave to us. Hoan says they own it themselves and take it on expeditions. Further up the coast is a large resort hotel for workers. It flies the national flag and is decorated with dozens of other small, colored flags with no special meaning, "for beauty." Next to it stands a pile of neatly stacked rocks, the relics of a bombed restaurant and air raid shelter. We pass an electric power station which I am told serves both irrigation and manufacturing works, and then head out to sea.

The bay is quietly beautiful in the morning mist, through which the sun breaks softly. Gulls soar over our heads. We thread our way through dozens of black rock islands of curious shape, some of which tower above us. Fishing barges bob along with their gaily colored fanshaped sails. Families live on them, says Khanh, and come ashore to sell their fish. Several groups wave and shout as we pass nearby.

Mrs. Tu dives into a picnic basket and we feast on peanuts, mandarin oranges, boiled tapioca, lemonade, and beer. The food comes from a women's garden in Mrs. Tu's agricultural cooperative. As we nibble away, my Hanoi and Quang Ninh friends get into a long, animated discussion of dragons, only bits of which are translated. I think they are comparing mythological stories from their respective childhoods in the provinces where they were born.

The bay we are sailing through is Bai Tu Long or "Bowing Dragon's Children," explains Khanh. (Hoan adds that presidents Tito and Ho Chi Minh swam here in 1963.) A mother dragon's children were kidnapped by a sea monster but she got them back with the help of fish in the bay. Hoan tells me Vietnamese dragons characteristically differ somewhat from those of China. They are gentler, she thinks, and are often mothers with children. I ask her why she thinks dragon stories are so widespread in the world. She says she feels sure it is because some such creatures lived in palaeolithic times and became woven into the legends of early men. Even today, many Vietnamese fisherfolk believe dragons save them from sea monsters and storms.

I ask Mrs. Linh about the mine she formerly worked in. It was bombed in the United States war, she says, but is fully restored; "90 percent" of the work is fully mechanized now. In general the coal mining areas of Quang Ninh underwent saturation bombing, as did the harbors. The district suffered notable atrocities, such as the slaughter, by bombing, of 500 people in Song Sang village. There is still a good deal of rebuilding to be done here, more than in Hanoi.

Mrs. Tu and Mrs. Linh say that nowadays mine workers' trade unions are able to buy quite a lot of communal property for their convenience and recreation. They are especially fond of boats in which they can take their families on trips.

Through Khanh, Miss Tinh tells me something of her wartime experiences with children. Her school in Ha Long Bay was split up and evacuated into the countryside in several small units to minimize the danger from bombing. In Miss Tinh's section no one was killed because, as she says, they were "clever and lucky." She says they followed the injunctions of President Ho Chi Minh, "to protect the lives of our children, who are our future, while also teaching them." It was a very intense time of love and struggle, with everyone trying their best to improve the life of the group and of the country. Ho Chi Minh's five principles of education figured prominently, and Miss Tinh quotes them:

1. Love the country and your compatriots. Hate the aggressor.
2. Constantly improve work and study.
3. Strengthen unity and observe discipline.
4. Practice hygiene.
5. Be modest, frank, and courageous.

Many schools were bombed in Quang Ninh and several teachers died while saving their pupils.

The sun shines as we get off the boat and climb a long flight of steps to the cave. We have seen a number of such caves along the coast, in many of which men and weapons have been hidden in wars over the past millennium, but this is the biggest and most famous. From a bend in the path there is a spectacular view of the ocean, the rocks, and the fishing boats, with our ferry in the foreground. We stop to photograph it and each other, with much posing and laughter.

The cave is enormous, with three main chambers. Trees and shrubs grow inside it near the entrance. Birds fly about and nest in them. There seem, however, to be no bats or rats; the place smells fresh and is surprisingly clean. There are several paths and rocky promontories to explore. Hoan and Khanh climb a steep rockface to get on to an upstairs platform where soldiers slept during wars.

The cave has a long and famous military history. The wooden spikes used to trap the Chinese invaders in the Bach Dang River in 1288 are believed to have been stored here; also perhaps those used earlier, in 938. The cave's dark depths hid men and weapons in several later invasions, in the Tay Son rebellion, and in the revolutionary war against the French in 1945-1954.

Hoan finds a piece of yellow quartz and gives it to me as a souvenir. This morning I am especially struck by the lively sense of their history all these friends display, their fascination with the relics of earlier resistance wars, and their high spirits on any kind of outing. Age does not matter; Mrs. Huong and Liên leap about with the rest and make several steep climbs, and soon I am joining them. We all have fun with the cave's resounding echoes.

In the late afternoon we make our second ferry expedition, across a bay north of Ha Long, to Hong Gai. Mrs. Huong was born here and our Quang Ninh hosts all live here now. A mountain rises up from the harbor, behind which are coal mines. The nearest is ten kilometers away. It is too late, wet, and cold to visit it; instead, Quyên drives us around Hong Gai port.

Above the ferry terminal is a vast red signboard: "Produce more coal for the Fatherland." Along the sea front, banners welcome the Fourth Congress and there are giant posters of miners, sailors, and fishermen at work.

The Hong Gai mines, docks, and workers' housing were among the worst bombed sites in the north. Much rebuilding has already been done; large buildings are restored and there are new rows of cottages painted a sunny yellow. But as we drive along the shore road I have my first glimpse of the kind of devastation that until recently was commonplace throughout Vietnam. Between the buildings are wide, grassy spaces where ruins have been hauled away. In one of them, under a makeshift roof, cement and machines have been assembled ready to build a block of workers' flats. A row of tall, old fashioned houses offers the most pitiful view I have seen in Vietnam. No doubt grim and dingy to start with, they are now sadly shattered. Upper floors dip and sag, staircases are smashed and panes broken, and there are gaping holes in the roofs and walls. Housing is so scarce that they are still occupied. An old man in a miner's coal-soiled smock stands beneath them. As I photograph them from across the road he stares blankly, with a look of despair.

The young here are hopeful, however. Two little boys and a girl run up to us, inquisitive and mischievous. They dance and tiptoe round us, pirouette, and peep at me from behind a lamp post. All have food in their hands; one boy is eating a kind of porridge with a spoon, and his large eyes regard me from behind his bowl. They wear jackets, pants, and sandals; although thinly clad for the rain, they don't seem to care—they are brimful of energy and joy of living. For once, Hoan lets me photograph this group.

Rain sheets down as we await the ferry. A young policeman is sitting in a pill box the size of a phone booth. These booths are found at intervals along all the roads, especially at terminals and on the borders of provinces. When we cross from one province to another, Hoan leaves the car to show my passport and explain my visit to the incumbent. This young man beckons Khanh and me in to shelter. We squeeze in beside him and he shakes our wet hands laughingly and asks my origins.

Across from the ferry terminal is an imposing but rather grim stone building, the old French prison, and next to it a large yellow building that Khanh says the French used solely to torture prisoners. Today they are trade union offices. Both were bombed and have been repaired since the war.

Three of our Quang Ninh friends say goodbye in Hong Gai; Mrs. Huong returns with us to Ha Long Bay for dinner. Her current work for the union is to travel about observing women workers' conditions. She inspects canteens, crèches, and workplaces, sees whether the party's programs are being carried out, and reports back to Hanoi.

In the evening Mrs. Huong recalls more scenes from her youth. If a man so much as broke a tree branch on land owned by the French, he had to pay a fine. If the man himself did not bring it, the director of mines would order his wife or daughter to be bound and brought to him, and would sometimes rape her. Many women mine workers were kidnapped by French officers for no reason at all, dragged into a building marked "storage," and raped there. To combat these atrocities, in 1930 the communists formed a Movement of Women Against Rape, one of the first of many popular fronts to become active in Hong Gai.

In spite of terrible repression, the communist flag was first briefly raised in Hong Gai in 1939, then again during the August revolution of 1945. The famine of 1945 was unusually horrible in this coastal region. The Japanese used rice as fuel, and when they knew they were defeated they deliberately burned large rice stocks. Thousands of corpses floated in Ha Long Bay, and there was bombing during the final struggle between the Japanese and the French. When French colonial troops returned in force a few months after the August revolution, they wrested Hong Gai and the coastal region from the Vietnamese and fortified them heavily. Late in the anti-French war, there was a major battle in Ha Long Bay in which Vietnamese troops defeated the French and then took over the coast again.

Affectionate and spontaneous, Mrs. Huong is a joy to be with. Although we cannot talk directly, she contacts me often through gestures, handclasps, and embraces, and tells me as much as Khanh and Liên can reasonably translate. As we ride home and I am silently pondering the years of massacre and bombing in Hong Gai, she says, "You are sad and thoughtful. You have a deep heart; I feel as if I'd known you a long time."

Mine worker, engineer, and administrator, Mrs. Huong is also a poet. In particular, she wrote poems to her husband during their long separations in the French and American wars. It is hard to say goodbye to this loving, imaginative woman. After a long embrace, she gives me three packets of picture postcards, prints of delicately executed watercolors, to take back to Canada.

As Khanh and I go upstairs after dinner, a young man from

the Soviet Union runs down. He greets us cheerily and asks if I speak Russian. Khanh tells him (in Russian) that I don't, I'm from Canada. She says he is probably a technician and that there are many in Vietnam. "They are very good, kind, and emotional," she adds. "They work and read hard. They are not at all fierce, as some noncommunists believe them to be."

14

Quang Ninh to Thai Binh

November 17. After breakfast Liên appears late, looking worried. Somehow, the hotel management has lost her identity card, which the law requires her to carry everywhere. Her inquiries prove fruitless, and we must leave at 8 A.M. She possesses another identity paper that she can use in emergencies, and she can obtain a new card, but the procedure is "very difficult." She is clearly much distressed but puts aside her anxiety so as not to spoil our day.

We drive back to Haiphong in the morning, then south along the coast to Thai Binh. We cross seven branches of the Red River, four by ferry and three over long bridges of iron and wooden piles. On the first ferry, women are crossing with baskets of parsnips, tapioca, and chickpeas, and hand carts of cabbages. Workers in blue overalls and soldiers in green uniforms also cross on their way to work. The soldiers are being dispatched to wherever they are most needed for construction.

Three Soviet cargo ships and one from East Germany have come into Haiphong since we left on Monday. Today the main square of the town is thronged with wheeled carts, barrows, and dozens of cycles. Flags and streamers herald the Fourth Party Congress. Schools, factories, trade unions, and cooperatives vie with one another to put up spectacular, flamboyant posters of working people, pictures of Ho Chi Minh, and banners welcoming the congress.

Quyên treats us to a love song on the radio, followed by a song about the Trung sisters repelling Chinese invaders (in 43 A.D.!). The music, featuring violins and flutes, seems more Western than I am accustomed to from India. The tunes are brisk and catchy, often martial in tone, and usually in the major mode. Quyên switches off a talk on agriculture that follows.

Along the roadside are many people with large reed baskets suspended from shoulder poles; they are used both to catch fish and to carry paddy or other commodities. On the banks of the estuaries and sheltered bays we see large "flying" fishing nets of the type used on the backwaters of Kerala in southwest India and introduced there by medieval voyagers from China. We pass dozens of fisherfolk's barges, and at quiet spots on the river banks, men and women fishing with lines. Khanh says shrimps are an important source of food along the coast.

At each of the ferry terminals is a village with mud or wood houses thatched with straw over wooden frames. Passengers stop at wayside stalls to drink tea and eat bananas, small rice cakes, tapioca, or peanuts. Pigeons, turkeys, ducks, and chickens scratch and peck by the roadsides. At one terminal a white samoyed stalks about importantly; at another, a child is carrying a small brown puppy—the only dogs I have seen in Vietnam. At one stop a young man on a Honda waits for the ferry. Each time we pull up, villagers gather round us, friendly and curious. They always assume I am from the Soviet Union, and are interested to know I'm from Canada.

My Hanoi friends behave courteously and affectionately to these villagers. At each stop they enter into conversation with peasants, soldiers, old people, and children, asking them about their lives, schools, families, and work. They explain our mission, and occasionally put an arm around an old woman's shoulders. Quyên, our driver, stops often to greet men he knows along our route. At the second terminal three barefoot children race up to examine us. Unlike most children I have seen they wear unwashed clothing and have streaked, dirty faces and tousled hair. They grin at us mischievously. Liên draws one to her and hugs her. "Just so dirty and so happy was I," she says.

At the last ferry stop a boy of twelve runs up carrying his small sister in his arms. He points me out to her and crows at her. A younger sister sidles up, takes the child over and, exactly as in India, settles her on her hip.

Khanh beckons me excitedly. A middle-aged village woman is waiting for her husband to come off the ferry; she has not seen him for ten years. Eagerly, my friends ask her story. They congratulate her and all of us shake hands and hug her. When the ferry arrives I lose sight of her in the crowd, but as we leave the shore I look back and think I can see her in the distance, walking away with a slight, straight figure in uniform.

On one of the ferries, as Liên and I lean over the rail, she points out to sea to some offshore islands. Oil is plentiful there and in the ocean itself, she says. Its extraction will eventually make life far better in Vietnam. Soviet technicians are currently exploring for oil off the coast of north Vietnam, Liên says, while Norwegians and French, and soon, perhaps, Canadians, will work in the south. "We thought it better to have the Soviet Union in north Vietnam and Western nationals in the south because they are more familiar there," she says. I cannot help finding this welcoming of Western foreign investment and technicians uncanny after the long period of French colonialism, the agony of the anti-French war, and the still more recent Canadian collusion with the United States occupation and devastation of south Vietnam.[1] I am also concerned at the prospect of investment by multinational corporations, whose profit extraction and unequal trade with the Third World are usually harmful. I indicate as much to Liên. She says she is confident the government will make only such arrangements as will benefit

Vietnam in the long run. She thinks the equipment and technical aid will be paid for in raw materials and will not involve permanent foreign ownership of installations.

Along the coast at frequent intervals, especially south of Haiphong, are Catholic churches, some of them large and imposing, some two to three centuries old. In the whole of north Vietnam about six hundred churches have been bombed and are under repair; we pass one still standing in ruins. Although many Catholics fled to the south under the influence of Ngô Dinh Diêm's propaganda in 1954, thousands remained. The churches operate freely, the priests and teachers living from the contributions of worshippers or from fields they till themselves. Liên says many young Christians are leaving the church for communism and that some have married former Buddhists. Over the years, Hoan tells me, the communists have had much trouble from "conspiratorial priests"; it is their opposition to the revolution, rather than their religion, that makes them objects of suspicion. Many priests favored the French in the anticolonial struggle, and some secretly tried to aid the United States forces and the Central Intelligence Agency in the recent conflict. Even today, priests in the south are occasionally caught distributing leaflets which oppose the revolutionary government, although the Catholic hierarchy as a whole, in both north and south Vietnam, has made the decision to cooperate with the government. Liên tells me, moreover, that the majority of Christians turned against the United States invaders when they saw American planes bombing churches, hospitals, and schools.

I tell Liên the Christian churches' imperialist and counter-revolutionary history is ironic in view of the fact that Jesus sought a classless society and was executed by the Romans as an anticolonial rebel, and that his central message was love, not conquest or hate. If he were alive today he would surely support the revolution in Vietnam. Liên seems a little worried by this weakness of mine for Jesus. She says she finds him a strange figure because he had no family or sexual life—"rather unhealthy," she says. Only later I remember that Ho Chi Minh had no family either.

Every mile or so south of Haiphong we pass *banquères,* circular towers of stone and earth about twenty feet high, from which French forces machine gunned the countryside during the anticolonial war. Each tower contains a room above ground with holes for observation and rifle fire. Below ground is a cellar to store weapons and ammunition. I am a trifle puzzled, when I think of it later on, to know why these towers have never been removed in the twenty-two years since the French departed. Possibly they were used as air raid shelters or as storage for ammunition in the anti-United States war. Today, grass and even small trees grow out of their flat roofs.

The Japanese were even more cruel than the French, says Hoan. They would open fire on the population at the slightest sign of disaffection and would beat and shoot people for small offenses, for example, stealing food for their children. But none of this stopped the revolutionary advance. In 1941–1945, while fighting went on mainly in the mountains, political resistance gathered strength steadily in the plains and cities.

Hoan and Liên say the famine was the worst period in both their lives. It resulted from drought, the Japanese export of rice, their policy of forcing the peasants to grow jute, their use of rice as fuel, their deliberate destruction of rice stocks toward the end of the war, and the Allied bombing which disrupted communications between the north and the south. Corpses cluttered the streets of Hanoi and Haiphong and floated in the rivers and bays. Hoan and Liên saw many agonizing deaths of friends and relatives. They would try to sleep in underground shelters and would come up each morning to find loads of corpses being carried off by truck.

Liên says, "In 1945 many people believed our revolution simply could not succeed, for we had no materials, no experience, a starving people, and very few leaders. But it did triumph, and to our own amazement we went on to fight two wars."

A cyclist suddenly rides from a side road across our path. Quyên swerves sharply, but hits him. We pull up and my friends run back to help the man to his feet. He is unhurt but shaken. They comfort him, then scold him mildly. Cyclists, both men and women, throng all the roads throughout the day. The men often carry a second adult or a child riding pillion.

Thai Binh has a population of half a million, in a province of 1.5 million inhabitants. Thai Binh province is the most fertile and productive region in north Vietnam. Its miles of flat wet-rice fields, irrigation channels from the Red River tributaries, and clumps of bananas and fruit trees remind me strongly of Thanjavur, the delta of the River Kaveri in southeast India where I have recently completed my study of changing agricultural relations. As a deltaic paddy-growing region that is undergoing agricultural modernization, Thai Binh is indeed the high point of my visit.[2] Like Thanjavur, it has a coastline used for intensive fishing. In both areas cyclones sometimes devastate the villages and cause the sea to flow inland.

Thai Binh town is a collection center for agricultural produce. Much of the province's paddy is husked here in modern rice mills and transported by truck or rail to Hanoi and other provinces. The town's broad streets, low modern buildings, and occasional corner gas stations remind me of a market town in the prairies of the United States.

We draw into the parking lot of the Hotel for Foreign Relations and are met by Mrs. Lê Thi Dinh, vice-president of the administrative committee of the province and an executive member of the Central Committee of the Women's Union. With her are Mrs. Lê Thi Biên Ninh, president of the Women's Union in the province, and Mrs. Pham Thi Nhân and Mrs. Doan Thi Chinh, both vice-presidents of the provincial union. A man of about forty whose name escapes me is here to represent the president of the province, who is busy with the provincial party congress of November 10 to 22. Mrs. Dinh is also attending the congress but has left it to welcome me.

Mrs. Dinh, the ranking member of the Thai Binh group, is a tall, rather stout, dignified woman of fifty-one. Over tea in the reception lounge she welcomes me and thanks me warmly for making my visit, asks after the members of my family, and sends them her greetings.

Mrs. Dinh was born in Thai Binh and, well before the revolution, became active in the women's movement. She was elected to the second National Assembly of North Vietnam and since then has twice been elected an executive member in the central committee of the Women's Union. She has a daughter studying in the University of Thai Binh. Her husband and two sons are still in the army, "far away."

Mrs. Ninh, president of the provincial Women's Union, was formerly a deputy in the fifth legislature of the National Assembly. One of her children is a teacher, one a soldier, and one attends the university.

Mrs. Nhân is the wife of a doctor. In fact, when I ask what the women do, I am told, "Her husband is a doctor"—the first time this has happened in Vietnam. Normally, a woman's own qualifications are given and her husband's are not referred to unless a special inquiry is made. Mrs. Nhân has two children in college, one studying agriculture and the other civil engineering.

Mrs. Chinh is a friendly, animated country woman. She has worked in the Women's Union most of her life. Her husband is in the army and her three daughters are all peasants. Mrs. Dinh asks me to note that none of these four women has had more than three children, which in their day was "the proper number." All four of these impressive middle-aged women were illiterate peasants at the time of the revolution in 1945, and have gained their education since.

We go off to our rooms to prepare for lunch. Finding them

turns into a hilarious scamper, the first sign I've seen of anything resembling disorder in Vietnam. Although the hotel was begun in 1960, because of the war it is still under construction. There are workers on ladders in all the corridors, and unattached toilets, baths of whitewash, piles of cement and bricks, and buckets of paint in unexpected places. A young woman rushes us and our luggage up four flights of stairs and along several corridors to rooms that turn out not to be ready. After a quick colloquy we run down again, then up again to the second floor; where a mystified young woman behind a desk reluctantly hands us keys from the board she is guarding. All of us are winded and Khanh and I are weak with laughter. We wash and run down again, bumping into several Russians on our way.

Lunch, a formal meal with our welcoming committee, opens with a thick soup of rice, carrot, and cabbage followed by cold roast chicken, bread, tasty meatballs with onion and tomato, and lots of beer. For dessert Mrs. Dinh proudly displays locally grown bananas and oranges, followed by tea with cigarettes and toffees (plain and chocolate), all made in Thai Binh.

Over lunch, with Khanh interpreting, Mrs. Dinh tells me the provincial congress of the Workers' Party is composed of several hundred delegates from Thai Binh. Out of these, twenty-six will be elected by those present to attend the Fourth Party Congress in Hanoi in December.

Thai Binh town, she says, was virtually destroyed by United States bombs, for the pilots regularly jettisoned them here when they flew in from the sea and could not or did not want to fly inland. Miraculously, this hotel (the only one) escaped, but almost every other structure has been rebuilt.

In spite of the war, Thai Binh has made extraordinary progress both in agriculture and handicrafts. In 1945 most rice fields produced only 1.5 metric tons of paddy per crop-hectare and grew only one crop a year. Now all fields grow two crops and many, three. Because of drought, this season's average yield is only 3.2 tons per crop-hectare, but last season's topped 4 tons. The province is the biggest supplier of rice in north Vietnam. Mrs. Dinh attributes most of the increase to improved irrigation and drainage, so far mainly achieved by redigging channels and redirecting natural flows. Electric pumpsets are, however, coming into use which permit still greater improvements, and many more are planned. The electricity comes from provinces further north and will be increased as new reservoirs are built.

Textiles are Thai Binh's main handicraft, especially carpets woven from imported wool. Ceramics are being developed. The hotel china comes from Czechoslovakia but quality china is now made in Thai Binh. Several delicate porcelain bowls are displayed in the hotel.

I mention to Khanh that the chicken is very tasty. Mrs. Dinh is delighted. "That is because it is an agricultural chicken," Khanh translates her reply, "and not an industrial one. Here we grow both, but the agricultural (farmyard) chickens taste much better. The peasants prefer them and like to keep them in their private gardens."

We talk of families. All the women present, like most young and middle-aged Vietnamese women, have been separated by war from their husbands and children most of their lives. Almost all able-bodied men in north Vietnam were in the armed forces or were posted to other war work during the anti-French war of 1945-1954 and again in the struggle against the United States and the puppet rulers of the south. The children of each family were scattered to different places in the countryside to minimize the danger of all of them being killed in a single bombing raid. Liên's children left her at the ages of nine, seven, and five respectively, and since 1965 she has been with her husband only one day and night each two weeks. In the same period, Hoan has seen her husband only ten days a year, except for 1972, when she did not see him at all. Apart from Mrs. Ninh, all these women's husbands are still away and all of the women long for their return.

15

Progress in Thai Binh

Mrs. Dinh has brought with her several sheets of notes. After lunch we settle down for a lecture on Thai Binh, with Khanh translating.

"You know, of course, that Thai Binh lies in the heart of the Red River delta on the east coast of north Vietnam. Being a delta, it is entirely flat—the only province without mountains in north Vietnam. It lies between Haiphong and Nam Ninh.

"Thai Binh is divided in two by the River Tra-ly. The province was formed about 2,000 years ago, mainly from alluvium, so our history is not as old as that of some parts of Vietnam. Today it comprises seven districts, 292 villages, and one town. Its area is 1,344 square kilometers, its population about 1,437,000, so as you can see, we have a very high density, about 1,095 per square kilometer.

"Our province is agricultural, our chief product being rice with subordinate crops and handicrafts. Before the revolution the land belonged to the landlords. Most landlords owned about fifty to a hundred hectares; some, less than fifty. The peasants were virtually landless, most of them being tenants and some, landless laborers."

I ask whether they were free laborers or hereditarily attached like serfs. Mrs. Dinh replies that they were free.

"The tenant's rent was usually about 30 percent of his

crop. Out of what remained, he had to pay his cultivation expenses. Usually tenants had to borrow each year in order to survive. After the harvest they would pay back their loans with 30 percent interest. Often they had nothing left and immediately went into debt again.

"So altogether most of our people were very poor, going in rags and patches. Old people often had to beg their food. The revolutionary movement was very strong here because of all this exploitation. Women, too, were oppressed by the feudal regime—most of them by the landlords and all of them by the feudal family. So women, too, took part in the revolution, for as Lenin said, 'Without women a revolution cannot succeed.'

"In Thai Binh we have a long history of resistance to aggression. As early as 139-142 A.D., two sisters of a Vietnamese general, called Dyên Ha and Bat Gan, helped their brother to drive out invaders from China. In 542 one of our kings, Ly Bi, recruited troops here and overthrew a foreign dynasty. Again in 1824-1827, a general named Ba-Vanh led a peasant uprising against the corrupt Nguyen dynasty. These are just a few instances of our military tradition, in which both men and women were prominent.

"Already in 1925, a Communist leader named Duc Canh mobilized people in Thai Binh to fight the colonialists. Yes!— we had communists even then, in the Youth Alliance, and in 1930 the party was formed. Early in the 1930s we had a huge demonstration of peasants at Tiên Hai to congratulate and encourage the peasant communists of Nghê An and Ha Tinh provinces who had set up soviets. That was one of the biggest demonstrations in the history of Vietnam.

"The 1930s brought terrible repression by the French of our revolutionary movement in the countryside. We have famous women alive today who struggled in that period; for example, the president of the Women's Union worked in Thai Binh then. Well, eventually we defeated the French in the revolution of August 1945.

"There was an appalling famine that year. In Thai Binh province alone about 200,000 died, for in their struggles to control us both the Japanese and the French had destroyed our dikes. After we took power, we had formidable problems of starvation and illiteracy. President Ho Chi Minh summoned our whole people to concentrate their efforts against these twin enemies. We had a slogan at that time, 'Each *ing* of land equals one *ing* of gold.'

"In those days almost everyone here was illiterate. You could count the literate on your fingers. All of them were landlords and all of them men. I could barely read in 1945 and knew very little; now I know somewhat more! We studied and set to work, built evening classes, and at the end of a year virtually everyone in Thai Binh could read and write. In the first election to the National Assembly of 1946, what a sight it was! Streams of women went to write their names and to vote at the polls. Women were slow compared to men because they had children to care for, but they succeeded, they had courage.

"We had a very short time of peace. Quite soon, the French were back and we had to fight as well as farm. We had no regular military force operating in Thai Binh, so everyone who was left here—old people, women, children—fought with their own weapons, which were poles, sticks, and swords. The women did marvelously; bands of them would attack the enemy posts at night. Thai Binh came out one of the best fighting provinces and produced the first Heroine of Fighting in all of Vietnam. Her name is Nguyen Thi Chiên; she was a peasant guerrilla. Yes, she's still living, and holds the title of Senior Colonel. Our government awarded many orders of merit to the women of Thai Binh.

"During the war against the U.S. imperialists we fought their planes as well as farming as hard as we could. All our seven districts were bombed and our city almost destroyed, also all our technical and scientific centers. Three of Thai Binh's women's artillery units were honored by the government, one with the highest title of 'Heroic Unit.' Twenty-three people received the titles of Heroes and Heroines. Altogether we shot down forty-four enemy aircraft in this province and captured two live pilots.

"We had heroines of production, too. A peasant woman, Nguyen Thi Mân, is one we are proud of. She was illiterate before but has finished the tenth standard now.

"Let me tell you now about our modern agriculture. You know, of course, that our land reforms gave land to the peasants. At first, beginning in 1954, we divided out the land to individuals. With so many people, everyone naturally received only a little land. After a short time we saw that it would be inadequate to improve the yield, for each peasant's capital and tools were far too poor, and all of them were growing different things. We went on like this for more than two years with separate plots. Then our government decided to organize the peasants into cooperatives to improve production. At that time each village of about 3,000 to 4,000 people was divided into two or three cooperatives; in each coop they had about a hundred hectares. All the old field boundaries were destroyed, roads were built at convenient points into the fields, and some tractors were gradually introduced. Before, we used pots to carry water, but now we even have electric pumps. Production has improved very much. Whereas before we had only 1 to 1.5 or 1.8 tons of paddy per crop-hectare and only one or occasionally two crops a year, now we produce up to 4 and even 5 tons per crop hectare and grow two or three crops a year. This year in spite of drought our average will be about 7 tons per hectare. In effect, in agriculture we have already moved from small-scale to large-scale production while missing out on the capitalist phase.

"Ninety-nine percent of the people of Thai Binh are in agriculture, so their organization has great importance. Since 1965, we have been joining small coops into larger ones, and this is still going on. Today a big coop may contain 300 hectares of wet paddy land; since 1971 we have even developed bigger ones of 500 hectares. The cooperative you will see tomorrow contains 300 hectares, about the size of a village.

"In addition to rice we grow a number of industrial crops, chiefly jute and rattan, also sugarcane, peanuts, green and black beans, bananas, and many other fruits and vegetables. Pig production is very important in Thai Binh, and we raise oxen and buffaloes for ploughing."

Answering my questions, Mrs. Dinh says the cattle eat grass, hay, and paddy bran, but not paddy straw as in Thanjavur. Straw is instead used for thatching or cut into pieces to make fertilizer. The milk yield of cows and buffaloes is very low and is fed to calves, the cattle being kept mainly for draft and meat. As in Thanjavur, their numbers have declined in the past decade with the introduction of tractors. A number of milk cows have, however, been introduced from Cuba and are being raised on state farms. Unlike Thanjavur, Thai Binh has neither goats nor sheep; these are found in more mountainous provinces.

The bigger coops, Mrs. Dinh tells me, use electricity for lighting, for radios, fans, and pumps, and for threshing and hulling machines. In peacetime, as in south India, plows and tractors are worked mainly by men. Both men and women sow the seed, weed the fields, and harvest; and women do the transplanting. Weeding was formerly done by hand as in Thanjavur, but now that the paddy seedlings are transplanted in rows it is done by hoe.

During the war, women carried out all the agricultural tasks including digging irrigation ditches and repairing the dikes after the bombing raids.

"Did women really take their rifles to the fields with them?"

"Yes, indeed! And we leaders took ours too—we never traveled by car without them."

Mrs. Dinh turns to education and culture.

"Before the revolution we had only one secondary school in Thai Binh; 99 percent of us were illiterate. Now we have a high school in every village and from two to three secondary schools. Altogether we have 400,000 pupils out of a population of fewer than 1,500,000. Some of our schools even have two or three stories.

"Our secondary schools are middle-level training schools where the students learn agriculture, communications, electrical engineering, crop management, etc. Those who attend have already finished eight to ten forms in the lower school, where they start at age five. We also have many night schools, and of course we had even more right after the revolution. And here in the provincial capital we have a medical university.

"We have two hospitals in each of the seven districts, each with 100 beds, and a larger one with 500 beds in the town. In addition, each village has a clinic with 12 or 20 beds, a fully trained doctor, a midwife, and two nurses. Before the revolution we had only one doctor who lived in Thai Binh, no midwives, and only one nurse in each district.

"The main point is that the revolution in our relations of production has made life happier and has increased the yield. This increases the goods we can sell, and means that we can afford to send sick people to hospital free of charge. It also means that our students do not pay fees—even at the university, books, pens, and classes are free. In each district we have two teams who tour the villages with portable films, and those, too, are free. And in each coop we have an art group for music, dancing, and singing, which all can enjoy."

Mrs. Dinh breaks off her lecture to return to the party congress. Our other hosts from Thai Binh take over, and Mrs. Chinh goes with me to my room. With no words but much laughter, we examine each other's clothes and I give Mrs. Chinh some small suits and dresses from India for children in Thai Binh. She is delighted, and pats me approvingly. She gazes for a long time at a photograph of my family and asks me to show with my fingers the height and age of my son. She replaces the gifts in my suitcase and indicates that they must be presented later to her whole group. With a hug, she leaves me to rest.

When it is finished the hotel will be well built and comfortable. My room has two beds, new blankets and padded quilts, a double wardrobe, a table with tea service, oranges, bananas, tea, and cigarettes, a desk and a chair, three low rattan chairs, and a washbasin. There are showers and toilets at the end of each corridor. Downstairs are several spacious, well furnished lounges, a director's office, and a courtyard with trees and potted plants. Young women in white uniforms serve at the long dining table, continually pouring out beer and tea. They are both hardworking and friendly. Eager to serve well, they greet the guests as equals and stop to chat with them. As in Hanoi, they sometimes wear curling pins.

Mrs. Ninh, President of the Thai Binh Women's Union, chats with me through Khanh and Liên over dinner. She emphasizes that most of the advances in agriculture have been made by women because of the absence of men (as well as some women) in the war. In the sixties and seventies women rose from 55 percent to 65 percent of the workforce in agriculture. They carried out the "Three Responsibilities"—to send men to the front, increase production, and fight when necessary. Thai Binh received the Third Order of Merit for sending and supporting fighters and the Second Order for production. The target of five tons per hectare per year, reached in 1972, was achieved mainly by women, as was the shooting down of several United States planes. Women learned to plow, use machinery, irrigate, and care for cattle. Each cooperative has a dozen or more experts, some of whom are women.

In agricultural cooperatives 5 percent of the land is given over to family plots on which houses are built, providing about 0.05 acres of private garden per family. The plots are used to grow vegetables and to breed chickens, pigeons, and a pig or two. The family owns the plot jointly and is responsible for working it, but women did most of the work in wartime and take most interest in raising and selling the produce. From the money they receive they buy extras for the family or save to build a better house. After the coop has reached the production target set by the state and has provided food both for its members and for sale to the government, it, too, may sell any surplus crops in the market and use the money as its members collectively decide. Ducks and duck eggs, unlike chickens, belong entirely to the public sector of the coop, the ducklings being raised in incubators.

The yield of husked rice from unhusked paddy is about 70 percent by weight in Thai Binh when hulled carefully with machinery, and about 50 percent by volume. The rice obtained is raw rice; paddy is not boiled before husking as it is in Thanjavur. This means that in addition to the higher yield of paddy per hectare and the greater acreage of double and triple cropping, more food value is obtained per unit of weight than in Thanjavur. There, rice is 66 percent to 68 percent the weight of paddy but part of the weight is water derived from preboiling the grain.

Mrs. Ninh confirms certain points that I have heard in Hanoi. One is that each house in a cooperative must have a well, a bathroom, and a latrine with two compartments. Another is that the cooperative constitution makes three important provisions for women: (1) pregnant women must work near their homes; (2) menstrual women must not work in cold water; and (3) weak persons must be given lighter tasks.

Women in the coop make most of their own clothing from cloth bought by the cooperative. They also make sanitary towels and mosquito nets, for themselves and for export to the city.

The living conditions of women have improved incomparably since the revolution. Mrs. Ninh particularly stresses day-care centers for babies and preschool children, midwifery, medical care in the clinics, especially during pregnancy and childbirth, and education. Food is plentiful, she says, but the women are very economical about not wasting it and about saving money.

Old people are encouraged to plant and tend young trees. Ho Chi Minh was especially keen on tree planting, which is done by everyone on New Year's Day. Roads have been turned into avenues of trees, and lines of fuel trees have been built around each cooperative which also afford shelter to the crops from storms.

In agriculture, Mrs. Ninh thinks that roads into the fields, together with the use of carts for transporting the crops (instead of shoulder poles) constitute one of the most important labor-saving measures. The other is the use of electric or diesel pumpsets to draw water from ponds, channels, and rivers for irrigation. Pumpsets are not, however, attached to tubewells or filter points as they are in Thanjavur, for surface water is said to be sufficiently plentiful.

16

An Agricultural Cooperative

The peasants rise at five and go to work at six. Mrs. Chinh says this is nothing; in the old days, the landlords sometimes forced them to start work at three or even 2 A.M.

At six on November 18, a gong is beaten in Thai Binh town and cheerful music starts up. My hosts say the gong gives the correct time so that people can adjust their watches, but it also no doubt calls some of them to work. At all events, I get up at six this morning, am summoned with hot water at 6:30, and am collected for breakfast at 6:45.

Breakfast is roast chicken in gravy, warm brown bread, and water, followed by rich hot chocolate. A Botticelli beauty with luminous eyes, soft hair, and a delicate skin serves and hovers over me tenderly. She repeats, "Canada *dong-chi!*" in tones of delight, pointing to me, until I realize this means "Canadian comrade." Her name is Dô Thi Tô. After breakfast I ask to take her photograph in the courtyard. She slips off to tidy her hair, and brings back a handsome soldier. Khanh arrives and tells me he is her fiancé. With shy smiles and blushes, they pose together.

Shortly after seven, we set off with driver Quyên, Mrs. Chinh, and Mrs. Nhân, to Vu Thang or Victory Cooperative about ten kilometers east of the town. On either side of the road are large paddy fields divided by paths, small rivers, or artificial canals with earthen dikes about four feet high. Some contain yellow stalks from the recent harvest. A few are still being harvested by groups of men and women with sickles. Others are being plowed by tractor, and some are already flooded in preparation for transplanting the February crop. In some newly plowed fields men and women are bringing loads of farmyard manure in containers suspended from shoulder poles.

As in India, small boys can be seen grazing water buffaloes on the banks of lush grass that border the smaller channels. Some are riding the buffaloes, and some animals have crows on their backs.

Mrs. Chinh says that deep trenches and bomb shelters were dug in all the fields in the war, but are now removed. Many dikes were bombed and were repaired immediately to protect irrigation and drainage. Here and there large bomb craters remain; most now form ponds. In one near the roadside, houses have been built and soil brought to make gardens.

We pass a cemetery containing large stone tombs and decorated urns. Khanh confirms that people here practice second burial: the body is interred in a grave or tomb until decomposition occurs, then the bones are collected and placed in an urn.

Not losing a minute, Mrs. Nhân tells me women are 50 percent of the members of the people's committees in this province, 25 percent of the members of communist party committees, and 51 percent of all students in schools and colleges.

We pass a street of small stores and thatch or tile roofed houses. In some of the stores women are selling vegetables, tea and rice cakes. Beyond the street, we cross a river over a newly built bridge.

We turn right along a wide dirt road and enter the cooperative lands. On our right is a threshing floor with straw stacks, to the left a small lake thickly covered with green algae. Mrs. Chinh says the lake is one of several bomb craters left over from the war against the French in the 1950s. In Vu Thang, all the craters have been turned into ponds or lakes for fish breeding. A stream pours clear water into one end of the lake, where a small boy practices rowing in a wooden tub.

The algae remind me of Thanjavur, where many village ponds have become thickly coated in the last few years. The villagers do not know why and regard the algae as a nuisance, for it prevents humans from bathing and makes it hard to wash the cattle. Animals simply push it aside to obtain drinking water. I remark to Mrs. Nhân, "I see you have a problem here too, with algae, as in India. Is it a nuisance?" When Khanh translates she laughs and says, "No, it is there on purpose; it is grown scientifically and is stored to provide fertilizer for the fields. The authorities wanted to use bomb craters to the best economic advantage. Fish and algae are their solution, and prove very profitable."

We drive up to the administrative center, a large tile roofed building with a verandah and a yard decorated with flower beds. An arch over the gate reads "Victory Cooperative." A welcoming committee of about a dozen men and women stands ready to greet us, with smiles and handshakes. They take us into the administrative center, where a feast of green tea, peanuts, fruits, sweets wrapped in rice paper, etc., is waiting. On the painted wall is a calendar showing a pretty girl watering brilliant beds of flowers.

Our hosts include Mr. Ding Quang Ngi, president of the cooperative, a stockily built, middle-aged man with a broad brown face, wearing an English (or Soviet?) style worker's cap and overalls. With him are Mrs. Noang Thi Thao, a member of the cooperative's administrative committee, Mrs. Dinh Thi Ngôn, president of the Vu Thang Women's Union, and a young woman, Mrs. Nguyen Thi Lê, secretary of the Youth Union.

Over refreshments, after the usual speeches of thanks and welcome, I ask my hosts whether Vu Thang was bombed during the United States war. It was, they tell me, although not until the "Christmas bombing" of 1972. There were two bombing raids, the first with "one very big bomb with many small bombs within it," the second, "two mother bombs and one of another kind." The bridge leading into the village was destroyed but was immediately rebuilt.

In 1945 Ding Quang Ngi was an illiterate youth of poor peasant family. After the revolution he studied and worked hard and was eventually elected president by the villagers. He has taken special courses at a provincial agricultural college in Thai Binh and has spent a year in the Soviet Union studying what Khanh translates as "business administration." Khanh goes on to interpret Ngi's lecture, which is carefully delivered from notes.

"Before the revolution," says Ding Quang Ngi, "the land here was clayey and waterlogged. It was saline and sour, for we are only twenty kilometers from the sea and our drainage was poor. In some years we receive up to 200 millimeters of rain in a single storm, which results in flooding and in backwashes from the ocean. When I was young our people were abysmally poor and often starved. Our poverty was caused by the French imperialists, who taxed us heavily, by natural calamities, and by the landlords. Women suffered especially, for they had no rights either in the family or in the wider society. Every year we had deaths from starvation, and sometimes even from thirst. We had many births, but few survivors. Out of a total of about 5,000 people, 200 to 300 died annually. We had no medicine and no education; all of us peasants were illiterate.

"Early in 1945 we experienced our worst famine in living memory. Seven hundred and seventy people died in this village in two months. Fifteen whole families were wiped out. You can imagine our hatred of the enemies who caused this calamity.

"After the August revolution, thanks to President Ho Chi Minh, our party, and our government, we ordinary people got the right to become masters of our country. In this village all the peasants, including the women, formed an organization. We turned over a new leaf, declaring equality between men and women. And the women lived up to it. Not only did they participate in public life and self-government; they also formed guerrilla units and underwent hard training. Along with us men, they joined the defense movement against the French and their local henchmen.

"In 1945 we had twenty-two noncultivating landlords in this village. Altogether, forty-one families (about 4 percent of the total population) were landowners. Sixty-five percent of the land was owned by 3.5 percent of the people. About 25 percent of the families were tenant cultivators, and about 70 percent, agricultural laborers. We also had a few artisans.

"You know, of course, about our war against the French colonialists. They built eight military posts or *banquères* around our village and set up a puppet administration. When we resisted it, they burned the village. Most of the landlords supported the French; when the French forces reinvaded Vietnam they hoisted white flags and waited for them to arrive. We peasants had to stop them from joining the French and surrendering the village, so we killed a few of the cruelest ones and immobilized the rest. Then the French bombed our village. In all, during the anti-French colonial war, tens of thousands of bombs were dropped.

"Even after they had signed the declaration agreeing to withdraw, the French came back and bombed this village, when all the other villages had peace. A hundred and fifty of our people died in that last bombing, and most of the lakes you see here were formed from the bomb craters made that day in 1954.

"Altogether during the anti-French war our villagers killed or captured 350 French soldiers, including 1 colonel, 1 captain, and 3 lieutenants. We destroyed three French posts and forced them to withdraw.

"Originally our village was called Dong Nhue, a very old name. Then it was renamed Cao Thang (Gold Teeth) after a peasant from here who led an uprising against the Nguyen dynasty in the eighteenth century. In 1956 our government renamed it Vu Thang or Victory village, and because of our exploits we were awarded the First Order of Resistance against the French colonialists.

"Now our economy. As you know, it is mainly rice; out of a total of 452 hectares of land, 300 are under paddy. Today, our population is about 4,000. In 1939 we produced a maximum of 2.5 tons of paddy per hectare from those fields that grew two crops, and that was our most prosperous year before the revolution. We used to harvest one crop in November and one in June. We tried to grow two crops in all the fields, but often we were prevented by floods. After the revolution, we were busy resisting the French, and that prevented us from improving our agriculture. In the most prosperous years of the anti-French war we got only 3 tons per hectare from two crops.

"Before the revolution each adult received only 3 kilograms (6.6 pounds) of rice per month. That's about 3.5 ounces per day; you can imagine our hunger. How did we live? Well, we grew a few green vegetables and water potatoes, and in the worst times we fled to the hills in neighboring provinces to get wild cassava and other roots. We very rarely saw any meat, and if we did get some we usually sold it to buy other food. In short, we tied up our waists.

"In 1956 we distributed all the land to the peasants. We took the land from the landlords, and took some land from those few rich peasants who had more than their share. We gave it to the landless laborers and poor peasants, leaving the middle peasants as they were.[1] We even left the rich peasants alone as much as possible, but some of them gave land voluntarily. Some of the landlords also gave willingly: those whose children had contributed to the resistance and others who wanted to progress and to change their lives."

"Were any landlords executed here during the land reform of 1956?" I ask.

"No, that was not necessary," replies Ding Quang Ngi. "We struggled against their ideology, not by beating or torturing them. We educated them through labor. Most of the landlords' families are still here as members of our cooperative.

"After dividing the land among all the adults in the village, both men and women, we cultivated with private plots until 1959. But it was clear that that method could not systematically increase production. In an effort to do this, we formed fourteen cooperatives in 1959, drawing into them as many peasants as we could persuade. At that time our peasants' ideology was such that we could form only small coops with their approval, in which they could carry on cultivating in ways familiar to them. By 1961, however, the peasants saw the benefits of cooperation and we managed to amalgamate the land into four bigger coops.

"After that we were able to start intensive cultivation with new irrigation. Before, we had had very small canals, many of them natural ditches. In 1961 we joined many fields into one and began to irrigate and to drain them systematically. We used mainly local labor, even in times of natural calamity; altogether we mobilized 2,000 peasants, men and women, for irrigation work. Although we had no pumps yet, we worked hard to drive the water out in floods, and in drought we poured in water instead of leaving it to the heavens.

"In 1961, we were harvesting 3 tons per hectare, 1.5 tons in each crop. In 1965, we joined the four cooperatives into one. Our aims were, first, to unite the labor force and apply techniques of intensive cultivation more thoroughly, and second, to see that every field was cultivated twice a year and fully harvested before the rains, a job that required strict management and discipline.

"In 1965 we bought our first diesel pumps. We use them to draw water out of the river, in drought or in flood. Since 1965 we have also gone in for modern intensive farming."

"What exactly do you mean by 'intensive farming'?" I ask. Khanh explains that I have been studying what is called the "green revolution" in a deltaic region of south India.

"Intensive farming involves deep plowing, deep harrowing, the use of chemical fertilizers, irrigation to provide plenty of water, and new varieties of improved hybrid seeds. The hybrid seeds are produced in quantity by a farm run by our provincial agricultural office. They develop them in a laboratory and then introduce them to the villages.

"As for fertilizer, we introduced chemical fertilizers in 1965. But we use 70 percent organic fertilizers and only 30 percent chemical, for the organic are cheaper and, we think, better for the soil. Our organic fertilizers are human and animal waste, all carefully collected and processed, algae, and green leaves. Our chemical fertilizers are mainly sulphate of ammonium and lime. The lime is to correct the sourness, which is also accomplished by better drainage. The sulphate of ammonium is produced in a plant owned by the state. Altogether, we use 200 kilograms of chemical fertilizer per hectare per year. We also use pesticides—we have a spraying machine.

"Since 1965 we have improved every year in methods and in yields. Gradually we increased the number of pumps, so that we now have twelve. Two of them are electric pumping stations, and ten are diesel; we use them both for irrigation and drainage. We have an electric threshing machine for the paddy, a rice hulling mill, and a food crusher for the pigs.

"I mentioned that in 1961 we were getting 3 tons of paddy per hectare per year. In 1966 we harvested 6.3 tons, and in 1970, 9.1 tons. Between 1970 and 1975 we increased the yield to 10 tons. We shall probably produce 11 tons this year. Moreover, the great increase over the last decade has to be attributed mainly to women, for women have formed 70 percent of our labor force since 1965, since most men were away in the army.

"Simultaneously, we have developed our stock breeding. Pigs are our most important livestock. Since 1970, we have increased the number of pigs owned collectively by the coop from 1,500 to 1,800. These are apart from the 2,000-odd pigs owned privately by families. We feed the pigs paddy, dry potatoes, and vegetables; with our increased yields we have had no problem about fodder. Nowadays we sell 80 to 100 tons of pork each year to the state trading corporation.

"We have, however, reduced our buffaloes. In 1965 we had about 200, mainly for plowing. Now with tractors coming in we have only 100. We keep very few oxen and no horses—those are not important here.

"Poultry and fish have increased in the last few years. The cooperative collectively owns 3,000 ducks for meat and 500 for eggs, also many geese and turkeys. Chickens and pigeons are private here; each family owns ten or more. As for fish, we now have forty hectares of ponds made from bomb craters. We have our own fish hatchery, produce ample fish for our own use, and sell 40 to 50 tons per year to the state.

"A big advantage of the coop is that we can plan the development of handicrafts, and in all seasons keep everyone at work. In Vu Thang we make mattresses, bricks, ceramics, roof tiles, ropes, mosquito nets, sanitary towels, and many other things for our own use; we also manufacture jute carpets for sale to the state.

"Since the revolution, our high yields have, of course, enormously improved our living conditions. For example, the average adult quota of paddy is now 25 kilograms per month, or about 17.5 kilograms of husked rice.[2] Children get smaller amounts according to age. Every year, our paddy yield has overfulfilled the target set by the state, so paddy is plentiful with us. Meat, fish and all kinds of food are plentiful now.

"Our cultural and spiritual life has improved immeasurably along with our material production. All our children now attend day nurseries, kindergartens, primary schools, and secondary schools free of charge. All our adults have had at least four years of primary education; many women have had ten. Adults of any age have the right to attend special adult classes two days a week; we hold night classes, too.

"Our cooperative owns a clinic for medical examinations and treating light illnesses. It has one doctor, three assistants, and five nurses. We also have specially trained women to take care of our day nurseries. Everyone in the coop has a medical record, and a health exam once a year.

"In the old days we had to go by boat between the villages much of the year because the land was low lying. Now we have modern roads through the villages and proper drainage. In Vu Thang we have a group of workers who deal especially with civil engineering and housing.

"Every month two films are shown here by cultural groups belonging to our district. We have our own art group too, for music, songs, and dancing.

"During our struggle against the United States aggressors our village performed many great exploits to build socialism and liberate the country. In 1975 we received the First Order of Resistance against the U.S. invaders, and on our National Day in 1975 we were awarded the First Order of Production. Altogether we have earned five Orders of Promotion from the state."

Mr. Ngi asks if I have any questions. I have!—far too many for a single morning.

"What about canteens? Do you serve meals collectively?"

"No," he replies. "Our peasants still prefer to cook and eat at home. We have discussed canteens, but each time we bring them up they vote them down. This is something that may come later, when people are ready."

"How do you use the 152 hectares of land in the cooperative that are not irrigated for paddy?"

"Forty hectares of bomb craters are now fish ponds. Houses and private gardens cover 5 percent of the total land or about 23 hectares—about 200 square meters or 0.05 acres per family. Then, of course, there are the threshing grounds, channels, piggery, craft shops, machine shops, storage sheds, dikes, roads, schools, hospitals, and administrative buildings. Some fields grow potatoes, cabbages, tomatoes, and various other vegetables and fruit trees. We also grow both China and Assam tea."

"Can you tell me something of your accounting? How much do you sell to the state, and how do you divide up the coop income?"

"Forty-five percent of our paddy is sold to the government.[3] It is husked in a mill in town and exported to other provinces. We eat the rest or feed it to the stock. We also sell pork, ducks, turkeys, geese, fish, and duck eggs to the state, and most of the jute carpets we manufacture. We receive cash for all these things. If we take the total income of the coop, in cash and kind, we calculate that we use 70 percent of it for wages and running expenses—small tools, jute to make carpets, repairs to machinery, etc. The bulk of that is wages, which are paid to each man and woman in cash and in kind. Another 20 percent of our product goes for new machinery, fertilizer, and civil engineering. Ten percent is left for social welfare, that is, housing, day-care centers, the schools, and the hospital."

"What are the wage differentials? How big are they? And do you pay the old and the sick?"

"Between the highest and the lowest payments there is only a difference of 20 percent. Those who can't produce still receive wages—the old or the disabled. We use social welfare to pay them. Women receive three months' fully paid maternity leave."

"How is the cooperative governed?"

"There is one director. Before 1972 we had a big management staff of seventeen people. Since 1972 we have had a staff of only five. We reorganized the management because we wanted a more efficient concentration of power. The director and management staff are elected by the members. In addition, we have a group of technical experts who help the staff. They deal with planning, social welfare, technical problems, and living conditions. They are trained here, but they attend courses in the provincial capital."

"Have the peasants any kind of union of their own?"

"The peasants have a collective organization with an elected council. This organization educates them about the policies of the party and the government. It represents the peasants' needs and aspirations to the cadres, and proposes policies. It controls the realization of policies for the peasants."

"What about the party? Where does it come in?"

"Party members are chosen from among the more progressive peasants. Their main job is to expound the line to the peasants and set a good example."

"Are the director and staff always party members?" As in the invalids' camp, this question provokes laughter.

"Well, they need not be—but they usually are."

We get up to tour the cooperative. "Now for the pigs," I say. Ding Quang Ngi looks worried and speaks to Khanh. She explains to me that, it being midday, the pigs are sleeping, and that they must not be disturbed. They have to sleep every afternoon after lunch as part of their regimen. I express disappointment. Can't an exception be made? After all I have come all the way from Vancouver. . . . Ngi grins and says, well, perhaps if we tiptoe. The last visitor to see the pigs asleep, he says, was Prime Minister Pham Van Dong!

The piggeries are open, airy buildings of extraordinary hygiene. The pigs are bathed daily from hoses, the floors swabbed clean and spread with straw. Huge, pink, and speckless, those in the first rows are sleeping peacefully, about four to a cubicle. An opening leads from each cabin to a passage with a trough behind, which has also been swilled down recently. The pigs are toilet trained! Quite young piglets, I am told, learn to use the trough to answer calls of nature, the waste being carefully collected for fertilizer. Sows with litters, and different grades of pigs intended for meat, are housed separately. In the far rows the pigs are still awake, grunting and squealing softly; they had lunch more recently.

In a nearby building huge vats of broken rice and vegetables are cooking over fires of paddy bran. The broken rice makes porridge for the baby pigs. The adult pigs are fed cooked rice flour with vegetables and "plenty of spinach." Fully grown pigs eat one kilogram of vegetables and four of rice flour for each kilogram of meat they produce.

Another building houses a small electric rice mill and an electric food crusher for the pigs. The paddy husk is removed for use as fertilizer; it is spread on top of farmyard manure in the fields. The bran is used as fuel or to feed the cattle. The rice mill amuses me for it is far smaller and simpler than the mills for husking and double-boiling paddy in Thanjavur, yet apparently it does the job. Both machines are made in Vietnam.

The same is true of the threshing machine. It is about eight feet long, five tall, and five across, seemingly little more than a toy, and is hooked up by a cable to an electric outlet on top of a slender pole. To please me, the director sets it going and pops in freshly cut paddy at one end; out comes straw at the other, while the grain falls into a vat below. Peasants gather around to watch and explain, and there is a good deal of excited chatter. A group of women is just arriving on the threshing floor from the fields with sheaves of newly cut paddy suspended from shoulder poles.

We take a walk down the main street of the coop. On one side is a fishpond with algae; on the other, a row of craft shops. One building houses about fifty sewing machines in small rooms where the peasants sew their own clothes. Two young men are mending tools in a blacksmith's shop with hammers and anvils, a small forge, and hand bellows like those used in many Indian villages. In a yard before another small building several older men are painting squares of woven rattan with red and green patterns; they will be sewn together to make carpets for local use. Another yard is stacked with roof tiles from the tile manufactory, and a third with bricks from brick kilns. We pass quickly through other buildings where towels, ropes, plain glazed pottery, jute carpets, and mattresses are being made.

Further down the main street a small stone temple stands on a plot of land. Formerly dedicated to a village god, it is now deserted, but, says Ngi, is left here out of respect for the past.

Tea bushes line the sides of several village paths like hedges. Through some bamboo trees we glimpse a small mud hut, half ruined, of the kind inhabited by landless laborers and other poor people in India. Khanh whispers, "Just think! People used to live in these!" I wonder aloud why it is there. She thinks, perhaps, as a memorial, or a toolshed, or because no one has bothered to remove it.

Down a lane to the clinic a little boy and girl dash up rolling a solid hoop of woven rattan. They run into me and look up flabbergasted, to everyone's amusement. These children and several others wear no shoes although the day is wet and cold.

The clinic stands in a large garden full of what Khanh calls "oriental medicinal plants." The doctor and his assistants and nurses, wearing long white gowns, greet us enthusiastically and show us around. A plaque on one of the two buildings reads, "Vu Thang Clinic, 1969." There are two main wards, each with half a dozen small rooms containing two single beds with blankets. No inpatients today, says the doctor, smiling—nothing but the usual colds. The walls of one room are hung with pictures of the human body showing points for acupuncture and acupressure, which are practiced frequently. In another room a table with stirrups is set up for gynecological examinations. A third ward is reserved for deliveries. Everything looks very bare but very clean.

The doctor takes us proudly to his dispensary to see his stock of medicines. Most of them have been grown by him and his staff in the clinic garden and processed on the premises. He shows us rows of jars full of substances for a variety of ailments—tonics, fortifiers, antibiotics, and powders or liquids to treat menstrual disorders, rheumatism, eye diseases, constipation, and dysentery. Other medicines are made from three different kinds of snake. The doctor is qualified both as a physician and as a surgeon; he removes tonsils here, and once did an emergency appendectomy.

I ask the doctor whether he has any cases of leprosy, which is still seen occasionally in Indian villages and quite frequently in the cities. He says no, leprosy can be cured now and has almost disappeared. A few seriously injured lepers remain in a special camp in north Vietnam.[4] A gentle, modest man, the doctor follows us back to the gate with his staff and warmly bids us farewell.

Our last call is to a "typical peasant house." It stands on a small street near three other houses belonging to the owner's three brothers. All are built spaciously of brick and have tiled roofs, like 70 percent of the houses in Vu Thang.[5] As I have often seen in India, paddy is spread out to dry on a patch of swept ground before the door of each house. Ngi tells me that before the revolution this joint family owned 1,000 square meters of land, or about a quarter of an acre.

We pass through a wicket gate and find bananas, tomatoes, green vegetables, and two fruit trees packed into a small garden. There are about a dozen chickens in a coop, and pigeons cooing in a pigeoncote set up about six feet high. Along one side of the yard is a pigsty with two fat pigs; I am amused to see that they have not caught the habits of the coop, but are wallowing in dirty straw. Attached to the sty at one end is a storeroom full of straw, firewood, and bran, and a fireplace for cooking the pigs' food.

Liên and Khanh lead me solemnly to the backhouse, and there, sure enough, is a neat double latrine with two holes in a wooden seat; one of the holes is stopped up with a small pile of stones. Next we go to the bathroom, a small outdoor room with a tub and scoop and a hatch through which to draw buckets of water from the household well. As in Indian villages, the well is built of bricks and concrete and is about six feet in diameter.

The owner and his wife come out to welcome us. They are

middle aged, their faces kind but rather sad. The mother leads me to the kitchen, where aluminum and earthenware cooking pots and pans lie around near a wood fire, much as in India. Next door is a storeroom full of jars and cans. There are two, or perhaps three, bedrooms with wooden bedsteads, mattresses, blankets, and quilts.

The main room is about fifteen by twenty-five feet. It is comfortable, tidy, and clean. In one corner stands a large wardrobe; in two others, double beds with gaily colored homemade quilts. A sideboard displays pretty china, pieces of bric-à-brac in brass and ceramics, stuffed birds, and wooden dolls. There are pictures and a clock on the wall, also a certificate of merit from the state. The house has electricity and a ceiling fan. In the center of the room is a dining table with a cloth, and six chairs. We are asked to sit down and are served tea in china bowls.

Khanh tells me that this couple lost a son in the war in south Vietnam. I tell them I am sorry, and feel that he died not only for Vietnam but for all mankind. The father bows gravely. I ask if they have other children, and he says yes, they have several. Many families in Vu Thang, Khanh says, sent every one of their sons and daughters to the front, and exactly one quarter of the families had one or more members killed.

We go back to the administrative center to say goodbye. On the walls I now notice many photographs of visiting dignitaries, including Ho Chi Minh, Lê Duân, and Pham Van Dong, and of members receiving trophies. As we drink our last cup of tea surrounded by a crowd of villagers, Ngi thanks me for coming and sends their warmest greetings to the workers and farmers of Canada. He introduces Nguyen Thi Lê, the young woman secretary of the Youth Union, and asks her to sing for us. In a lovely, melodious voice, full of passion, she sings a ballad of love and praise for Vietnam, its mountains and rivers, green fields, birds, and beauty, and the steadfastness of its people. Everyone gazes at Lê in silence; it is a deeply emotional scene. Afterwards we take a final group photograph, and drive off amid shouts of farewell.

As we return to Thai Binh, Mrs. Nhân tells me that during the war each province in north Vietnam had a sister province in the south to which it sent soldiers, technicians, equipment, and food for the liberated zone. "Mothers who had already lost their husbands sent their sons." In Thai Binh each peasant family would contribute as much as 100 kilograms of rice in a single food drive. The richer cooperatives in the north, like Vu Thang, helped subsidize the poorer ones as well as the front.

When I return to Canada I learn that several foreign guests have been taken to Vu Thang. It is clearly a model cooperative with a higher yield and more modern facilities than most in north Vietnam. Nevertheless, it is amazing that Vietnam can unveil a model cooperative at all after so many years of destruction, and Vu Thang is by no means unique in Thai Binh. What I saw of other villages while traveling suggests, moreover, that the people are equally well nourished and the villages equally clean, egalitarian, and cooperative, although in some cases less prosperous than Vu Thang in terms of such facilities as tiled roofs, electric lighting, and fans.

Both the similarities and the contrasts between Vu Thang cooperative and the Thanjavur villages where I have worked are striking. Both areas are irrigated deltas affording intensive rice agriculture with subsidiary crops. Both had land reform legislation in the 1950s and have experienced the introduction of chemical fertilizers, pesticides, tractors, hybrid seeds, and pumpsets since 1965. Both had low yields of about 1.5 to 1.7 tons of paddy per hectare per year in the late 1940s. Both, at that date, had steeply stratified class structures composed of landlords, tenant farmers, artisans, and landless laborers.

Although Thanjavur's rice yield has more than doubled since 1951, the annual average yield per hectare has increased to only 4.1 tons per year as against 10 to 11 tons in Vu Thang and about 8 in Thai Binh as a whole. In spite of the intensive use of pumpsets and filter points, Thanjavur's improvements in irrigation have been piecemeal, and the district even now grows two paddy crops a year on only 30 percent of its irrigated land.

The most distressing difference from Thai Binh lies in the evolving class structure of Thanjavur and the increasing poverty of at least half of its people. Although Thanjavur's paddy production has increased at least five times as much as its population since 1951, the main impact of both the land reforms and the green revolution has been bad for most of the smallholders, the cultivating tenants, and the agricultural laborers—for all, in fact, except the bigger merchants and landlords, a small number of industrialists who are also often landlords or merchants, and a small number of more enterprising rich peasants. On the whole, landlords have used their local and statewide power to evade the land "ceiling" of fifteen acres per family: there remain many family estates of one to two hundred acres, and a few of one to three thousand. During two decades of inflation many smallholders have sold their plots, so that today only about 20 percent of the agriculturalists own rice fields, compared with about 30 percent in 1951. At the same time, landlords have evicted their tenants in order to avoid granting fixity of tenure and to cultivate with modern methods. As a result, only about a quarter of Thanjavur's land is now under cultivating tenures, whereas about half the land was leased to cultivators in the early 1950s.

The result of all this is a vast increase in the number and proportion of landless or near-landless agricultural laborers in Thanjavur. Agricultural laborers, about 40 percent of the agricultural workforce in 1951, are now over 60 percent, and up to 74 percent in some of the more densely populated coastal villages. Lacking industry to absorb them, they are severely underemployed. They work only about 90 to 140 days a year, and can eat two meals a day only for about six weeks after each of the two harvests. The rest of the time they subsist on a handful of grain, salt, a few chilies, and the rats or small fish they can catch in the paddy fields.[6]

These marked differences in prosperity and employment exist in spite of the fact that Thanjavur today has a population density of only 398 per square kilometer, whereas Thai Binh has 1,095. No clearer demonstration could be provided of the fact that it is not population, but the political economy, which causes poverty in the "underdeveloped" countries of the capitalist world.

The underlying difference between Thai Binh and Thanjavur is, of course, that India has not had a revolution and is not proceeding to socialism. In spite of its "socialist" rhetoric, it is following a path of dependent, state capitalist development. Both industry and agriculture are hampered by inadequate planning, unequal trade with the industrial nations, the continuing private ownership of land and most industry, and by the fact that the private profit of a few is the main goal of production and distribution. Seeing Vu Thang cooperative after living for five years in rural south India convinced me that only a revolution leading to socialism could transform India's villages into similarly healthy, cooperative, busy, and egalitarian communities, and bring their people the kind of happiness that I saw in Vu Thang.

Top left: Children in Vu Thang Cooperative, Thai Binh province. *Top right:* The clinic, Vu Thang Cooperative. *Bottom:* Street scene in Thai Binh.

Top: Siesta, Vu Thang Cooperative. *Bottom:* Threshing at Vu Thang.

17

Sightseeing in Thai Binh

Our hosts would like me to see everything in Thai Binh. Time being short, they settle on the Revolutionary Museum, a carpet factory, and the public library.

As we walk down Main Street at 3 P.M. on November 18, a picture palace is showing a film on the liberation of south Vietnam. Speakers broadcast music much of the day in Thai Binh town. This would soon irritate and weary me but is evidently liked by the people, as it is in villages of south India. Mrs. Chinh tells me a pioneer palace will soon be built for cultural events and sports.

All this time, the provincial party congress is proceeding in the meeting house of the Workers' Party. It is discussing the draft program for the national congress, already published in *Nhân Dân*. Suggestions for amendments have been prepared by leading cadres and will be debated and voted on at each of the provincial congresses.

Each province of north Vietnam has its own revolutionary museum, a small version of the national museum in Hanoi, depicting the exploits and sufferings of the people of that province. Thai Binh's museum contains three rooms, covering (1) from prehistoric times until 1945; (2) the famine of 1945, the Japanese departure, the August revolution, the French war, and the subsequent regroupment of communists from south to north Vietnam in 1954–1955; and (3) the land reform of 1956, through the period of United States war crimes against Thai Binh, to 1975 and the end of the war in the south. A friendly director, a member of the Workers' Party, shows us each exhibit and keeps up a running commentary, translated by the redoubtable Khanh. Here are just a few of the highlights.

From the exhibits in Room 1, one sees that Thai Binh has been an especially significant site of peasant uprisings from the early eighteenth century to 1954. This may have resulted from its being a densely populated agricultural region with a steeply hierarchical class structure, and a prime target of coastal attacks by foreign invaders. Pictures and weapons are displayed of thirty years of almost continuous warfare against the French conquerors in the late nineteenth century. Later we see photographs of Thai Binh communist cadres of the Youth Movement in the 1920s, and of houses used as secret bases of cadres when the party was being formed in 1930.

Room 2 opens with the famine of 1945, especially ferocious in Thai Binh. Two hundred and eighty thousand people, or a quarter of the province's population, starved to death in two months; there are photographs of starving, skeletal children and of bodies piled in the streets. There follow pictures of bases for revolutionary struggle against the Japanese and of peasant uprisings against their landlords. Then a painting commemorates the triumphal celebration of the August revolution by Thai Binh peasants.

From the anti-French colonial war that followed, there is a photograph of the Thai Binh marketplace crowded with Vietnamese prisoners behind barbed wire. There is a large glass case full of weapons used by the French to torture prisoners, including nails driven into their skulls. For the first time I learn that the French, as well as the Americans who followed them, used napalm in Vietnam; there are photographs of flaming and badly burned people from this period. There are many pictures of Nguyen Thi Chiên, the peasant fighter and heroine of Thai Binh, and a pistol given to her by Ho Chi Minh. Finally, there are photographs of the movement and arrival of communists from south Vietnam in 1954, including fighters from Thai Binh.

Room 3 presents paintings by local artists of scenes from the land reform of 1956 and of agricultural production. There is a flag used as a common symbol by Thai Binh and Vinh Tra. This is the south Vietnamese province to which Thai Binh sent aid and fighters from 1960, when the South Vietnamese National Liberation Front was formed, to 1975 when the south was liberated. There are photographs of Thai Binh peasants ceremonially handing over rice and slaughtered pigs to government representatives for transport to Vinh Tra. From the 1966 Congress of Emulation Fighters, there are photos of young men and women of Thai Binh honored for their military exploits in the south.

The period of the "Johnson war" of 1965–1968 shows fearsome evidence of the bombing of Thai Binh. In all, this period saw 1,064 bombing raids on 173 villages. Twenty occurred during five months in 1965, 295 in 1966, 653 in 1967, and 96 in the first three months of 1968 before the bombing halt. As the photographs show, the raids of 1966 mainly destroyed irrigation works. Many of those of 1967 also broke dams and destroyed stocks of rice. Mementos of the period include a plastic case containing the hair of a small girl who was flung into a tree and killed by a bomb in 1966. There are knapsacks of people killed in bombing raids. There is the shirt of a newborn infant injured with his mother by a fragmentation bomb; the mother died, but the son is living. There is a handkerchief taken from one of 31 pupils killed by a United States bomb in a school in Thuy Dân village on October 21, 1966. On the brighter side, there is a gun used for shooting down United States bombers, a fragment of a plane, and several thick straw hats of the kind everyone wore for protection against shrapnel. There are pictures of Thai Binh women defusing bombs in order to carry on cultivation.

There is a photo of Pham Van Dong, the prime minister, holding rice in his hands while visiting Vu Thang to honor it for exemplary production. In 1972, President Nixon resumed the bombing of north Vietnam in a last ditch effort to stem the flow of aid from north to south and to influence the outcome of the peace negotiations in Paris. Nine months of bombing of the coastal areas culminated in the atrocious "Christmas bombing" of all of north Vietnam between December 18 and 30, 1972, the last phase of direct United States attacks on the north. During these nine months, 542 bombing raids were carried out over Thai Binh province, equal to half those in the whole period of the Johnson war of 1965–1968. A total of 2,750 ordinary bombs, 454 "mother bombs," 50 rockets, and 642 delayed bombs, was sent against 207 villages. The gates of Thai Binh's main dam were attacked fifty-five times, Thai Binh town sixteen times, its storage areas eleven times, and two particular villages forty-four times. A single bridge was attacked thirteen times. Seventy-four percent of the 1972 raids took place at night.

With a sad smile, Khanh points to a United States pilot's suit and equipment lying in the center of the floor of this room. It includes a torch, a water flask, handguns and knives, and a white flag with words in twelve languages requesting food and protection.

From this period there is a photograph of three women's artillery units using antiaircraft guns. There are the metal mugs from which they drank water, and some of the fans presented to them as awards by a grateful people. There is the rifle that shot down United States plane No. IAD6 with 8 bullets on July 6, 1972. From the same period there is a picture of a musical troupe from Thai Binh whose members volunteered to work along with the fighters of south Vietnam, and of Thai Binh troops fighting near the Laotian border against troops of the United States-supported puppet government of Laos.

Room 3 continues with maps and charts of Thai Binh's growing agricultural production in the 1960s and 1970s. The most recent show paddy production figures for 1975-1976 for all the cooperatives, ranging from 7 to 10 tons per hectare per year. There are photos of the presentation of a central government award to Thai Binh province for first producing seven tons of paddy per hectare in 1966-1967. Other photos show members of the Women's Union receiving awards for production and for serving the battle front, and of groups of women building new irrigation ditches in 1975.

The exhibits end with Thai Binh's role in the final victory in south Vietnam. They culminate with the entry of Thai Binh fighters into Saigon's Presidential Palace (now the Independence Palace of Ho Chi Minh City) on April 30, 1975.

The carpet factory contains 300 young women working in three rooms. They are hand weaving wool carpets, chiefly for export, following patterns many of which have been supplied with orders from the Soviet Union and East Germany. Seated on stools, the women work two to a frame. The designs are intricate, mainly of flowers, with geometric borders; the colors are bright blue, green, white, and yellow. To me, the work looks hard on the eyes and likely to produce backache, but the women are young and seem cheerful, and their surroundings are clean, light, and airy.

The factory opened in 1973 and the women have received technical training in Hanoi. Most of them are eighteen or nineteen years old. Four women technical assistants supervise their work. Carpet making is old in Vietnam, but a new effort is being made to boost and diversify production for the export trade. At present most of the trade is with the Soviet Union and Eastern Europe, but markets are eagerly sought in the capitalist countries as well, for only by increasing its foreign exchange through exports can Vietnam afford much needed machinery from the industrial countries. Exports to Canada will begin in 1977. Formerly, I am told, this factory

produced wooden clogs. Nowadays, plastic footware is preferred both to clogs and to rubber sandals, large numbers of
which were made during the war, partly from the tires of
captured United States vehicles.

We enter the warehouse, which is stacked with finished
products. On the wall hangs a rug, beautifully executed but
to me rather garish, featuring President Ho Chi Minh. This
rug and another like it have been made specially for the party
congress. Another represents the president's mausoleum, and
a third, his cave by the Lenin River.

We drink tea with the woman manager (a party member)
and a group of women workers. They work a forty-hour
week, Monday to Friday, and on Saturday do marketing and
household chores. "What do you do on Sundays? Political
meetings?" I ask. There is a ripple of laughter when Khanh
translates. The manager smiles gently. "On Sundays we go for
walks and relax with our families," she says.

A young woman technical assistant is asked to sing for us.
She has a strong, tender, throbbing voice. She sings, first, a
song in praise of Vietnam and of its fighters; second, the song
of a woman parting from her lover as he goes to war. As in
the cooperative this morning, the quality and passion of her
voice move me. Such sincerity and such unity of commit-
ment and artistic feeling seem far more common in Vietnam
that I have ever found elsewhere. Everyone murmurs and
applauds. Then another ripple of laughter: someone has no-
ticed our young driver Quyên, the only man in the room; he
is blushing deeply because of the love song. The women cheer
him goodnaturedly.

Thai Binh is proud of its library, a large, impressive modern building. We are met and shown around by the head
librarian, a party member, and several leading cadres, who are
eager to show their collection. It contains about 100,000
volumes. Downstairs is a reading room with dozens of magazines and newspapers in Vietnamese, Russian, French, and

English, and a loan section of Vietnamese books. These cover all fields of science including archaeology and anthropology, modern agriculture and green revolution techniques, as well as history, fiction, and poetry.

Upstairs is the reference library, available to party cadres and others in the province engaged in specialized research. Most of the books here are foreign and have been donated or ordered from abroad. They include many Soviet works on agriculture, chemistry, physics, mathematics, and communist history, and some Russian fiction. Other books are in French, and a few in English. There are no Chinese books, but the foreign language section features grammars and dictionaries for Vietnamese readers in Chinese as well as in Russian, French, and English. The journals in the reference library are mainly Russian. One in French deals with the International Federation of Women. On the third floor, a microfilm section has recently been begun.

As we walk round the library I ask Liên whether the International Relations section of the Women's Union has anyone who speaks and translates from Chinese. Rather hesitantly, she says, "No. There was one person formerly, but she has left us." Although bordered by China, Laos, and Cambodia, Vietnam's cultural and scholarly relations seem at present to be overwhelmingly with the Soviet Union and Eastern Europe.

The library staff comes to see us off and laughingly agrees to be photographed on the steps of their building. In front of it is a small public park with topiary animatedly representing a dog, deer, lions, and elephants. Beyond the park is a pagoda-like memorial to dead fighters of the province.

Our final dinner in the Foreign Relations Hotel in Thai Binh is a grand and ceremonious event. Mrs. Dinh has returned from the party congress. Commanding and dignified in an embroidered, dark satin gown, she presides over the function. Present are our three other hosts from the Thai

Binh Women's Union, my women friends from Hanoi, driver
Quyên, the hotel manager (who was lamed, and I think lost a
leg, in the war), a man introduced as a "leading cadre" of
Thai Binh province, and a young man representing the provincial Youth Union.

Before dinner the "leading cadre" questions me on the
conditions of workers in Canada. Through Khanh, I tell him
that the standard of living of unionized workers is rather
high; poverty is mainly among the unemployed, some of the
old, some nonunionized manual workers, and the ethnic
minorities, especially the Native Canadians. Workers suffer
mainly from periodic unemployment, the psychic alienation
of industrial life, the dominance of United States companies
over Canadian industry, and the fact that real wages have
fallen in recent years. I say I see no prospect of a revolutionary upsurge in the short run, and that the labor unions
are mainly economist and conservative. He says that since
Canada is capitalist, there must be some grievances, some
unhappiness, that would form a basis for organizing among
workers, and that he suspects there is more poverty than I am
aware of. I agree that this may be true. In any case, he tells
me, it is necessary to work for the dictatorship of the
proletariat in Canada as in all countries. To do that one must
have a strong and united vanguard party. One of the women
seconds this. "The party is like the brains in the body," she
says.

As often happens, I am asked for my impression of all I
have seen. I say I am deeply moved by all the progress in
spite of the war and destruction. My hosts emphasize that the
achievements are mostly small-scale, and that above all they
must develop large-scale industry. Do I know about Vietnam's potential for offshore oil mining, and its need for
foreign collaboration? I say I do, and that I have been reading
about the Paracel Islands and understand they are claimed as
part of Vietnam. There is a chorus of affirmation and some
rather grim smiles. "That is certain," they say. They tell me

that Soviet technicians have just extracted 200 liters of oil
from the sea off the coast of north Vietnam, as is reported
in *Nhân Dân* today.

When we are seated at dinner there are formal speeches of
welcome and good wishes before the meal. Some twenty-five
dishes are served, mainly of meat and fish, including pâtés,
egg salad, egg rolls with spiced meat, barbecued pork, rice,
soup, roast chicken, cold fried fish, sweet rice, and rice
pudding. The whole is delicately flavored and delicious, and
is accompanied by several white and red wines, beer, coffee,
tea, and a lemon liqueur.

During dinner Mrs. Dinh addresses me across the table,
with Khanh beside me to translate. She asks what most
impressed me about Vu Thang today. Answering sponta-
neously, I say the piggeries—their cleanliness and the fact that
the pigs are toilet trained. Mrs. Dinh is offended, and says
that she would prefer not to hear of such things at the dinner
table. I realize I have made a serious *faux pas,* probably as
much by not stressing human effort and achievement as by
introducing a distasteful subject. Mrs. Dinh's displeasure is
momentary, and she is soon recalling incidents from the
modern history of Vietnam. It is clear, however, that this
rather grand lady will not brook levity!

Mrs. Dinh stresses the need to analyze and seize upon
contradictions both regionally and in the world in order to
carry out a successful revolution. As an example, she points to
the Vietnamese success in seizing the revolutionary opportunity in 1945 when the Japanese and the French were
fighting each other over their territory. She refers insistently
to the belief—for her, an incontrovertible fact—that the
Soviet Union is the main, safe base for revolutions leading to
socialism.

I ask her why, then, the Soviet Union supports and arms
the reactionary government of Indira Gandhi in India. She
says that this aid is, in her opinion, not to support counter-
revolutionary forces but to keep the United States at bay,

and she asks me, "Who are the main enemies of revolution in India?" I reply that I think they are the Indian big bourgeoisie and the landlords, supported chiefly by Western imperialism (with which she agrees), but that they are also substantially upheld by Soviet military aid and sales and by Soviet investment in the Indian public sector. She passes over this point and simply concludes, "Remember that revolutions are fought to rescue people from *misery*. You must first see where the misery is, and then who is causing it." She reminds me, too, that a revolution cannot succeed without a strong and united vanguard party and without the full participation of women, and that it can only be begun and won from within the country, never from foreign lands.

As course follows course, I cannot help silently contrasting this banquet with the spartan existence that I know is the everyday lot of the Vietnamese communists—their one-room apartments, sparse clothing, and simple food. With extraordinary generosity, they appear to reserve a substantial part of their meager surplus to entertain foreign guests and assistants who have aided their country; perhaps also to show their pride in their capabilities. I remember that the peasants and workers, too, hold feasts for marriages and festivals. The long travail of the Vietnamese, with all its shortages and agony, seems only to have enhanced their capacity for joy in living.

We rise for toasts to the peace movement and the workers and farmers of Canada. Very graciously, Mrs. Dinh presents me with two silk cushion covers embroidered in Thai Binh, a badge commemorating the first achievement of five tons of paddy per hectare in this province, and a ring decorated with a dragon, made from the wreckage of a United States plane. With a warm hug she kisses me on both cheeks. Reluctantly, I say goodbye to my Thai Binh hosts.

18

The Bach Mai Hospital

November 19. We drive quickly to Hanoi through a morning drizzle, and at noon drop Khanh at her apartment building on the outskirts of the city. For nine days she has worked at my side, interpreting all the lectures and almost all the conversations recorded in this book. On several occasions she has translated patiently and faithfully for fifteen consecutive hours. By now Khanh is longing to see and nurse her baby again. She bids us a cheery farewell and promises to be back this evening.

At 2 P.M. Liên, Hoan, and I visit the famous Bach Mai Children's Hospital in Hanoi. We are met by the medical head of the hospital, Dr. Dai, a gentle and modest man of middle age, and the vice-head, a woman of forty who represents the Workers' Party and is concerned with social and political policies.

The stone steps leading upstairs to the head's office and the reception room are still partly destroyed as a result of the bombing of 1972. The old fashioned elevator is immobilized, its shaft blocked by debris.

The reception room is small, with armchairs and an occasional table in one half, and a table of equipment in the other. When we enter, two nurses are folding linen, for the hospital is acutely short of space.

The head and vice-head serve us tea and describe their

hospital. It has 110 beds and a staff of 200, 65 percent of whom are women. The staff includes 47 doctors and pediatricians and 4 pharmacy experts.

"The layout of our hospital is old-fashioned," explains the head, with Liên interpreting, "really not at all suitable for children. It was built in 1920 and has never been improved. During the recent war it was bombed twice, the second time by B-52s during the Christmas bombing of 1972. A new children's hospital is now being built four kilometers away. Our medical equipment was mostly destroyed in the bombing, our glassware all broken, and our electrical equipment badly damaged. Because of these damages our labs are still not in good order. Our Ministry of Health cannot yet provide all that is necessary, for it has many other hospitals to care for.

"Our hospital has four functions. The first is the treatment of children under fifteen who have serious, special illnesses. They come from all over north Vietnam, and include both newborns and babies. Second, we are concerned with the formation of cadres, that is, the training of doctors and nurses. Every day fifty students in pediatrics come to work here and fifty in general medicine, in addition to postgraduate students preparing for medical training in the universities, and nurses in training. Third, we are involved in public education for motherhood, especially through radio and TV broadcasts. And finally, we carry on scientific research—everything to do with children's diseases.

"In spite of all our difficulties during the war, we made a number of advances of which we are rather proud. For example, we managed to concoct a substitute for milk for our patients during the U.S. blockade. It's made out of a flour derived from fish, rice, and soya beans, and is all right, even for infants. We have done significant research in social diseases such as diseases of the thyroid gland and pulmonary inflammations, also on the growth of children."

I ask the head whether it is true, as was reported to Wilfred

Burchett,[1] that a substitute was found for blood plasma during the war. "It is true, although is was rarely used," he says. "It was obtained from coconut milk and was used in very dire cases in south Vietnam when blood was not available. Although not entirely satisfactory, it saved some lives.

"Producing artificial limbs and organs is one of our main activities," continues Dr. Dai. "We produce kidney machines for the treatment of chronic nephritis, and isotopes for investigating throat diseases. We also make pacemakers to correct heart function and respirators for artificial respiration. As far as possible we use modern techniques, but unfortunately much of the equipment we need is too expensive."

I ask the head and vice-head to tell me more about the bombing. The vice-head replies, "The first bombing was in June 1972. In that raid only one department out of ten was destroyed and no one was killed. The B-52 raid on December 22, 1972, was far more atrocious. This room was entirely crushed, for example. The buildings in the pediatrics section received five bombs, and our dermatology and ear, nose, and throat sections were totally destroyed.

"Fortunately, none of our regular child patients was killed, for we had already evacuated them. We did have some emergency patients whom we rushed to the center of the hospital. One of those patients died. Forty of our staff were killed, and also sixteen people—neighbors and children of the staff— who had come to the hospital's underground shelter. We had to dig out the bodies. They had come here because the hospital bore a red cross, and even after the bombing of June 1972, which we thought accidental, no one really imagined it would be deliberately attacked. Altogether, ten children of the staff and neighbors were killed, and a total of fifty-seven people." The head and vice-head speak calmly, without anger, but their eyes and faces show suffering.

While the vice-head is speaking, the head has unrolled a screen on the wall and placed a projector on the table. He shows a short film shot soon after the bombing, which reveals the damage to various sections of the hospital. The film goes on to show the visits of several dignitaries, the construction carried out since the bombing, and the resumption of medical work in the damaged buildings. There is a plan of the hospital showing the exact placement of the thirty-six bombs dropped on it. Each large bomb was accompanied by four smaller ones. Among the visitors are Prince Sihanouk and Princess Monique of Cambodia with Prime Minister Pham Van Dong paying tribute to those who died in the attack, and movie star Jane Fonda, who visited Hanoi while the hospital was being rebuilt.

We make a tour of the hospital. It has ten sections: surgical, pediatrics, cardiology, respiratory, endocrinology, digestive system, hematology, nephrology, reanimation, and dietetics. The dermatology and ear, nose, and throat sections, and the X-ray lab are not yet rebuilt. There are laboratories for biochemistry, microbiology, and pharmacology. A doctor heads each section, with three or four junior doctors and seven to ten nurses in the section.

Pediatrics comprises two rooms with about a dozen sick babies in cribs. Some are in intensive care in incubators, with tubes in their mouths. One has had a cerebral hemorrhage; one is premature and is minute. A machine in the room makes a loud, irritating noise, but I doubt if the babies can hear it through their cocoons of cloth and their glass containers.

The room for heart patients has about twenty beds, one of them behind a screen. The windows are wide open and it is cold. The patients look sad. A stoical little girl of about ten sits crosslegged on her bed wearing a man's gray winter overcoat. A boy has recently had heart surgery. A very pale, stout boy of about eight gazes at us with large eyes as we pass. Nurses are gently tending the children.

The laboratories are small and poorly equipped. I cannot understand most of the equipment, but it is clear that almost all of it is ancient, and that several essential machines are missing since the bombing. The head shows me one machine contributed by the World Federation of Women which is greatly prized. I examine a very ancient Beckman photometer used for testing infants' blood; a new one is badly needed. The head tells me that international and foreign relief groups have contributed a total of $500,000 since the bombing but that it is quite inadequate. Some necessary machines, in addition, can be obtained from abroad only with great difficulty. The head lists the following as being urgently required; I have added some current prices in Canada.

1. Apparatus for measuring the pH of blood,
   blood gas, Astrup type, 1 @ $8,500
2. Flame photometer, 1 @   4,000
3. Beckman colormeter, 1 @   800
4. Centrifugal machine, 3000 revolutions per minute, 2 @   800
5. Apparatus for sterilizing medical instruments, 1 @   12,000
6. Thromboelastrograph   ?
7. Dishwasher, 1 @   420
8. Slide projector and screen, 1@   175

The staff rooms are tiny; each is shared by the personnel of two sections. The head says mildly that they really need one per section. From those I meet and talk to, I have the impression that the staff is doing a heroic job under woefully inadequate conditions.

We walk across the hospital yard to see the bomb sites. At one end of the complex of buildings, two wards, upstairs and downstairs, which were once the dermatology and the ear, nose, and throat sections, are completely ripped off. About fifteen yards away is a pile of rubble, bricks, twisted wire, and part of a bedstead, near a mound which marks the site of an air raid shelter where sixteen neighbors and staff children were killed. Across the quadrangle a large corner of a building has been blown away, revealing the ruined X-ray section, not yet rebuilt.

We return to the reception room, where tea, fruits, short-breads, cakes, and a bouquet of white chrysanthemums are waiting. I ask about the running of the hospital. As usual, the party, the staff's trade union, the youth union, and the women's union are significant political organs. The staff of each unit carry on daily criticism and self-criticism "with the aim of solidary, collective responsibility," I am told. Between the trade union and the hospital administration criticism is "mutual and frequent," says the vice-head, "all, of course, toward the improved care of the patients." Every week, the head tours all the departments and exchanges ideas and criticisms. One day a week is devoted to collective diagnoses of the most critical cases. Once a week there is scientific discussion of some new research or invention.

Bach Mai is the saddest place I have visited in Vietnam. The children are so ill, the bomb damage so extensive, the equipment and the international aid so pitifully inadequate. Yet here as everywhere I see the same ingenuity, the same indomitable determination and courage. As the head and vice-head bid goodbye to us in the courtyard, I feel that here are people the like of whom one seldom meets.

At 4 P.M., Liên and Hoan take me to Hanoi's Reunification Park. It lies on the shore of Lake Mãu, is extensive, and contains beautiful trees, shrubs, and walks. Hoan asks two uniformed high school girls to accompany us as guides, for she and Liên have not been here for several years. Usually they have no time, they say, and when their husbands are away they do not feel much like coming. The park is a special haunt of young lovers, and by 6 P.M. becomes *"très animé."*

"Did you name it when Vietnam was reunited this year?" I ask.

"No, indeed!" says Liên. "We named it in 1954, when our country was first temporarily divided by the Geneva Accords. It expressed the determination to reunify Vietnam and rebuild it after the anti-French colonial struggle."

The park was a garbage dump and a shanty town under the French, they tell me, one of Hanoi's worst eyesores. Nowadays, garbage is taken far from the city and processed for fertilizer or recycled for industrial use. The trees were planted gradually after the liberation of north Vietnam. Liên and her pupils used to come here on Saturdays to plant them in the late 1950s.

Like everything else I have seen in Hanoi, the park is a model of neatness. The walks are constantly swept clean, the flower beds weeded. Not a single cigarette packet or piece of paper is in sight. Our young guides lead us through a children's playground with swings, seesaws, and the like, to an aviary of brilliantly colored parrots and other birds. The parrots' tongues are split to make them talk. We go from there to an orchestra stand where concerts of classical music are given by the Hanoi orchestra.

I cannot imagine a pleasanter place to spend my last twilight than Reunification Park, with two of the friends I have come to love. The birds, trees, and flowers, the gently lapping lake, the schoolgirls, and the young lovers, betoken hope, life, and peace.

My last evening. Vô Thi Thê, Liên, Little Liên, Hoan, and Khanh are with me and have ordered a final, sumptuous dinner. Eel soup is followed by frogs' legs, pork and green beans with onions, rice, fish sauce, delicious meatballs in thin, crisp batter, fruit salad, vin rosé, beer, tea, and coffee. For me, the meal is both sad and happy; I am wondering whether I shall ever see these kind friends again.

We chat about all I have seen and done in the past ten days, about our families, and about women's groups in North America and other possible visitors to Vietnam. We touch once more on India. I say that because I have come from there and feel loyalty to the people of India, I want to state, one last time, that I do not agree with Soviet aid to the Gandhi government, with Vietnamese verbal support for it, or with the view that that government is in any meaningful sense anti-imperialist. It has carried on too much repression of revolutionaries and of poor people. My friends listen in silence and we turn to other matters.

As we rise, Liên lightly touches my arm. "We are sorry that we could not answer all your questions, Kathleen," she says. I realize she is referring to the many questions I have posed about China, the Soviet Union, Soviet and Vietnamese policy to India, and so on. I tell Liên I think I understand that their wish to reunify the socialist camp prevents them from freely discussing foreign affairs, that I appreciate their discretion and hope they do not mind my having tried to raise questions that have troubled me.

Over coffee, Vô Thi Thê presents me with an ivory necklace bearing a pendant with the Buddha of a thousand eyes and thousand hands, and two other necklaces for friends in the peace movement in North America. With warm speeches and embraces, we say goodnight.

19

Farewell to Hanoi

November 20. At 7 A.M. Little Liên appears with a box and string to pack the many books I am taking back to India or to Canada. During breakfast, Hoan and Khanh arrive. They want to take me sightseeing around Hanoi before we leave for the airport at noon, and to fulfill my earlier request to visit a pagoda.

We drive down Dien Bien Phu Street, past Ba Dinh Square with the National Assembly building and the presidential mausoleum. Soon we reach the Lake of White Silk, one of Hanoi's five largest stretches of water.[1] Across it in the distance is a beautiful pagoda, together with buildings traditionally occupied by silk weavers, after whom the lake is named.

A few miles from the city we reach the splendid Victory Hotel, funded by the Cuban government and built by Cuban technicians and workmen as a gift to Vietnam. The buildings are large and graceful, with a swimming pool and a lake nearby. The decor reminds me of Hawaii; the reception hall is an indoor garden with a stream, a fountain, and trees. Half a dozen Cuban workers, one of them black, lean chatting against the rail of the verandah; they exchange cheery greetings with my hosts. The hotel is reserved mainly for foreign guests. Liên says the rooms are very expensive—60 dong or U.S. $12 a day! The food, of course, is much less, she says, but the whole cost is fabulous. Liên is astonished when I tell her rooms in a similar hotel in North America might be $40 a day, and meals of equal price.

Our next stop is a Buddhist pagoda dating from 1624, also beside a lake. It has a Chinese style roof and is adorned with inscriptions in the ancient script. Hoan and Liên tell me pagodas are dedicated to the Buddha; temples, to human heroes of the past. Workers are building a drain between the temple and the lake and are using the entrance hall for their wheelbarrow and cement. An empty alcove in the hall may once have contained a statue. On one side the hall opens on to a wide veranda with seats, designed as a lecture hall, where religious elders give sermons on holy days. Liên says that nowadays mainly old people attend. Hoan asks the caretaker, an old woman, to open the main, locked room on the other side of the entrance hall, where regular worship is carried on. It is filled with bronze and stone statues, with a large and beautiful Buddha in marble as the central figure. Incense is burning and fresh flowers have been offered before several of the figures.

As we leave, two young men are fishing in the lake with rods and lines. Hoan goes and speaks to them gently, her hand on the shoulder of one of them. They at once pack up their gear and depart. Private fishing is illegal, says Khanh. The government has the lake fished once a year for sale to the public. Poaching is a minor offense that still has to be eradicated.

We drive to a temple dedicated to Lê Loi, the general who led the Vietnamese against the Ming invaders in 1427 and later became king. The building, three stories high, has a gateway with four stone pillars bearing sculptures of dogs and dragons in relief. Inscriptions adorn the front of the temple. The interior is delicate and beautiful, with screens inlaid with colored wood and mother-of-pearl, mother-of-pearl inscriptions, and many ornate bronze and gold vases, statues, and lamps. The central figure in the entrance hall is a large, painted statue of the general. His boots and weapons are laid before him. In the shrine behind this hall is an immense statue of the Buddha in black bronze, and, in a side hall, a small figure of the sculptor. A large room to the rear contains many images, with holders for offerings.

A Soviet party is being shown around by a guide as we enter. Worshippers pass to and fro through the rooms and some of them leave incense and flowers.

Liên and Hoan tell me they have a limited knowledge of the temples and pagodas, derived from their historical studies; they have little interest in religious beliefs and rites. Hoan says, however, that the temples, unlike the churches, were valuable hiding places and centers of propaganda for their party in the war against the French, as most of the priests were patriotic. Both Buddhism and Christianity now have cordial relations with the state in Vietnam. Premier Pham Van Dong, for example, formally received Cardinal Trinh Nue Khue on August 31, 1976, when he returned from his consecration in the Vatican.

Back at the hotel, Hoan says, "Again we are sorry, Kathleen, that we could not answer all your questions. We have learned from experience that we must not comment freely on foreign states or parties with which we have fraternal or cooperative relations. In that way we retain the respect of all."[2] I thank her and again say that I see the value of this policy, and of reserving full discussion to representatives of fraternal parties.

Vô Thi Thê, Khanh, and Little Liên are waiting. I distribute parting gifts to all my friends—clumsily wrapped packages of various personal items, new and old, which they receive appreciatively. They are worried in case I am hungry before reaching Rangoon, so at eleven I am served a second breakfast, thus in one morning consuming six fried eggs in melted butter! My friends eat too, then we set off. I give my fountain pen to a rather startled Quyên, wanting to hug him but not quite daring.

At the airport I tell Hoan it is hard, now that I'm leaving, to believe I have really been in Vietnam. "For so long, it has had a mythical quality. It's difficult for us to take in all you have been through and accomplished."

"We, too, can sometimes scarcely realize our great success," she says.

We talk of families, especially mine, and I thank Vô Thi Thê for my visit. She asks me how I found her younger comrades; was I pleased with them? I say I was, beyond expression, and her face lights up.

Hoan unpins the small blue badge of Vietnam that she has worn since the anti-French war and gives it to me. Her simple gesture touches me very deeply. Like herself, it is such a small, delicate object, representing thirty years of hard struggle, suffering, and courage. We all embrace quickly. As I climb the steps of the plane, they are on the roof of the building, waving. My heart is shaken with tears of gratitude and love.

In Vientiane I meet a French doctor returning to Paris. Although lame and elderly, he has spent six weeks in both north and south Vietnam visiting hospitals and finding out about needed supplies. He stresses the doctors' courage and inventiveness, but also their lack of equipment and medicines, and especially what he regards as the poor state of the rural clinics. He blames the French government for not helping, and the United States for not paying its reparations and for reimposing its veto on United Nations membership for Vietnam. The Norwegians and Canadians, and perhaps also the French, he says, have contracted to explore for oil in south Vietnam. The Vietnamese would like to pay for the technology in raw materials, he says, but the terms have not yet been made public.

The doctor is not very sanguine about the immediate future of Indochina. There are a million unemployed on the streets of Ho Chi Minh City, he says. They were formerly involved in the black market, prostitution, gambling, the import trade, or serving the puppet regime or the Americans. The government is gradually settling many of them on 2,000 square meters of land per person and encouraging them to form farming cooperatives or at least, work exchange teams, but he says that many are unwilling to cooperate. He stresses the huge problems in the south, and his belief that it will take at least two years to settle down. The factories and machines left behind by the Americans are not very useful, he says, because no spare parts are available.

Meanwhile, my companion sees serious strains between Cambodia and Vietnam. The Cambodians expelled 150,000 Vietnamese after their revolution, he says, and there have been border clashes between Cambodia and Vietnam and a dispute over the ownership of islands in the Gulf of Thailand.[3] Laos, also, is in difficulties, with its sparse population and shortage of industry.

The Chinese, this observer says, have refused to attend the Fourth Congress of the Workers' Party, "probably because Brezhnev is going."[4] He confirms my impression, however, that the Vietnamese hope for better relations with China in the wake of the arrest of the "gang of four."

A young West German woman reporter has spent two weeks as a tourist in Vietnam. She thinks there is a food problem, and especially a shortage of protein because there is little milk. I tell her that I cannot speak about conditions in dislocated or devastated areas of the south, but that the rice ration is considerably higher than the amount available to the poor in south India, and that in Hanoi, Quang Ninh, and Thai Binh, protein was reported to be adequate in the form of meat, poultry, eggs, fish, and peanuts.

Having just left Vietnam, I realize anew how important in any descriptive account are one's preconceptions and the people one has talked to. Here already are two people who, although sympathetic, because of their particular experiences and standards of comparison have left Vietnam with a prevailing sense of a mountain of problems and dangers. By contrast, because I am comparing Vietnam with India and because I have been in the company of people confident of their nation's future, I am leaving with some understanding of the problems but, most of all, excited by the achievements and potential of Vietnam. I can only report what I have heard and seen.

Epilogue

Notwithstanding the discretion of my friends in the Women's Union, I met several members of the Communist Party of Vietnam who made comments or answered questions, both on internal policies and on foreign affairs. Apart from the interview with Comrade Hoang Tung (see chapter 10), I have chosen to assemble these comments here rather than attributing them to particular people and places, and have added to them certain information from the press and some few conclusions of my own. The viewpoints that follow are very limited and are not necessarily held by all communists in Vietnam, but as most of them were expressed by several people, in different places, they are probably characteristic. Most of the comments I heard referred to the Soviet Union, China, or India, the three countries about which I made most inquiries.

The Soviet Union: It seemed clear that despite an effort in public to deal evenhandedly with all member countries of what the Vietnamese still insist on calling "the socialist camp," the Soviet Union was by far their most important ally in November 1976. Soviet trucks, technicians, and machinery were widely prevalent. Soviet planes flew most frequently into and out of Hanoi. Thousands of Vietnamese students receive higher education in the Soviet Union, which is often referred to as "our friend, the Soviet Union." Only "our friend, Cuba" seemed to occupy a similar place in the hearts of the people I met; I did not hear this phrase applied to other countries.

The organization of production appears to reflect Soviet rather than recent Chinese influence. As Comrade Hoang Tung indicated, the Vietnamese firmly believe in the value and justice of material incentives to boost production, as is seen in their use of bonuses and of special prizes of consumer goods to workers who win emulation contests. The view was expressed that the Chinese had erred in the period of the Cultural Revolution by giving up bonuses and paying insufficient attention to wage differentials, and that they were now realizing their mistake.

The management of factories and cooperatives in Vietnam in recent years may show the effects of Soviet influence. Most, if not all of them, have one-person directorships, although the director shares his or her responsibilities with, and can be checked by, a small elected managerial committee. As Comrade Ding Quang Ngi, the director of Vu Thang, indicated, the managerial staff had been reduced from seventeen to six since 1972. Others reported that such recently increased centralization of management is general in enterprises in north Vietnam.

Some Soviet influence may also, perhaps, be seen in the emphasis on careful cost accounting in state and cooperative enterprises, in the insistence that enterprises should make, or at least aim to make, a profit, and in the continuing reliance on the "law of value" in the economy of Vietnam.

The following statement by Lê Duân in 1970 outlines the Vietnamese approach to cost accounting, material incentives, and profits in relation to socialist management of the economy:

The practice of economic construction in our own and other socialist countries proves that economic management must *correctly utilize certain levers*, such as prices, wages, profits, and credit, and fully enforce the system of cost accounting and the socialist mode of business. The commodity-money relationship is the result of history and is closely related to a given level of development of production. When this relationship develops on the basis of private ownership, it is accompanied by class differentiation and accelerates the division of society into rich and poor. However, once the economic levers are in the hands of the proletarian state, the exploiting classes have been abolished, and the small producers have turned towards collective work, then a judicious and rational development of the commodity-money relationship, along with a redivision of labor and a technical revolution, will become a positive factor in promoting the growth of production and the organization of a new life. Therefore, to bring into play the law of value, cost accounting, and the levers of profit, wages, prices, and credit is an extremely important economic problem. The law of value and the practice of cost accounting make it possible to gauge the effectiveness of economic and technical measures and to assess the quality of work in each enterprise, region, branch, and level. They permit the mobilization of latent economic potentialities and the encouragement of innovation, thriftiness, and industriousness in the interests of the state and nation. The work of economic construction in a poor country such as ours, with low labor productivity and limited financial resources, demands an intensive preoccupation with business efficiency if we are to satisfy our immediate needs while achieving extended reproduction. Indeed, we must accumulate profits for extended reproduction on a national scale, as well as within each branch, level, and basic economic unit. All branches, levels, and units must show definite progress after each production cycle. However, profits and losses should not be viewed with the petty mentality of a small individual producer. In our present conditions, the greatest profit lies in extended reproduction, a multiplication of branches and trades, an increase in the quantity of products, and the raising of labor productivity in each branch and the entire national economy. Only on this basis can we speak of profits and reconcile profit making with the socialist nature of our economy. Thus, on the one hand, we must make profits in each branch and period whenever possible. On the other hand, if we take into consideration the development of the entire economy over a long period, then we can comprehensively examine the question of profits and losses.[1]

The emphases in this approach are somewhat different from those found in China during the Cultural Revolution, where less emphasis was placed on profit making by individual branches and units. Although each enterprise was expected to make a profit (unless there had been a deliberate plan to expand production on the basis of state subsidy), all industrial profits went into the state coffers rather than being partially retained within the enterprise as a whole, or distributed as bonuses to individual workers.[2] In Vietnam, by contrast, although the state sets the wages in particular industries and types of enterprise for all of north Vietnam, part of the profits of a successful industry are retained and distributed as overall rewards or as individual bonuses.

The Vietnamese explanation of their use of the market and of material incentives is the usual one, that these are essential in the lower stage of transition to socialism when the productive forces are backward, but will become unnecessary later when heavy industry has developed, there is plenty for all, and the transition to communism has become possible. When I pointed out that material incentives were far more prominent in the Soviet Union, with its relatively high productivity, than in China with its low level, the response was that (a) the Soviet Union had not yet embarked on the "higher stage," (b) it had permitted too severe a development of income differentials, but, it was thought, was at present reducing them, and (c) China had disregarded material incentives too much and too early, to the detriment of its economy, and was now being obliged to backtrack.

Perhaps the most significant view on internal relations which, in 1976, aligned Vietnam with the Soviet Union rather than with China was the belief that no class struggle exists in socialist societies—nor, presumably, to use Hoang Tung's term, in societies that are "proceeding to socialism." This view, expressed by Hoang Tung himself, was repeated by several other Vietnamese whom I met.

There appears to be some change in this respect from the

view expressed by Comrade Lê Duân in 1970, although the change may be one of phraseology rather than of substance. In *The Vietnamese Revolution,* Lê Duân wrote:

> After the seizure of power and the establishment of the dictatorship of the proletariat, the class struggle against the bourgeoisie and other reactionary forces will continue with unabated ferocity in various forms, "sanguinary and bloodless, violent and peaceful, military and economic, educational and administrative," in order to build socialism.[3]

Lê Duân saw the class struggle in societies advancing to socialism as one "to abolish the capitalist sector and all other forms of exploitation, to stem the trend of small production toward spontaneous capitalist development, to suppress all attempts at disruption by hostile elements, and to assure order, security and a strong potential for national defense." He also saw class struggle in a society moving to socialism not only as the abolition of the capitalist economic sector and all other forms of exploitation, but as "the simultaneous implementation of the triple revolution: revolution in relations of production, technical revolution, and ideological and cultural revolution."

By 1970, however, Lê Duân already saw the struggle between the socialist and capitalist paths in north Vietnam as

> primarily a struggle to raise small production to the level of large-scale production. The basic content of the class struggle in the period of transition to socialism is to adhere firmly to the dictatorship of the proletariat in order simultaneously to develop the *three revolutions,* with the technical revolution as the keystone (italics as in the original).[4]

This emphasis on "the technical revolution as the keystone" was repeated in 1976 by Lê Duân in his speeches to the National Assembly and the Fourth Congress of the Workers' Party, in which he stressed the central need to develop the productive forces, especially heavy industry, in Vietnam.[5]

Therefore, although the term "class struggle" has been

used in the past in relation to the evolution of socialism in Vietnam, it has evidently not referred to mass struggles on the part of the people against those in the Communist Party itself who may proceed to reestablish undue hierarchy, privilege, arbitrary use of power, or gross material inequalities, as it came to do during the Cultural Revolution in China.[6] Lê Duân and others in the Vietnamese party have, both recently and in the past, inveighed against these evils, but have represented them as dangers that the party itself must correct, with the aid of regular but peaceful criticism and suggestions by the masses through their collective organs such as the trade unions. They have apparently not foreseen as an ever present danger the growth of the party itself, or a sizable section of it, into a privileged class which exercises power at least partly for its own material and psychic aggrandizement. This is evidently not foreseen, or even admitted, as a possibility in Vietnam, because the party itself is viewed as the embodiment of the dictatorship of the proletariat, and its unity and internal discipline as the essential ingredients for maintaining that dictatorship. On this point Vietnamese theory dovetails with that of the Soviet Union, although in practice the Communist Party of Vietnam seems to be much closer to the proletariat and the peasants, both in lifestyle and aspirations, than is the case in the Soviet Union.

In many respects the Vietnamese also agree with Soviet interpretations of world politics and ideology. Those who expressed opinions regarded the idea that capitalism is being restored in the Soviet Union as ridiculous, and, as Comrade Hoang Tung put it, made declarations to the effect that they had "not seen social imperialism in this world." Everyone who expressed an opinion thought that, in spite of various deviations at various times, the Soviet Union was still the main bastion of world socialism on which other revolutionary movements could rely. Vietnam's warm support for Cuba, for the MPLA in Angola, and for the revolution in Mozambique, conformed to Soviet rather than to Chinese foreign policy, as did their firm opposition to the present dictatorial regime in Chile.

So also did Vietnam's verbal support for the government of Indira Gandhi in India, its eagerness to trade with India, and its willingness to receive foreign aid in such forms as an experimental rice producing station from India. Again, Vietnam's participation in the Conference of Non-Aligned Nations in Sri Lanka in August 1976, was in conformity with that of other Third World nations which in fact have close ties with either the Soviet Union or the Western nations or both; this conference was not endorsed or attended by China.

On the other hand, it seemed clear that Vietnam was trying to follow a path toward socialism that differed in some major respects from that followed by the Soviet Union. Several Vietnamese expressed the view, for example, that Soviet income differentials were far too great. Differences of twenty-five times, and even of a hundred times, were mentioned, whereas in Vietnamese enterprises differences of five or six times seemed to be the norm. As I have mentioned, however, the belief was expressed that the Soviet Union was engaged in reducing its income differentials.

Obliquely, moreover, it was indicated that Vietnam's development would differ from that of the Soviet Union in not forcing collectivization on the peasants against their will, and in not "squeezing" the countryside to pay for the development of industry and of the cities. Indeed, although the cash wages of industrial workers are higher than those in the agricultural cooperatives, the view was expressed that people in the countryside are actually better off than are most in the cities, certainly in terms of housing and food supply.

In spite of the prevalence of one-person directorships in enterprises, moreover, the Vietnamese emphasis on the "collective mastery" of the people and on their training for self-government was greater than has been reported for the Soviet Union. In the vital roles accorded to the trade unions, the Youth Union, and the Women's Union, and in the use of these organs as conveyor belts for information and criticism from the people to the leaders, and vice versa, it seemed that democratic processes were very active in Vietnam.

The general outlook I found in this respect was well expressed by Prime Minister Pham Van Dong in an interview with a special correspondent of *Le Monde* on April 16, 1977:

> Important progress has been made in the fight against bureaucracy, and this is thanks to the active participation of the people.
>
> Bureaucracy is the enemy of socialism. Socialism must be the work of the people. That is why people's power must be set up, for the people and by the people, under the leadership of the working class. This is what we call the right to collective mastery in our socialist society.
>
> To combat bureaucracy is really to fight for the removal of all obstacles to the real exercise of power by the people at all levels, from the base to the top of the State structures.

Similarly, the Political Report of the Party Central Committee to the Fourth Congress contains a statement by Lê Duân emphasizing the need to strengthen "collective mastery" by enhancing the powers of the National Assembly, People's Councils, Trade Unions, Youth Unions, and Women's Union.[7]

Although my observations were necessarily superficial, I received a similar impression of flourishing democratic processes from the fact that the management staffs and often the directors of enterprises are elected by the workers and can be recalled, and that, especially in recent years, there has been a strong effort to recruit workers and peasants into the Communist Party.

Again, although enterprises in Vietnam are expected to make a profit, and despite bonuses and other forms of material incentive, the Vietnamese state evidently does operate to even out the basic incomes of workers in more and less prosperous enterprises of the same character throughout north Vietnam. It was further reported that state enterprises had no opportunity to trade with one another, as they reportedly do in the Soviet Union. In their approach to the "law of value," as in the matter of material incentives, of enterprise management, of mass criticism and participation in management, and of the struggle against bureaucratism and commandism, the Vietnamese in actual fact seemed to be trying to steer a course between those of the Soviet Union and of China in recent years—a course based on their own conditions and experience.

In their assessment of foreign countries and revolutionary movements, too, the Vietnamese differed at several points from the official statements of the Soviet Union. The possibility that most Third World nations could make a peaceful transition to socialism seemed, for example, to be thought unlikely by those Vietnamese I questioned who ventured an opinion.

It was already clear in November 1976 that Vietnam had no intention of becoming entirely dependent on the Soviet Union, but was striving to maintain independence through diversified trade, investments, and foreign aid agreements with as many nations as was feasible. The Vietnamese decision to join the World Bank, the Asian Development Bank, and the International Monetary Fund, to seek foreign private investment in oil, mining, and other industrial and metallurgical fields from Western Europe, Japan, and Canada as well as from the Soviet Union, and their grateful acceptance of foreign aid from the Scandinavian countries, indicated this desire for flexibility in foreign relations. So did their quest for trade relations with Western Europe, Japan, Canada, Hong Kong, the Middle East, and other regions.[8]

Since November 1976 the Vietnamese appear to have taken further steps toward diversifying their foreign economic relations and perhaps toward differentiating their foreign policy from that of the Soviet Union. Despite Soviet pressures, for example, Vietnam did not invite the Communist Party of India (a strongly pro-Soviet party) to attend the Fourth Congress of the Workers' Party in December 1976. On the other hand, Vietnam continued to defend the government of Indira Gandhi even after a breach had occurred in its relations with the Soviet Union.[9]

In February 1977, the former French ambassador to Hanoi reported to a correspondent of the *Far Eastern Economic Review* that in the future, Vietnam wished to strengthen its nonalignment by having the Soviet Union and China provide half its foreign aid, and Western Europe, Japan, and Canada the other half. This would be a marked departure from the state of affairs at that time, in which the Soviet bloc provided some 40 to 50 percent of Vietnam's foreign aid (about U.S. $487 million) and China and Albania the equivalent of $329 million, while total aid from the noncommunist nations for 1976–1977 was estimated at $162.1 million.[10] In the same month it was reported that officials in Hanoi requested a visiting United Nations Development Program team for assistance in oil exploration in north Vietnam.[11] While plans for United States investment in Vietnam have not yet been entered into, their possibility has been discussed.[12] Hanoi's relations with four of the five states of the Association of South East Asian Nations (the Philippines, Singapore, Malaysia, and Indonesia), although not with the dictatorship of Thailand, were also relaxed during 1977, in contrast to the Soviet Union's continuing hostility to this U.S.-backed coalition, and trade relations have been established.[13]

At least some of Vietnam's increasing autonomy has been forced upon it by the new policies of both China and the Soviet Union in the postwar period, for Vietnam not only must now pay for its imports from these countries, but also, reportedly, must repay past debts.[14] In late 1976 Nguyen Duy Trinh, an authority on state planning, stated: "We must quickly and clearly realize the changes in international cooperation and, on this basis, more strongly emphasize our policy of being self-reliant . . . making every effort to produce a large volume of export goods."[15] In September 1977, Communist Party Secretary Lê Duân made a much more forthright acknowledgment: "During our anti-U.S. resistance, fraternal countries helped us by giving us weapons and food. By so doing, they promoted common interests, ensured the survival of socialism, and fulfilled their international duties. But during the construction period, aid will be limited, and the principal thing will be cooperation on the basis of mutual interest."[16]

The reduction of aid from the Soviet Union and Eastern Europe, as well as from China, accounts at least in part for Vietnam's search for investment capital from the Western industrial nations and Japan. Together with bad weather, it also accounts for the fact that whereas in 1975–1976 emphasis was placed on developing heavy industry as rapidly as possible, Vietnam's economic plan for 1976–1980, announced in November 1976, scaled down the goals for heavy industry and instead placed prime emphasis on agriculture and light industry.[17] By this means it is hoped to afford improved living conditions to the people and to step up exports so as to acquire needed capital for future investment. Thirty percent of development funding was thus accorded to agriculture in 1977 as against 17.4 percent in 1976, and 35 percent to industry as against 41 percent in 1976, while targets for 1977 provided for a 55 percent increase in exports over the previous year.[18]

Meanwhile, Vietnam drew $35 million from the International Monetary Fund in January 1977, and was reported to have relaxed its conditions for the reception of foreign investment from the industrial capitalist nations in April 1977 and again in September.[19] Agreements for offshore oil exploration have been signed with the government-owned Elf-Aquitaine of France and Petro-Can of Canada, and Japanese aid is expected to be forthcoming for Vietnam's first oil refinery and processing base. Other foreign investment ventures have been approved with governments or firms in France, Denmark, Norway, and Sweden. Vietnam also wishes for trade, aid, and investment from the United States. Although these are not yet forthcoming, President Carter's expressed wish for "normalization" of relations with Vietnam, and the lifting of the United States veto on Vietnam's joining the United Nations, may have paved the way.

Time will tell whether these ventures will have overall beneficial or deleterious effects on Vietnam's economy and society. At present, it seems clear that the duty of socialists in the West is to press the United States government to make reparations to Vietnam for its extraordinary war damage, as was promised in the Paris Agreement of 1973, rather than to criticize Vietnam for seeking sorely needed capital for reconstruction wherever it may be found. Certainly, Vietnam's leaders are confident that, relying mainly on their own efforts but with a variety of forms of minor aid and investment from many sources, they can maintain their revolutionary principles and socialist goals, and establish an independent stance in world affairs. The entry of Vietnam into the United Nations in September 1977 may enhance Vietnam's ability to offer an example of independent socialist construction and policies.

China: While only a few hints were dropped, it was obvious that Vietnam's relations with the People's Republic of China were strained at the time of my visit. Although some Chinese aid, development projects, and trade continued, and some Vietnamese students were training in China, far fewer instances of Chinese than of Soviet cooperation were evident. Chinese aid on the Red River bridge to New Hanoi, and on several other technical projects, had reportedly flagged in the previous two years. Especially bitter were the disputes over the Paracel Islands off Vietnam's northern coast, currently held by China, and the Spratly Islands off its southern coast, currently held by Vietnam, all of which are claimed by both countries. Chinese exports of 500,000 tons of free rice a year to Vietnam had been halted, and the Vietnamese were aware that they must in the future pay world market prices for imports from China.[20]

242 Ten Times More Beautiful

In November 1976 I found the Vietnamese attitude to the Cultural Revolution in China lukewarm and at least in some respects disapproving. The official stance was, "We did not really know much about it; we were too busy fighting the war." This rather ironic statement contains an essential point, for Vietnam has not yet experienced the need for an upsurge among the people to cleanse its own bureaucracy and party, engrossed as it has been in thirty years of revolutionary conflict against external enemies.[21] It remains to be seen whether some form of concerted renewal from below will prove necessary in Vietnam, as it apparently did in China after two decades of peace.

Even so, Vietnamese objections to certain developments in China up to late 1976 were more than mere differences of timing and priorities. For example, the Vietnamese official view, as I have mentioned, favors the use of bonuses and other material incentives to increase production, and does not acknowledge the need for any form of class struggle in socialist societies.

More generally, the Vietnamese do not appear to recognize, or at least to emphasize, the need for "two-line struggles" within their party. The unity of the party appears to be more important to them than struggles within it. They pride themselves on never having had a split, or even any large public commotion, within their party, and apparently rely on the method of majority decision-making and strict party discipline, together with tolerance for minority opinions. Again, although they have enforced the combination of labor with study among intellectuals since 1958, the Vietnamese have apparently never had a struggle concerning "redness" versus "expertise."[22] Their attitude toward their own history, art, and literature, finally, seems to be far less iconoclastic than that of the Chinese has been during the period of the Cultural Revolution. Like the Chinese, the Vietnamese select and emphasize themes from the past which reinforce their present ideology, for example, those concerning rebellions and wars against invaders, popular uprisings against feudal corruption, or the struggles of women against foreign and patriarchal domination. At the same time they seem inclined to try to select what is appropriate from past philosophies rather than to reject them outright. For example, the Vietnamese have never had an anti-Confucian campaign, but instead attempt to reform and purify the Confucian tradition while maintaining such ideals as selfless moral rectitude and loyal obedience to a regime that one finds morally acceptable.[23]

In late 1976 the Vietnamese disagreed profoundly with several facets of Chinese ideology and foreign policy in recent years. They regarded the whole concept of "social imperialism" as erroneous, and needless to say, deplored the Chinese view that the Soviet Union was the main enemy of world revolutionary developments proceeding to socialism. Nor did they accept the Chinese division of the world into (a) two superpowers (the United States and Soviet Union), (b) industrial nations that are not superpowers, and (c) underdeveloped nations oppressed or exploited by the superpowers; for this in their view ignored the primary distinction between the socialist and capitalist world camps and between revolutionary and counter-revolutionary governments and movements. In their eyes, United States imperialism was still the main enemy of world revolution, in spite of their wish to normalize trade and diplomatic relations with that country as with all other countries.

These differences between Vietnam and China were recently stated by Nguyen Khac Vien, director of the Foreign Languages Publishing House and editor of *Vietnamese Studies* and *Vietnam Courier,* more openly than has been usual in public discussions:

> On certain serious matters, especially concerning the international role of the United States imperialists, we are at odds with the policy of the Chinese leaders. We think that the number one enemy of humanity is U.S. imperialism, and this is a serious

disagreement. Whatever material difficulties we may have, we will continue to affirm this position and warn other peoples of the world of United States imperialism and U.S. neocolonialism. On the other hand, if the United States wants to have good relations with the Vietnamese people, we will not refuse. But politically, from a revolutionary point of view, our position in the near future is intransigent.[24]

Vietnam's experience of severe strain with China goes back at least to the Nixon and Kissinger visits to China in 1971-1972, and the normalization of relations between the two governments that occurred at the height of the U.S. bombing of Vietnam. Officially, the Vietnamese state that China's and the Soviet Union's reception of President Nixon during the bombing was their own business and did not affect Vietnam's war effort. But when I expressed the view that the visits *were* harmful, at least to world opinion about the war and about socialist solidarity, one person silently took my hand, and another murmured, "We were *weeping.*"

The Vietnamese who made comments approved of the arrest of the "gang of four," seeing it as "one first small step" in the right direction. Some stated that they hoped especially for a change in Chinese policy in view of the death of Chairman Mao Tsetung. One person in authority declined to discuss Chairman Mao's contribution to communist theory and practice, saying only that his life and experience "were very rich and full, and no one can assess him yet."

While the Vietnamese I spoke to denied any signs of the restoration of capitalist relations in the Soviet Union, some thought that the "gang of four" might well have been bent on restoring bourgeois right in China, and thought that they had a large following which would make the struggle against their influence a serious one. Some expressed the hope that the arrest of the four would presage a very gradual rapprochement between China and the Soviet Union, "first," as one put it, "on the state level, and then lower down, among the people." The reunification of the socialist camp was an ardent desire of all who spoke about the differences between China and the Soviet Union, and several quoted President Ho Chi Minh's last testament on this subject. They saw the disunity and rivalry between these powers as an inexpressibly tragic setback to the world communist movement and to revolution in particular countries.

During 1977 Vietnam's relations with China appear to have become a little warmer. In February, Chinese technicians were reported to have resumed work on the new Red River bridge and other constructional projects. In March, a medical delegation from Vietnam paid a friendship visit to Peking and entered into an agreement on medical cooperation, and a team of economic experts made an extended tour of China, the first of its kind for many years.[25] I have no knowledge of Vietnamese reactions to more recent events in China, for example, the expulsion of a number of leading figures in the Communist Party and its Central Committee, the reported execution of twelve party members in Honan in August 1977,[26] the restoration of Teng Hsiao-ping, and the reported reduction in the powers of trade unions, the Youth Front, and the Women's Association in China.[27] Presumably, the Vietnamese approve of the restoration of material incentives in production relations in China, but are disappointed that the profound changes in Chinese politics in 1977 have not so far brought any sign of rapprochement with the Soviet Union, but rather continuing deterioration in their relations.[28]

India: Vietnam's official relations with the government of Mrs. Indira Gandhi were cordial and cooperative in 1976, involving increasing trade and the promise of aid projects from India to Vietnam. India was, for example, constructing an experimental paddy-producing station near Hanoi, and had promised water buffaloes to supplement Vietnam's depleted stocks.

During the Emergency in India from mid-1975 to March

1977, the Vietnamese gave verbal support to Mrs. Gandhi, condemning those who wished to oust her as "reactionary rightists" and proimperialist elements, who, defeated in the elections of the early 1970s, were trying to slander and drive her out of office.[29] When I questioned Vietnamese about this and about the massive Soviet aid and sale of weapons to India, the response of those who answered was that Soviet aid was not designed to uphold counter-revolution in India but to support the progressive elements in the government and the Congress Party and to prevent India from falling completely into the imperialist camp. The Gandhi government, they said, was opposed to United States imperialism to some extent; it was not, for example, comparable to that of Suharto of Indonesia. In these respects the Vietnamese view paralleled that of the Soviet Union and of the Communist Party of India, both before and during the Emergency.

When I pointed to the violent repression of peasants, workers, and revolutionaries carried out over the past decade by the Congress government in India, some persons appeared troubled and remained silent. Others said that, of course, it would be marvelous if India had a socialist revolution. All who commented made it clear that they were not deceived into thinking that Mrs. Gandhi would bring socialism to India, and that they thought it unlikely or impossible that India could make a peaceful transition to socialism. "We are speaking of scientific socialism, of course," said one, "not Mrs. Gandhi's type of socialism." Another statement was, "I do not believe in the peaceful transition to socialism in India unless the United States, Canada, Western Europe, and Japan all go socialist first." The Vietnamese view that a revolution was necessary in India and that it would probably involve protracted fighting contrasted with the Soviet view that India under Indira Gandhi was engaged in peaceful transition to socialism.

In late 1976 the Vietnamese government parted company from the Soviet Union by refusing to invite the Communist

Party of India to the Fourth Congress of the Workers' Party. They thereby presumably refused to single it out as *the* Communist Party as opposed to the Communist Party of India (Marxist), India's other parliamentary communist party which had opposed Mrs. Gandhi and the Indian National Congress Party for more than a decade. When I asked which of the several communist groups in India the Vietnamese thought most correct or most promising, their response was, "At a time when the revolution has not broken out in India, how can we choose a party to support?"

In general, it was said, all the communist groups in India were too small, weak, and disunited; India's tragedy was that it did not have a strong and unified communist movement. Opposition was also expressed to the view of some Maoists in India that the Soviet Union is the main enemy of the Indian revolution; this view was characterized as "reactionary." It was hoped that the recent events in China, by bringing about a détente in hostilities between China and the Soviet Union, would make greater unity, or at least less antagonism, possible among the Indian communists. Above all, it was stressed that revolution in any country can come only from within; it is impossible to influence it from foreign countries and undesirable to try. "If Gus Hall can't make a revolution in the United States," quipped one, "even Giap can't."

Because I think that it is more responsible to try to evaluate policies, however inadequately, rather than simply to report them, I will state briefly my agreement or disagreement with the positions outlined above.

Vietnamese support for and loyalty to the Soviet Union seem understandable and legitimate. It has been their chief mentor and revolutionary example since the Russian revolution, and gave them essential aid that they can never forget during their wars against the French colonialists and the United States invaders. For Vietnam to receive aid from, and to trade intensively with, the Soviet Union and the Eastern

European countries today seems inevitable and probably essential, given Vietnam's history, its grave need for capital, and the meager resources available elsewhere. There is, moreover, ample evidence that, even at the risk of endangering the aid they receive when they disagree with the Soviet Union, the Vietnamese quietly go their own way, as they did, for example, during the United States invasion of Cambodia in 1971, by cooperating with the Cambodian liberation movement at a time when the Soviet Union was supporting the proimperialist dictator Lon Nol.

I also agree with the Vietnamese communists that whatever else is happening in the Soviet Union, it is not, or not at present, capitalism that is being restored there, and that the Soviet Union is not an imperialist power in the sense of regularly and continuously engaging in the economic exploitation of weaker countries around the globe. I think, however, that the Vietnamese underestimate the degrees of hierarchy, conservatism, and repression of dissidents that exist in the Soviet Union, even though they do object to certain features such as the disparities in incomes. The Vietnamese view that the Soviet Union is still the bastion of world socialism certainly ignores the growth of an entrenched privileged ruling class in that country, whether it be termed "state capitalist" or a "ruling class of bureaucrats."[30]

The Vietnamese also appear to ignore, at least in public, the Soviet Union's counter-revolutionary role in several countries, notably in Bangladesh and Sri Lanka as well as India. It is true, of course, that there was little or nothing that Vietnam could have done about Soviet actions toward such countries during the past decade, but their public silence in itself carries weight, and will increasingly do so as they emerge from their own revolutionary conflict and take their place as the third most powerful socialist country. I agree with the Vietnamese, however, that the Soviet Union has been a reliable ally in the struggle for socialism in Vietnam, Laos, Angola, Mozambique, Cuba, Chile, and other regions.

On the question of material incentives, one-person directorships, the general running of the economy, and the role of the market, I had doubts before going to Vietnam, having been influenced by strongly favorable reports of the reduction of material incentives and the stress on moral incentives during the Cultural Revolution in China. I left Vietnam, however, believing that as far as I could see and had heard, in Vietnam in its present and recent conditions the current organization of production works effectively and has the enthusiastic support of the people. My experience in Vietnam reminded me forcefully that there are no across-the-board rules for the development of production relations in a socialist society. Each country must work them out in terms of its own circumstances and its people's traditions, needs, and level of development, as well as in terms of the dangers to which it is exposed and the external demands made upon it.

My present belief is that something resembling class struggle does seem to be necessary in socialist societies, and that even Lê Duân's statement, quoted above, did not cover all contingencies of socialist class struggle. The difference between the Vietnamese view, as expressed by Comrade Hoang Tung and others, and my own may, however, be only one of choice of words.

Present day socialist societies are states, and are likely to remain so into the foreseeable future. There is no prospect at present of the "withering away" of the socialist state. Because they must first win the revolutionary war and then suppress the conquered classes and reeducate the counter-revolutionaries, they are necessarily strongly disciplined states at the outset. They have a self-recruiting ruling stratum in the form of the communist party, which appoints the holders of many offices and nominates others for election. Although the ruling stratum governs on behalf of the proletariat and the peasants and is ideally (but actually only in part) drawn from them, the members of the government and the leaders of the party are not themselves workers or peasants and, in the nature of the case, cannot be. They are only symbolically a "dictatorship of the proletariat." Their work, powers, and responsibilities are different from those of the proletariat. Over time it is possible that their interests might diverge from those of the mass of the people whom they govern, hence the need for the people themselves to keep a check on them and to struggle against any tendency on their part to develop into a ruling class. "Class struggle" in a socialist society seems to me therefore to be a preventive struggle against the re-formation of a ruling class, once the conquered classes have been abolished.

During the revolutionary war such struggles of the masses against erring sections of the revolutionary party are likely to be minimal or unnecessary, for the revolutionary war is itself a gigantic class struggle against the imperialist bourgeoisie and their representatives—the invading forces, the puppet rulers, and their supporters among the landlords, the comprador bourgeoisie, and other elements. Even long after the war is won and the society consolidated, struggle to overthrow part or all of the governing stratum and replace it with a new one and a different system is of course not necessary, provided that those in power continue to govern for the welfare of the proletariat and are responsible to it. In that sense, indeed, there is no class struggle in a genuinely socialist society. Socialist states do, therefore, contrast sharply with capitalist states, in which the built-in character of exploitation requires that, when the time is ripe, the ruling class must be overthrown in favor of a nonexploitative, socialist system.

Nevertheless, in socialist societies that have passed the period of their revolutionary war, some kind of "class struggle" seems essential in the form of organs and methods for the proletariat and the peasants (who over time turn into proletarians) to criticize and if necessary remove individuals or segments of the party in power who fail to govern according to their mandate, usurp powers or wealth not accorded to them by the people, or fail to promulgate reforms as these become necessary. The experiences of China and the Soviet Union since their revolutions suggest that in postrevolutionary societies there is always a possibility that the communist party, or a portion of its leadership, will develop into an exploitative ruling class unless struggles are waged by the common people to see that this does not happen.

Although the Cultural Revolution in China may not have carried out such struggles to the best advantage and may have resulted in needless chaos and sectarianism, the issues it addressed—bureaucratism, elitism, undue privilege, hardening of social strata, commandism, corruption, and usurpation of powers—were surely real ones, and will continue to be real today under the new Chinese dispensation.

It may be that the government and the Communist Party of Vietnam have provided adequate channels for struggle from below against such tendencies, in the form of the trade unions, the Peasant Union, the Youth Union, and the Women's Union, in the recruitment and internal organization of the Communist Party itself, and in the methods of regular criticism and self-criticism they have adopted, apparently with great success. If the state is to remain devoted to the interests of the working people and ultimately to be controlled by them, struggles of this kind must presumably be institutionalized so that those who do manual work and lack direct governmental powers can keep a check on those who govern and who command the means of production and the system of distribution. As political education develops and the people achieve "collective mastery," such popular vigilance can presumably supplement periodic campaigns within the party to ensure its members' dedication to the people's cause.

With regard to their views about China, I agree with the Vietnamese in rejecting the Chinese formulation of "three worlds," in their implied disapproval of Chinese policies toward Angola and Chile, and in their rejection of the Chinese belief that the government of the Soviet Union is the main enemy of world revolution. On the limited evidence available, it seems likely that those Vietnamese were correct who took the view that the "gang of four" were sectarian leaders who produced much unnecessary conflict and perhaps engaged in conspiracy, and that their arrest was justified. But I disagree, on the evidence available, that they were bent on restoring *capitalist* relations in China, and I was disturbed by the character assassination and apparent lack of orderly production of legal evidence against them. During 1977 I have been still more disturbed by the apparently large numbers of leaders expelled from the Communist Party of China and by the seeming weakening of the powers of trade unions, the Youth Union, and the Women's Union. I have no way of knowing the Vietnamese reaction to these events.

With reference to India, I agree with those Vietnamese who disbelieve in the peaceful transition to socialism and in the Congress Party's ability or will to bring socialism to India. After thirty years of the postcolonial state in India the facts speak to the contrary. For that very reason, however, I disagree with the view I heard in Vietnam that Soviet aid was justified by preventing India from falling completely into the imperialist camp. The alliance that prevailed between India and the Soviet Union in 1971–1976 showed no sign of reducing the exploitation of India by United States and other Western corporations. When, moreover, a people is as exploited, poverty stricken, and wretched as are the majority in India, and when they suffer from political repression of the kind exercised against dissidents during 1975–1977 (and against communist revolutionaries and many workers and peasants long before), it does not matter which camp they are in. It was with regard to this view and to the Vietnamese government's verbal support for Mrs. Gandhi's Emergency that I had the most—indeed the only profound—disagreement with some of those I met in Vietnam.

This disagreement must, however, be kept in perspective. The Vietnamese were not actively aiding the government of India in its repressive measures, but were merely publishing opinions, and those of a very limited character. They were, moreover, in my view justified in believing that the dominant opposition to the Congress Party would not bring political or economic gains in the long run either, and might lead India into still further dependence on and exploitation by United States capital. Finally, I agree with them that revolution in India as in any country can come only from within.

During 1977 reconstruction and development in Vietnam have proceeded in the face of serious problems imposed by both human and environmental factors. An unusually severe and prolonged cold spell began in north Vietnam in December 1976, while the south experienced its worst drought in thirty years.[31] These misfortunes affected crops in both regions. As a result, the Vietnamese had to resort to more stringent rationing and have experienced some shortage of food. Since, in any case, the cultivated acreage as a result of the war was only five million hectares for a population of fifty million,[32] the food problem has loomed large in 1977. The fact that Vietnam no longer receives free rice imports from China has compounded the difficulty.[33]

Foreign capital for reconstruction and development has proved hard to come by. According to Bank of America figures, in the two years preceding September 1977, Vietnam was able to raise only U.S. $270 million in commercial loans from the capitalist nations, a far cry from the $3.5 billion of "aid" (actually, war reparations) promised by the United States in the Paris agreements, not to mention the $150 billion spent by the United States in its war against Vietnam. Some of the commercial aid recently raised has had to be earmarked for imports of food. Meanwhile, Vietnam was reported to have had an overall trade deficit equivalent to U.S. $714 million in 1976.[34]

Despite these formidable obstacles, agricultural and industrial development are proceeding apace and much has been accomplished internally to "heal the wounds of war" and to rehabilitate devastated lands, cities, and people. A few examples will be given.

In the south nearly a million demobilized soldiers of the

former Thieu army are clearing land along with teams of young volunteers from the city. They are removing bombs and mines from formerly cultivated areas while also opening up New Economic Zones in the highlands that will relieve population pressure in the cities and the Red River delta. Since the liberation of the south, more than 600,000 hectares of new land have been cleared for cultivation. Two million more hectares are planned for the coming decade, 1 million of them during the first five-year plan. The government's goal is to produce 21 million tons of rice by 1980 instead of the 12.7 million produced in 1976.[35]

Dozens of agricultural research units, and hundreds of experimental stations, employing 20,000 people, have been set up; investments in irrigation in 1977 are double those of 1976; the supply of electricity to agriculture is being increased by 30 percent, and modern machinery is being applied to 33 percent of the tilled acreage throughout Vietnam.[36] Thousands of United States M-13 tanks abandoned in south Vietnam have been turned into plowing machines, a modern instance of "swords into plowshares."[37] Socially, Vietnam is solving its food problem by extending to the south the land reforms, cooperative farming, rationing of grains, and state trading in foods that have already proved successful in the north.

The United States' bombing of the countryside and forced urbanization policy changed the south from an area with 85 percent of its population in the rural areas in 1960 to one with only 35 percent rural inhabitants in 1974. Many of the refugees were herded into or around Saigon, which grew from 1 million in 1953 to between 3.5 and 4 million in 1975. On liberation day in 1975 this city alone contained over 1 million unemployed, more than 300,000 prostitutes, more than 200,000 drug addicts, 200,000 vagrants, 330,000 suffering from venereal diseases, 200,000 with tuberculosis, and 1 million destitute. Smaller cities like Hue, Da Nang, Can Tho, Qui Nong, and Vung Tau had experienced similar growth with the same kinds of problems.[38]

Notes

Preface

1. *Hanoi Diary, Economic and Political Weekly*, Bombay, 1975.
2. The Vietnamese, of course, refer to *Vietnam* rather than to *North Vietnam* and *South Vietnam*. Throughout this book, therefore, the terms *north* and *south* are used as geographical designations only, except in occasional historical references to the divided country.

Chapter 1: Rangoon to Hanoi

1. I have added the figures from Alexander B. Woodside, *Community and Revolution in Vietnam* (Boston: Houghton Mifflin, 1976), p. 261.
2. *The Socialist Republic of Vietnam, Structure and Bases* (Hanoi: Foreign Language Publishing House, 1976), p. 22.
3. Nayan Chanda, "Hanoi's Joint Venture Plan," *Far Eastern Economic Review*, September 24, 1976, pp. 55-56. At that date Vietnam was reportedly interested in joint ventures with foreign private capital in the textile, readymade clothing, electrical appliances, and food-processing industries and in the production of chemicals based on local mine output (offshore oil, tin, tungsten, apatite, phosphate, and anthracite). Negotiations in several capitalist countries made progress after the time of my visit, and by August 1977 Vietnam was receiving government aid and/or private foreign investment from Japan, the Philippines, Hong Kong, France, Norway, Denmark,

Sweden, and Canada; was receiving loans from the World Bank, the Asian Development Bank, and the International Monetary Fund; and was holding talks with the United States on the resumption of normal trade and the transfer of technology. Despite congressional opposition to direct aid or reparations to Hanoi, the United States was estimated to be contributing $34 million to Vietnam during 1977 through UN agencies and international banks, and United States companies were especially interested in exploring for offshore oil. In July 1977 the United States finally lifted its opposition to Vietnam's admission to the United Nations. See, e.g., Nayan Chanda's articles on Vietnam in the *Far Eastern Economic Review,* December 17 and 31, 1976, and February 25, March 4, March 18, April 1, and June 17, 1977.

4. The Workers' Party was renamed the Communist Party of Vietnam at the Fourth Party Congress in December 1976.

5. A brief account of Vô Thi Thê's life and of her participation in the Vancouver Conference in 1971 is contained in the *Bulletin of Concerned Asian Scholars* 3, nos. 3-4 (Summer-Fall 1971).

6. Aid on this bridge, called the Thang Long or Soaring Dragon bridge, had been provided from China as part of a contribution by about 1,000 Chinese technicians and experts in building and repairing over a dozen projects during the past three years, but in 1976 the work slowed almost to a halt, presumably because of the deteriorating relations between China and Vietnam. In February 1977, however, it was reported that progress on the bridge had been resumed (*Far Eastern Economic Review,* February 25, 1977, p. 18).

Chapter 2: History of the Workers' Party

1. Vietnam has long had a shortage of oxen for the tasks required of them, and many have been killed in wars. Before the revolution women were frequently required to pull carts or plows in place of oxen, and some still do so voluntarily. Both in Hanoi and in the countryside I saw a number of women in peasant dress, some of them quite old, pulling light carts of vegetables. As the vegetables that are sold privately by peasants in Hanoi and other towns come from the peasants' private family plots, I assumed they were being brought for sale by old, retired family members while the young were at work in the cooperative.

2. This standard Marxist phrase refers, of course, to a socialist government by and for the working class. For discussion, see Chapter 9, "Death and Spiritual Life," and the Epilogue.

Chapter 3: A Revolutionary Museum

1. For the events to which the museum exhibits refer, see especially *Vietnam: a Historical Sketch*, 1974; *An Outline History of the Vietnam Workers' Party*, 1976; and *President Ho Chi Minh, Beloved Leader of the Vietnamese People*, 1966, all published by Foreign Languages Publishing House, Hanoi.

2. Knowing that the Vietnamese would suffer from a prolonged military conflict, the government of the Democratic Republic made a temporary accord with the French on March 6, 1946, accepting the return of French troops for a five-year period but providing for a referendum on the question of reuniting Cochin China, Annam, and Tonkin—a question already settled in theory by the creation of the Democratic Republic in 1945, but opened again by the French reoccupation of Cochin China. As Ho's and Giap's speeches on the occasion show, however, the Vietnamese government did not expect the French to fulfill the accord, but used it to gain time until the country had recovered from the famine and the fighting forces had been strengthened. It was in fact only a matter of weeks before the Vietnamese were engaged in open warfare with the French forces. See, e.g., Russell Stetler's introduction to his edition of General Vo Nguyen Giap, *The Military Art of People's War* (New York: Monthly Review Press, 1970), for details of this period.

3. See Felix Greene, *Vietnam! Vietnam!* (Palo Alto, California: Fulton Press, 1966), for Nguyen Van Troi's story.

4. Hanoi's army daily, *Nhân Dân*, like the Soviet Union, interpreted the disturbances that preceded Indira Gandhi's institution of the Emergency in June 1975 as caused by "reactionary rightists" who were trying to slander and drive Prime Minister Gandhi out of office. Vietnam's stances have not, however, precisely duplicated those of the Soviet Union. Despite Soviet lobbying, the Vietnamese refused to invite the pro-Moscow Communist Party of India to their Fourth Party Congress in December 1976. On the other hand, the Vietnamese appear to have supported Mrs. Gandhi even longer than did Moscow. In spite of the CPI's and the Soviet Union's brushes with her late in 1976 and 1977, a *Nhân Dân* editorial in early 1977 said that "with the support of the patriotic and democratic forces, India has defeated many schemes of sabotage of imperialism and reaction" (*Far Eastern Economic Review*, February 25, 1977, p. 20).

5. The agricultural laborers' union of the Communist Party of India (Marxist) had been battling for several months for permanent employment for laborers, higher wages, lower rents, damages for dismissed laborers, and a stoppage to the introduction of tractors at a

time of severe underemployment. Massive demonstrations had been staged and several Communists and laborers had been murdered. The Kilvenmani dispute, however, arose over the workers' refusal to quit the Communist union and join a bogus union started by the landlords' so-called Paddy Producers' Association. The massacre was spearheaded by the president of this association even though he did not himself employ Kilvenmani workers.

Chapter 4: "We Know Why We Are Crippled"

1. *Far Eastern Economic Review*, December 31, 1976, p. 11.

Chapter 5: Agriculture and Handicrafts

1. *Far Eastern Economic Review*, August 20, 1976.
2. *India: A Reference Annual, 1976*, Ministry of Education and Broadcasting, Government of India, pp. 179-80; *Statistical Handbook of Tamilnadu, 1972*, Madras: Department of Statistics, p. 94.
3. *Season and Crop Reports of the Government of Tamilnadu,* July 1976.

Chapter 6: Women in Revolution

1. Especially useful on women are Arlene Eisen Bergman, *Women of Vietnam* (San Francisco: People's Press, 1974), and Margaret Randall, *Spirit of the People* (Vancouver: New Star Books, 1975).
2. Bergman, *Women of Vietnam*, p. 31.
3. Ibid., p. 47.
4. Ibid.
5. Ibid., pp. 49-50.
6. Ibid., p. 53.
7. Lê Thi Rieng, vice-president of the Women's Union for South Vietnam, was arrested in Saigon in 1967 and had all ten fingers bandaged, dipped in gasoline, and burned one by one. She was shot with two other women after the Tet offensive of 1968. Rieng was one of thousands of women tortured and killed by the puppet regime and the United States invaders. The torture and heroism of some of these women are described by Randall, *Spirit of the People*, p. 52 and elsewhere; Bergman, *Women of Vietnam*, pp. 98-107; and in the *Bulletin of Concerned Asian Scholars* 3, nos. 3-4 (Summer-Fall 1971): 14-16.

Chapter 7: Vietnamese Women Today

1. Margaret Randall, *Spirit of the People* (Vancouver: New Star Books, 1975), p. 22.
2. *Bulletin of Concerned Asian Scholars* 3, nos. 3-4 (Summer-Fall, 1971): 16-17.
3. Data for Canada are taken from the *Report of the Royal Commission on the Status of Women in Canada* (Ottawa: Information Canada, 1970) and the *Canada Year Book, 1969* (Ottawa: Dominion Bureau of Statistics, 1970); for India from the *Census of India,* 1971, and for Vietnam from Lê Thi, who was citing the Census of North Vietnam for 1972.
4. "Viet-Nam Workers' Party Fourth Congress Opened," *Women of Vietnam* 4, Supplement (Hanoi: Foreign Languages Publishing House.

Chapter 8: A Hanoi Textile Mill

1. Alexander B. Woodside, *Community and Revolution in Modern Vietnam* (Boston: Houghton-Mifflin, 1976), p. 305.

Chapter 9: Death and Spiritual Life

1. *Far Eastern Economic Review, Asia Yearbook, 1976,* Hong Kong, p. 318.
2. Julian Huxley, *Religion Without Revelation* (New York: Mentor, 1959).
3. See, e.g., Alexander B. Woodside, *Community and Revolution in Modern Vietnam* (Boston: Houghton-Mifflin, 1976), pp. 203-06, 305.
4. Ibid., p. 2; the report of the cartoon was contained in *Van Nghe* (Literature and the Arts), Hanoi, October 30, 1964, p. 10.
5. See especially the work of Georges Condominas; for example *We Have Eaten the Forest, The Story of a Montagnard Village in the Central Highlands of Vietnam* (New York: Hill and Wang, 1977).
6. *Vietnam: A Historical Sketch* (Hanoi: Foreign Languages Publishing House, 1974), p. 54.
7. Ibid.

Chapter 10: A Hanoi Interview

1. This interview has been published in *Monthly Review* 29, no. 1 (May 1977) and *Social Scientist*, Trivandrum, March 1977.
2. Of the people I met in Vietnam, only Khanh, the two Liêns, and Duyên spoke enough English to be willing to converse without an interpreter. French and Russian are more widely spoken.
3. Report to the First Session of the National Assembly of Vietnam, quoted in *Vietnam*, Special Issue, July 1976.
4. Quotation from Lê Duân's Report to the First Session of the National Assembly of Vietnam, June 24, 1976.
5. This statement echoes that of President Ho Chi Minh in his Testament, and of First Secretary Lê Duân in his Report to the First National Assembly, June 24, 1976.

Chapter 11: Hanoi to Quang Ninh

1. The work was finished by December 6, 1976, in time for the Fourth Party Congress.
2. Among my Vietnamese hosts, Khanh, Little Liên, and Duyên, the younger members, wear their hair to their shoulders; the older women wear buns.

Chapter 14: Quang Ninh to Thai Binh

1. See, e.g., Claire Culhane, *Why Is Canada in Vietnam? The Truth About Our Foreign Aid* (Toronto: NC Press, 1972).
2. For a comparison of agricultural relations in southeast India and north Vietnam, see my article, "The Green Revolution in Southeast India and North Vietnam," *Social Scientist* 61, Trivandrum, August 1977.

Chapter 16: An Agricultural Cooperative

1. Dinh Quang Ngi uses the standard Marxist terminology to describe the agricultural classes. In this terminology landlords are those who own land but do not cultivate it themselves, leasing it out to tenants; rich peasants own more land than they can cultivate, and hire laborers to work for them; middle peasants own just enough land to cultivate themselves and provide for their families; poor peasants

own or lease less than they require, and must hire themselves out part-time to earn a living; laborers own little or no land and hire themselves out all or most of the time.

2. This compares favorably with the thirteen kilograms per adult per month mentioned by Hoang Tung as the current basic ration throughout Vietnam. Evidently, the members of rich cooperatives do enjoy a better food supply than city people or people in poor coops, even though they supply rice to other provinces and also help subsidize the poorer coops.

3. Hoang Tung stated that 20 percent was the highest amount sold to the state by individual cooperatives, so Vu Thang must be quite exceptional. This again is evidence of the unusual prosperity of this cooperative. As I do not know what proportion of the fish, pork, poultry, etc. of Vu Thang is sold to the state, I cannot be sure of the exact percentage of the total product sold and retained.

4. North Vietnam's main leper hospital, the Quyn Lap Leprosy Research Center with 2,500 beds, was, however, completely destroyed by bombing. In all, 350 hospitals and 1,500 infirmaries and maternity hospitals in north Vietnam were destroyed or damaged in the anti-United States war (*Vietnam: Destruction, War Damage* [Hanoi: Foreign Languages Publishing House, 1977], pp. 30-31). My figure of 600 bombed churches in North Vietnam, mentioned in chapter 14, is taken from this same document.

5. Professor Alexander B. Woodside has told me, however, that according to Vietnamese newspapers in the north, Thai Binh province had only 16 percent of its houses roofed with tiles in 1976 (*Hoc tap 4*, 1976, p.19), about the same percentage as Thanjavur in that year.

6. For more detail on Thanjavur see "Changing Agrarian Relations in Thanjavur, 1951-76," in *Essays in Honour of A. Aiyappan*, Special Issue of the *Kerala Sociological Review*, Trivandrum, 1977.

Chapter 18: The Bach Mai Hospital

1. Wilfred Burchett, *Vietnam: Inside Story of the Guerrilla War* (New York: International Publishers, 1965).

Chapter 19: Farewell to Hanoi

1. The other four are West Lake, the Lake of the Restored Sword, Lake Bay Mau near Reunification Park, and Lake Thuyen Quang.

2. This policy was well stated by Nguyen Khac Vien, director of Hanoi's Foreign Languages Publishing House, in an interview with Peter Limqueco in 1977:

Our policy is a policy of independence, that is, we think that every Communist Party, according to the national circumstances and according to its own analysis, may have a point of view that differs from that of another state or another party. Between us we discuss issues frankly and openly, but we do not do it in newspapers or on radio, etc., because we always assess the possibility of working for the establishment of a common solidarity and fraternity between the different Communist Parties of the world. It is in this spirit that we are working. The spirit of independence and fraternity may at a given moment contradict the national interest. For instance, someone may say to us that they cannot provide us with technical or material support, and we have to accept this. After all, it is the respect of certain principles that enables us to work with a long perspective, even if at moments we have to make sacrifices. This was especially true during the war, which made the war much harder, and longer. But we accept that in the spirit of hoping that someday we will re-establish the great fraternity between the Communist Parties of the world and the socialist states. (*Journal of Contemporary Asia* 7, no. 2 [1977] : 217-18.)

Nguyen Khac Vien then went on to discuss the fact that in some respects Vietnam is at odds with the policies of the Chinese leaders (see Epilogue).

3. According to diplomatic sources in Hanoi, Vietnam returned at least some of the disputed islands to Kampuchea (Cambodia) and agreed to settle border disputes peacefully (*Far Eastern Economic Review, Asia Yearbook*, 1977, p. 330). There were renewed clashes on the Kampuchea-Vietnam border on land between May and August 1977, and disputes concerning ocean rights in the gulf. The government of Vietnam was confident that the disputes could be settled by negotiation (*Far Eastern Economic Review*, August 19, 1977, p. 11). One version of the exit of Vietnamese after the victory in Kampuchea is that they left peacefully on the agreement of both governments, as part of an effort to solve Kampuchea's serious problems of population relocation and reconstruction (*Far Eastern Economic Review, Asia Yearbook*, 1977, p. 330).

4. A somewhat different explanation by a recent visitor to China is that the Communist Party of China has not sent delegates to any national communist party congress in recent years because of international and in some cases internal splits among communist parties, and the Chinese belief that at the present stage each party should settle its own policies internally.

Epilogue

1. Lê Duân, *The Vietnamese Revolution* (New York: International Publishers, 1971), pp. 101-02.
2. Paul M. Sweezy, "Contrasts with Capitalism,"*Monthly Review* 27, no. 3 (July-August 1975), p. 3.
3. This and the next two quotations are from Lê Duân, *The Vietnamese Revolution*, p. 64. The quote is from V. I. Lenin, *Left Wing Communism, an Infantile Disorder* (New York: International Publishers, 1940), p. 29.
4. Ibid.
5. "Lê Duân's Report of the First Session of the National Assembly of Vietnam," *Viet Nam* 17, no. 2 (July 1976), Embassy of the Socialist Republic of Vietnam, New Delhi, p. 20; and Lê Duân, "Line for Socialist Revolution in the New Stage," in *Political Report of the Party Central Committee to the Fourth National Congress,* presented by Comrade Lê Duân, First Secretary of the Party Central Committee, Hanoi, December 1976, p. 39.
6. For the different meanings of the term *class struggle* in a socialist society, see Paul Sweezy, "Theory and Practice in the Mao Period," *Monthly Review* 28, no. 9 (February 1977), p. 9. For a more extended discussion, see Charles Bettelheim, *Class Struggles in the USSR, 1917-1923* (New York: Monthly Review Press, 1976). See also, e.g., Mao Tsetung, "Speech at the Tenth Plenum of the Eighth Central Committee, September 24, 1962," in Stuart Schram, ed., *Chairman Mao Talks to the People: Talks and Letters, 1956-1971* (New York: Pantheon, 1975), pp. 188-96.
7. "To Strengthen the Socialist State, to Enhance the Role of the Mass Organizations, to Fulfill the Work among the Masses," in *Political Report to the Fourth National Congress,* p. 129.
8. *Far Eastern Economic Review, Asia Yearbook, 1976,* pp. 331-32.
9. Nayan Chanda, "Vietnam Opts for Broad Approach," *Far Eastern Economic Review,* February 25, 1977, p. 20.
10. *Far Eastern Economic Review,* February 4, 1977, p. 29.
11. *Far Eastern Economic Review,* February 25, 1977, p. 20.
12. *Far Eastern Economic Review,* June 3, 1977, p. 44.
13. *Far Eastern Economic Review,* June 24, 1977, pp. 18-19.
14. *Far Eastern Economic Review,* February 4, 1977, p. 33.
15. *Far Eastern Economic Review,* February 4, 1977, p. 32.
16. *Far Eastern Economic Review,* September 23, 1977, p. 30.
17. *Far Eastern Economic Review,* February 4, 1977, p. 28.
18. *Far Eastern Economic Review,* August 29, 1977, p. 48.

19. *Far Eastern Economic Review*, May 13, 1977, p. 40, and September 16, 1977, p. 62.
20. *Far Eastern Economic Review*, August 20, 1977, p. 48.
21. The Communist Party of Vietnam did, however, expel some party members in late 1976 and punished some cadres in the course of a campaign to cleanse the party and administration, maintain unity in the party, combat rightist tendencies, and get rid of "bad elements." Some of those punished were convicted of corruption in the course of liberating south Vietnam. As far as I am aware, however, no popular upsurge occurred or was encouraged against such elements and tendencies in the party. Arrogance, bureaucratism, and "commandism" were among the offenses mentioned (*Far Eastern Economic Review*, December 3, 1976, pp. 15-16, and December 31, 1976, pp. 11-12).
22. Alexander B. Woodside, *Community and Revolution in Modern Vietnam* (Boston: Houghton Mifflin, 1976), pp. 269-70.
23. Ibid., pp. 265-66.
24. *Journal of Contemporary Asia* 7, no. 2 (1977), p. 218.
25. *Far Eastern Economic Review*, February 25, 1977, p. 18.
26. *Far Eastern Economic Review*, August 19, 1977, p. 8.
27. *Far Eastern Economic Review*, September 2, 1977, pp. 8-10.
28. *Far Eastern Economic Review*, June 17, 1977, p. 14.
29. *Far Eastern Economic Review, Asia Yearbook, 1976*, p. 318.
30. For discussion of this subject, see Bettelheim, *Class Struggles in the USSR;* Bernard Chavance and Paul M. Sweezy, "Production Relations in the USSR," *Monthly Review* 29, no. 1 (May 1977), pp. 1-19; Ross Gandy, "The East European Social Formation," *Monthly Review* 29, no. 3 (July-August 1977), pp. 82-88.
31. *Far Eastern Economic Review*, August 19, 1977, p. 30, and *Vietnam Courier* (Hanoi) May 1977, p. 1.
32. Compared, for example, with Poland's 31 million hectares for 33 million people, Roumania's 23.7 million hectares for 21 million people, or even India's 162 million hectares for 570 million people. China's arable land is, however, some 105 to 120 million hectares for about 900 million people, approaching the low ratio in Vietnam. See *Vietnam Courier*, May 1977, p. 1, and Harry Magdoff, "China: Contrasts with the USSR," *Monthly Review* 28, no. 3 (July-August 1976), p. 14.
33. Under the former Saigon regime, 450,000 to 700,000 tons of rice were imported to South Vietnam in any given year, and in North Vietnam some 500,000 tons were imported free from China, in addition to some wheat imported at low cost from the Soviet Union (*Far Eastern Economic Review*, August 20, 1976, p. 48).

34. *Far Eastern Economic Review,* September 16, 1977, p. 82.
35. George C. Hildebrand, "Vietnamese Focus on Food and Health," *The Guardian,* September 14, 1977, p. 19.
36. *Vietnam Courier,* May 1977, p. 2.
37. Hildebrand, "Vietnamese Focus," p. 19.
38. *Vietnam: Destruction, War Damage* (Hanoi: Foreign Relations Publishing House, 1977), pp. 64-65.
39. *Vietnam Courier,* July 1977, p. 10.
40. *Vietnam Courier,* April 1977, p. 24.
41. *Vietnam Courier,* May 1977, p. 3.
42. *Vietnam Courier,* July 1976, p. 10.
43. *Vietnam Courier,* May 1977, p. 5.

Index